LETTERS IN BLACK AND WHITE

LETTERS IN BLACK AND WHITE

A New Correspondence on Race in America

WINKFIELD TWYMAN, JR. AND JENNIFER RICHMOND

Foreword by Erec Smith
Afterword by Izabella Tabarovsky

PITCHSTONE PUBLISHING
DURHAM, NORTH CAROLINA

Pitchstone Publishing
www.pitchstonebooks.com

Parts of Letters 46, 47, and 75 were previously published on the *Truth in Between* page on *Medium*. Parts of Letters 66 and 67 were adapted from Jennifer Richmond and W. F. Twyman, Jr., "Nothing to Talk About: Affinity in the Age of Diversity," *Areo Magazine*, September 11, 2020. Part of Letter 70 was adapted from Jennifer Richmond and W. F. Twyman, Jr., "The Golden Age of Slogans," *Areo Magazine*, April 6, 2021. Parts of Letter 74 were originally published in W. F. Twyman, Jr., "Commentary: We Must Let Go of the Grudges from Slavery," *Chicago Tribune*, November 6, 2017, and W. F. Twyman, Jr., "The Turning Point of Self-Loathing," *Richmond Times-Dispatch*, September 28, 2017. The essay by Jennifer Richmond that appears in Appendix I, "Diversity Drop-Out," was originally published in *Areo Magazine* on April 24, 2019.

Library of Congress Cataloging-in-Publication Data

Names: Twyman, Winkfield, Jr. author. | Richmond, Jennifer, author. |
  Smith, Erec, writer of foreword. | Tabarovsky, Izabella, writer of
  afterword.
Title: Letters in black and white : a new correspondence on race /
  Winkfield Twyman, Jr. and Jennifer Richmond ; foreword by Erec Smith ;
  afterword by Izabella Tabarovsky.
Description: [Durham] : Pitchstone Publishing, [2023] | Includes
  bibliographical references and index. | Summary: "Winkfield Twyman, Jr.
  and Jennifer Richmond - a black man and a white woman - share their
  years-long correspondence about race in the United States"— Provided by
  publisher.
Identifiers: LCCN 2022026613 (print) | LCCN 2022026614 (ebook) | ISBN
  9781634312363 (hardcover) | ISBN 9781634312370 (ebook)
Subjects: LCSH: United States—Race relations. | Twyman, Winkfield,
  Jr.—Correspondence. | Richmond, Jennifer—Correspondence. | African
  Americans—Social conditions. | African Americans—History—Anecdotes. |
  Anti-racism—United States | BISAC: SOCIAL SCIENCE / Race & Ethnic
  Relations | BIOGRAPHY & AUTOBIOGRAPHY / Cultural, Ethnic & Regional /
  African American & Black
Classification: LCC E185.61 .T94 2023 (print) | LCC E185.61 (ebook) | DDC
  305.896/073—dc23/eng/20220616
LC record available at https://lccn.loc.gov/2022026613
LC ebook record available at https://lccn.loc.gov/2022026614

ISBN 978-1-63431-299-8 (pbk.)

For

Winkfield Franklin Twyman, Sr.

In Memory of

Daniel Brown, 1833–1885
Rosa Nell Brown Twyman Jackson, 1897–1983
Lourine Womack Twyman, 1940–1990

And

Finnegan Gray Higginbotham, the next generation.

It is difficult to make a man miserable
while he feels he is worthy of himself,
and claims kindred to the great God who made him.
Thus, they have schooled themselves to labor and to wait
in the hope of the coming of a better time.

George Boyer Vashon, August 1862

Contents

Preface

Dear Reader,

As we've come to appreciate over the course of our letters, nothing is ever black and white. Things are really shades of gray when one gets right down to it.

We began to exchange letters after Jennifer Richmond, or Jen for short, voluntarily attended a diversity-training program sponsored by the City of Austin, Texas. As a white American woman, she hoped to learn how to nurture and advance social connections so that all Americans might build a genuinely diverse and egalitarian society *together*, but she left the training feeling despondent and disappointed. She set fingers to keyboard to write about the training's reliance on tropes, stereotypes, and caricatures that only served to divide rather than unite. On April 24, 2019, Jen published an essay about her diversity-training experience in *Areo Magazine*.*

The following morning before work, Winkfield F. Twyman, Jr., or Wink for short, came across Jen's essay, read it with interest, and discovered that Jen invited correspondence from others to learn about their own experiences and to have a meaningful dialogue about race. At the time, Wink had been working on a novel about the first black lawyer in the United States. As a black American man, he was motivated to write in large part due to many of the same tropes, caricatures, and stereotypes that commonly define all public discussions about race in America—and

---

* To read the article, see appendix I.

so he reached out to Jen that same day.*

Wink's first letter to Jen ended with a simple truth: "There are over 40 million black Americans. That means there are over 40 million different perspectives, life stories, and personalities. Painting with a broad brush strays from truth, a truth that is always nuanced and complex." Extending that point here, we further note that there are nearly 250 million white Americans in the United States and over 40 million people of mixed or other races, with life stories equally nuanced and complex.

No human in one lifetime could ever know all there is to know about everyone in their life—let alone about tens or even hundreds of millions of people. It is an impossible task. As a result, we are susceptible to caricatures and popular stereotypes about many things, including race. But we can get to see and know others as individuals, and there is no better path for finding common ground and understanding than by speaking plainly and listening attentively.

These truths guided our decision to commit to a written exchange. Yes, for purposes of convenience, we communicated mostly via email, but we approached our correspondence with the same thoughtfulness, faithfulness, and sincerity you might find in any old-fashioned epistle. Before social media and the Internet, there was a time when letters were the prime means of sharing one's deepest feelings, affections, and convictions. The correspondence of Commander George Washington conveyed to his generals the deepest gratitude for unimaginable sacrifices and contributed to the fortitude that made a nation out of thirteen ragtag colonies. The written word from the Civil War battlefields at Cold Harbor and Vicksburg gave comfort to the young brides and families back home. And, of course, the open letter Dr. Martin Luther King, Jr., penned to fellow clergymen as he sat in a solitary jail cell in Birmingham anchored the Civil Rights Movement in nonviolence. In this tradition, we refer to our written exchanges as letters.

You will find there is no corruption of plain English in our letters.

---

* Disclaimer: As you will discover in this book, my views toward race and culture differ from those of my immediate family members. Further, the descriptions of events and recollections of conversations that I shared with Jennifer Richmond are based solely on my own memory and perceptions. Thus, my wife, children, and others whom I referenced in my correspondence do not necessarily agree with anything I have written. (NB: My wife and children made me write this!) —Winkfield Twyman, Jr.

To the greatest extent possible, we both avoid words and phrases drained of real meaning, such as *white privilege, white fragility, oppression, anti-racism, systemic racism, institutional racism, white supremacy, ally,* and *woke.* These words are clumsy, slippery, and manipulated beyond recognition. These words have themselves become caricatures. They mask real life in Middle America. We choose instead to use our brains and describe real moments drawing on the other three hundred thousand words in the English language.

We wanted to look past the tropes and stereotypes that often seek to divide—so that we might discover what draws us together. Some of our letters were written over days. Other letters were written in minutes. Some letters required sustained research and deliberation. Others flowed quickly and with emotion. For the purposes of this volume, we've curated the letters for purposes of length and to save the reader from moments of needless repetition. Letters have also been lightly edited, and notes have been added to some letters, either to reflect a link that one of us shared or to simply add a bit of extra context for the reader. Beyond these changes, the letters remain largely intact, and they track the evolution of our thoughts, ideas, and relationships. Although the last letter in this book was written in the fall of 2022, our exchange is ongoing.

As the letters reflect a private correspondence between two individuals, they sometimes tend toward the personal. Some readers may wonder how we found the courage—perhaps an imperfect word for this context—to publish those elements of the letters that might reveal too much—or that might not always meet the approval of those we know in the real world, whether coworkers and colleagues or close relatives and loved ones. Speaking honestly means fidelity to what has been lived and what we believe to be true. Anything else would be inauthentic. We shared things with one another in the letters that we might not normally share or say publicly. We're writing life, not a fairy tale. While our primary approach was to emulate the long letter-writing tradition that today sheds much-needed light on the past, we also found ourselves following in the tradition of contemporary writers like Thomas Chatterton Williams, who plunged into the meaning of a blond-haired, blue-eyed daughter of a black dad in *Unlearning Race: Self-Portrait in Black and White*; Ta-Nehisi Coates, who divined purpose in the most intimate details of his son's life in *Between the World and Me*; and Karl Ove Knausgard, who laid bare moments of his family's life in *My Struggle*. We are well aware we are opening ourselves to judgment. Still, we find comfort in knowing we will be judged on our own terms—not on some stereotype or caricature based on our bios, skin color, or gender.

We share our letters with the hope that others might better understand not only us but also their own family members, coworkers, neighbors, and fellow Americans—that everyone might start seeing the gray where once they saw only black and white. Yet, we also realize that ours are just two stories, and we speak only for ourselves. Millions of people cannot talk or correspond with millions of people. However, one person can correspond with another person and achieve meaningful truth. Thus, continuing with Jen's initial invitation for discussion, we hope our letters will inspire others to join the dialogue as individuals. Together, let us discover a universal story—our story.

Wink & Jen

Foreword

As a rhetorician, I am especially sensitive to the failures in communication across difference that are beginning to define American society, if not Western Civilization, as a whole. I have my theories about this communicative breakdown that could be reduced to xenophobia, tribalism, and the misunderstanding of others' values. When considering all of this, I often feel like I am drowning in negativity and hopelessness. However, every once in a while, I am thrown a lifeline. *Letters in Black and White* is that lifeline.

This book's authors, Winkfield Twyman, Jr. and Jennifer Richmond, provide a much-needed paradigm in our current culture war of race: simple and honest dialogue between two good-faith interlocutors. The fact that one correspondent is a black male and the other is a white woman is not an insignificant factor; it models ideal communication and saves the ability to dialogue across differences from becoming a lost art.

But these contributions to race relations are easy to discern. What people may miss in reading this book is its tacit promotion of collaboration at the local level. As the authors put it in their preface, "Millions of people cannot talk or correspond with millions of people. However, one person can correspond with another person and achieve meaningful truth." This is one of those situations in which less is more. Changing minds *en masse* is a very tall order that takes time and energy many don't have. However, starting small, addressing the issue in small groups, even only as a pair, can produce long strides in mutual understanding, tolerance, and equality. And if those conversations can be chronicled, like they are in this book, readers can be shown the way and follow the direction in which these strides can move us toward what the authors call the "Blessed Society."

I want to be clear. I am not saying that Twyman and Richmond represent *the* black and white experience, respectively. They are two individuals with unique perspectives. However, what I am saying is that this book is both a source of key insights, considerations, and facts *and* a model performance of what dialogue can be. We've lost sight of the efficacy of dialogue in the midst of social media and the confinement of 280 characters. This book can remind us of what good-faith conversation about difficult topics can look like. It can drive home the fact that racial congeniality is a superordinate goal—one that is important for the well-being of all involved, regardless of skin color, class, gender, etc.

Twyman and Richmond provide us with profound lessons: the power of immersion into cultural pluralities that shed light on our commonalities while appreciating our differences; the detriments of dogma and empty sloganeering; the necessity to define ourselves by our present and not our past; the importance of a black history that celebrates triumph as much as tragedy, etc. I could go on—and the reader will no doubt uncover their own lessons—but my main point is that a dialogue between two people can hold a trove of insights, considerations, and facts that power us toward that Blessed Society.

Personally, I find this book to be both familiar and novel. Regarding familiarity, I see significant parallels between my life and Twyman's. We were both black males who found ourselves in predominantly white spaces at a very young age. We have both been insulted for our optimism and seen as too naïve to see what's *really* going on between races. We are both seen as overachievers, by both blacks and whites, in ways that shroud us in suspicion. We are both unafraid of the full history of black Americans. I do not want to reveal any more here, for fear that the reader will lose the sense of discovery I had reading the book, but I will say that ultimately, we are both personified antitheses to the preferred narrative of black suffering: "Blackness Is All About Oppression. Nothing Else Matters." These words, which you will encounter in the pages that follow, continue to ring in my ears long after having read the book. I personally take such a belief to be defeatist and unnecessarily hopeless, and I am willing to stand by that conviction despite the social, professional, and even familial risks. Before you form your own opinion one way or another, I would only encourage the reader to consider Twyman's trenchant, powerful, and personal response to this statement.

Richmond's life experiences, on the other hand, were often quite foreign to me. In fact, they were foreign in a very literal sense. Richmond's experiences abroad as a child and teen not only affected her career choice but also inadvertently immersed her in a cultural plurality that opened her eyes to the fact that, at the end of the day, we are all human regardless of race, ethnicity, or nationality. She brings this insight into both her correspondence with Twyman and her dealings with the world at large. Because of her experiences, she sees current trends in antiracism—trends that, I believe, rest on a foundation of tribalism, resentment, and learned helplessness—as profound and tragically unnecessary phenomena. I couldn't agree more with her views on this current trend, and I think the reader will find many of her comments and insights persuasive.

Perhaps the authors' biggest contribution to contemporary race relations is their willingness to address how their views on race affect their personal lives. Both Twyman and Richmond recount times in which their viewpoints—for example, disagreeing with some tactical aspects of antiracist activism—either ended relationships or caused significant contentiousness with family members. Both authors expose to us how close to home these issues are for them. Both authors have my admiration and respect for talking about this openly and, again, modeling what it takes to negotiate these issues effectively.

Let me close by saying that I am glad you are reading this book. I truly believe that it is exactly what we need at this moment in the American culture war of race relations. Not only does it provide perspectives one does not get from mainstream accounts of "whiteness" and "blackness," but it also shows the benefits of mature and honest dialogue, the need to embrace America's virtues in the face of its vices, and the promise of classical liberal values. But please don't take my word for it. Turn the page and discover for yourselves.

Erec Smith
Co-Founder and President, Free Black Thought

EPISTOLARY I

Letter 1

Dear Ms. Richmond,

I came across your essay this morning on the *Areo Magazine* website, which I read on a regular basis because of the exceptional insights one can find from time to time. I concur with your complaint that diversity programs won't have an enduring (positive) effect. As you note, they tend to advance "a familiar echo chamber unable to resonate outside [their] narrow (and, dare I say, privileged) confines." I understand you are looking to exchange letters as a conversation starter on questions of race. I like your idea.

Here's why: Whenever I come across a highly touted "conversation about race" in the media, it always seems to be a conversation among the same handful of people echoing the same boilerplate script written for a public audience. All the while, these individuals act as though they are speaking for whatever race they happen to belong to and corrupt the English language for their own specific agenda. Such an approach might be good for their book sales or consulting fees, but when it comes to conversations that might actually create a meaningful difference that improves the Black Experience in America—and that might actually unite rather than divide—private grassroots conversations between individuals will bear the most fruit. This would be especially true if the conversations were between what I call "Old Americans."

Let me explain what I mean.

One of my buddies is a recent immigrant from Hong Kong. "Julia" is very conservative on race. She has been a U.S. citizen for about ten years. When one starts talking about slavery from the 1660s and 1790s, one loses Julia, and rightly so. She has no felt lived experience or history relating to the subject—no dog in that hunt. Her lack of empathy is genuine and sincere, not contrived with malice. She reads her own immigrant experience and perceives the Black Experience through the lens of high expectations, higher education, and duty to achieve out of respect for ancestral suffering. She would not be an ideal interlocutor for such a project—at least not in its early stages.

If the intent is to work toward a unified American future in which history is understood as history and not as present—and reconciliation is reached through honest, unfiltered discussion and truth-telling—the descendants of American slavery should first be having direct and genuine conversations with white descendants of the slave system. Old Families dating back to the 1600s and 1700s are the logical listeners, because white descendants of slavery get it—or at least they should. They know the guilt as a family stain. They recognize familiar family names in black faces. They know they are related to black Americans as 4th, 5th, and 6th cousins. That's the natural market for a race conversation driven by the Black Experience.

And let's not forget, there is no one "Black Experience." There are over 40 million black Americans. That means there are over 40 million different perspectives, life stories, and personalities. Painting with a broad brush strays from truth, a truth that is always nuanced and complex, which I'm sure you can appreciate. A person wouldn't know this if they relied only on today's diversity-training programs for their "education." Such programs are so often wrong and offensive precisely because they put people like me—and you—in a box. The differences found within any given extended family are greater than any average difference found between races, however the term is defined.

I recently wrote a short manuscript about my own family's attempt at truth and reconciliation. Although I come from a black family, we trace our bloodline and family name back to George Twyman I (1661–1703), an English immigrant who settled in Jamaica, Middlesex County, Virginia in 1677.[*] Perhaps you might find an exchange with me of some value?

---

[*] Family historian Dr. James Edwin Smith III notes that George Twyman I was born in 1661. See his book *Migrations: Our Family's Immigrations to America, From All Over the World* (p.

A Blessed Society is over the horizon for now, but your call for direct conversation is an important step, so regardless, I wish you well on the journey.

Regards,

W. F. Twyman, Jr.

---

138). Nathan W. Twyman, in his *American Twyman*, gives a different birth year: "If George was this son of Nicholas (Twyman), he was born in 1663, and his parents and siblings had died by the time he was six years old" (p. 3).

Letter 2

Dear W. F. Twyman, Jr.,

Thank you for responding to my diversity-training article. Discussing race in the public square has become such a minefield. I certainly agree that more private discussions out of the public spotlight should occur. But even as I sit down to write to you, I don't know where to start.

Let me first say I approach the whole issue with hesitation. I bristle at the new terms and ideas that have spread widely over the past few years—*white privilege, white guilt*, etc. I see them as blunt tools used to silence voices and stymie conversation. Likewise, the term *racist* has become a popular weapon to shut down anyone who could be considered disagreeable, and in some cases, the accusation has even had professional ramifications for the supposed offender.

When trying to understand these new trends, I work to put myself in another's shoes. But not having grown up in a black ghetto or having had to navigate the streets that Ta-Nehisi Coates describes in his book *Between the World and Me*, I honestly have trouble doing so. My parents and grandparents didn't have to face segregation or other discriminatory policies that would have impacted their ability to generate and hold on to wealth. And yet, I can't help but feel that the current discussions are not meant to level the playing field, so to speak, but rather to assign blame and even to relieve people of any personal responsibility for their own decisions and actions. They are often exercises in excuse-making and finger-pointing that deny people their agency and dignity. None of this is to say that we shouldn't take a hard look at America's past injustices, but it seems that instead of grappling honestly with our past, we are, in reality, reviving and reliving it.

I'm often uncomfortable speaking these truths. As you know from reading my article on the City of Austin diversity-training program that I attended, when I did speak up about my concerns, people of all colors immediately sought to create actual physical distance from me. Admittedly, I have never studied race relations or American history in great depth. As an international relations specialist who grew up in various Asian countries, perhaps I see the American experience from a different angle than most. The people in the countries in which I lived held America in such high esteem—particularly its ideals and promise. The "American Dream," that a little grit and determination could lead to success, was a completely novel idea cherished by so many.

I wonder, do you think that as a black American you are freer than someone like me to explore these issues publicly? I'm sure that you could be labeled a race traitor or some of the more colorful names I've only recently learned. I believe Coleman Hughes was publicly called a "coon" after his congressional testimony on reparations.* I'm not really even sure what that means, but it doesn't sound good. Do you worry that creating such a reputation would impact your relationships with friends or family, or even your professional life?

I avoid these conversations at home. My husband is a Law Enforcement Officer (LEO) who sees everything through the lens of crime and criminality only. There is no nuance. No complexity. It is truly only and always black and white. I know there is more to every story, which is one of the reasons I started this exploration, so I could better grasp the gray—or the truth in between—about race and race relations in the United States. Meanwhile, however, I refrain from having these conversations

---

* Coleman Hughes is a young public intellectual who has written extensively on issues of race in the United States. A distant relative of Sally Hemings from Monticello in Charlottesville, Virginia, Hughes has testified before a U.S. House Judiciary Subcommittee against reparations for American slavery. See Victor Morton, "Rae Sanni Calls Coleman Hughes 'Coon' for Opposing Reparations," *Washington Times*, June 19, 2019, www.washingtontimes.com/news/2019/jun/19/rae-sanni-calls-coleman-hughes-coon-opposing-repar/; and Sahil Handa, "In Defense of Coleman Hughes," *National Review*, June 21, 2019, www.nationalreview.com/corner/coleman-hughes-slavery-reparations-defense/.

at home. They are an effort in futility. I cannot change his life experiences that have led him to such a binary perspective. He used to work as a detective in New Orleans, a city where the majority of the population is black and that is often referred to as the "murder capital" of the United States. I only hope that through my research and writing, perhaps by osmosis, the many shades of gray (ha—the title of a naughty and somewhat taboo novel, and indeed we are treading into the taboo) may seep in to blur the black-and-white mindset that he, and so many others, desperately cling onto to make sense of the world.

It takes courage to bare your soul to another person—never mind to the world. What if the world—or perhaps worse, those around or even closest to you—don't like what they hear? Of course, it goes without saying that no one is immune to critics, but on the topic of race, it seems the critics are especially active and influential. Anyone speaking and writing in good faith can be easily trampled for some perceived sin in our outrage-driven milieu. Perhaps the bigger and better question is, if we truly feel that we, as a society, are walking down a dangerous path, can we afford to be quiet? Do we do a disservice to the next generation if we cower in the face of difficult conversations? And so, I guess that's where we are, you and me. On the edge of a courageous conversation.

Okay, okay, I just had to laugh at that—courageous conversation. That is the premise of diversity training—to have "courageous conversations." In those circumstances, courageous conversations entail the courage to face the predetermined conclusion that white people suck. If you are brave enough to stand against this dogma, your courageous conversation will get you the boot. You will wear your *white privilege* score like a scarlet letter, as I did in the City of Austin's diversity training, so people will know to avoid any engagement with you lest they become similarly tainted.

We have different truths in our lived experiences. We see and approach the world in novel ways. Do we have the courage to share our authentic selves as we tackle the dogma that seeks to sloganize the way we interact?

To our future correspondence,

Jen

Letter 3

Dear Jennifer,

So, do we have a go at a courageous conversation? I don't know, but if I had any hesitation, it would not be because of what the world or public square might think.

Before I explain and as a housekeeping matter, I normally write under the pen name "W. F. Twyman, Jr." I do so for several reasons. First, I grew up in the South and developed an affinity for using initials when one meant business. I am a Southern writer in that regard. Second, I always use "Jr." because I am a Jr., and this separates me from my dad and me from my son. We recycle names in my family. The Jr. reminds me that I am merely the latest link of a chain of men with my family name dating back to August 24, 1893, when my Great Uncle Winkfield Twyman was born. Names matter. We do not use Scrabble pieces for names in my family.

Moving beyond names to your sincere anxiety about where to start . . . how would you start a discussion with anyone? If you met someone on the bus or at the bookstore or in the checkout line at the grocery store, how would you start a conversation? Maybe you're overthinking a simple task made *writ large* due to fear about race.

It is okay to accept a conversation with hesitation as long as your reasons for said hesitation are well-reasoned and conveyed in a spirit of understanding and truth-finding. I really think that is all we can expect of anyone in a conversation. I certainly agree that certain slogan words are used to silence conversation, but I have zero interest in that type of correspondence. I suspect you feel the same. It is interesting that I do not think in these terms of hesitation. Perhaps my desire for authenticity and animus against falsehoods in the public square steels my resolve to write.

I appreciate your empathy. It is interesting that, as you show your empathy, you reference not growing up in a black ghetto or having street experiences like Coates. The same goes for me, too, you know. I view black ghettos and the streets of Coates's prose as alien places. So, I should share your same difficulty in understanding these new slogan words, *non*? In your attempt to understand this trend, I was curious why you didn't try to put yourself in the shoes of upper-middle-class black families? Would you similarly have difficulty seeing the world from the perspective of a married black lawyer whose dad was a lawyer and mom was a dentist? Whose uncle was a lawyer, aunt was a doctor, and grandfather was a doctor? Why doesn't this slice of life come into your mind as you attempt to put yourself in another person's shoes? Asking for a friend.

And by the way, who wants a level playing field—at least in the broadest and strictest sense? We should try to lift people up, but there are more than 300 million Americans and 7 billion people on the planet. No two people are equal in every respect, so how could the playing field ever be equal for everyone? Some people are smart, and others are less intelligent. Some people are disciplined, and others are impulsive. Some people are conscientious, and others are devil-may-care in their lives.

There is already too much blaming and shirking of responsibility in the public square. I view this as almost a truism. It shouldn't require the courage of a Greek god to state the obvious. Maybe the inability to speak reality against the bullying force of theory and ideology is the deeper problem.

Are you today uncomfortable speaking your truths due to your experience with diversity training? Hmmm . . . There's an old song that goes "you can't please everyone, so you got to please yourself."* There's a lot of truth in that song. I grew up in a Southern suburb where I was almost always the only black kid in my class from third grade through my senior year in high school. I learned very quickly to know who I was and

---

* "Garden Party" by Ricky Nelson (1972).

what I thought. If the world accepted my opinions and thoughts, great. If not, I was still going to believe what I believed and voice my opinions. Isn't it odd that public school integration gave me the sense of self to be myself, but diversity training robbed you of your ability to be yourself in the public square? That is a ghastly outcome. Did it ever occur to you that the "people of all colors" who sought to create actual physical distance with you were schoolyard bullies? One doesn't engage bullies. One keeps one's distance from bullies. Maybe you should have been the one keeping your actual physical distance from bullies?

I will say writing is wonderful therapy. Any unresolved conflicts and wounds bullies inflicted upon you will excise themselves as you write more and more about race. I think so. This gives me hope and inspires me to accept your offer of a correspondence.

The world is full of damaged souls. If you decide to write, you have to accept that not everyone will accept what you say. And that is cool since everyone doesn't have to perceive life the same way. That's not your purpose for writing, is it? So, I hear your fear, and the best antidote to fear about risks is just writing through the fear. Maybe the whole world will not stop just because Jennifer from Austin, Texas, has an opinion. Suppose you wrote your opinion, and no one cared? Would your fears seem silly in retrospect?

You refer to me as a black American. That is not quite right. While it is true I was born and grew to adulthood as a black American, circumstances have caused me to retire from blackness. I now consider myself an American native to Virginia. We can talk about the reasons for my decision later in this correspondence, but simply put, outside forces have attempted to impose dogma on me as a black American. I reject any dogma all the time. Thus, blackness was no longer working for me as a self-concept. (See *Unlearning Race: Self Portrait in Black and White* by Thomas Chatterton Williams.)

So, to answer your question, I have no thoughts as a black American. As an American native to Virginia, I am as free to explore these issues publicly, just as you are. See how that works? The artist Adrian Piper and writer Thomas Chatterton Williams would be proud. How can I be cast as a race traitor if I have retired from blackness? I don't engage bullies in any event, so questions and concerns about name-calling don't register for me. That is a benefit of growing up as the only black kid in a Southern suburban class in the 1970s. I am resilient. I can think for myself. As for family and friends, there's nothing new to see here, I suspect. My views are known.

You ask, what if the world doesn't like what it sees? Been there, done that. I have been on a Black History Month panel with black professors at UC San Diego. I have expressed my dissident views and been ignored. I suspect being ignored is the easier path for those who don't dig what I write. Why engage me and my views? That would give me credibility. So, I really suspect silence will be a probable response more than criticism and a few harsh words on social media. I don't do Twitter since I already lean anxious in my genetic makeup.

You are correct about the bigger questions. We need to write because, if we are silent, others will weaponize words like *white privilege*, *white fragility*, and *white supremacy*. If that happens, we are all that much closer to struggle sessions like those witnessed in Communist China. Struggle sessions were not tea and crumpet affairs. That is my visceral fear—struggle sessions in corporate America and higher education.

If you're up for a courageous conversation, I'm up for a courageous conversation. I just wonder if you're overstating the courage to write.

We will see,

W. F. Twyman, Jr.
An American Native to Virginia

Letter 4

Dear W. F. Twyman, Jr.,

It must be nice to retire from race. Maybe I'll try it too! I think you make it sound too simple, though. Could it be your black *privilege* speaking? In our current cultural climate, where the pedagogy of racial essentialism has crept into so many of our institutions and even personal interactions, to retire from whiteness would likely be interpreted as hiding from history.

You asked why I mentioned Coates and the black ghetto and not an "average" black upper-middle-class family. When it comes to discussions about race in the public square, I think we tend to focus on the struggles of lower-income black populations. But you bring up a very interesting and revelatory point. Of the 40 million black individuals and experiences, how many see through the lens that Coates offers, and how many, instead, lean toward Thomas Chatterton Williams' point of view? Despite the fact that there are more black Americans total in the middle- and upper-income brackets than in the lower-income bracket, there's a tendency to focus on the ghetto as the "typical" black American experience. As you infer, that doesn't align with the reality of most black Americans. Why the need to lump black Americans into a singular experience of a race predestined to live out their lives according to Coates's ghetto illustration?

I think that is, in many ways, exactly the problem I have with the "diversity-training" view of the world. The blanket classifications not only needlessly pit races against each other but also steal agency from black Americans, casting them always as the *oppressed* underclass, with whites lumped together as the *oppressor* class.

I think distinguishing between equity and equality helps here. The word *equity* is a new slogan word that refers to equality of outcome. The real goal should be equality of opportunity—making sure all people have the same opportunity—and I do believe we still have a ways to go to realize this objective. However, like you, I don't believe we should strive for *equity*. That word smacks of the gray conformity of Marxism, which would repress our differences to banal homogeneity.

Let me tell you a story of *equity*. Back in the early 1990s, I was living in China. China had just begun to open up to the world, but the idea of the *iron rice bowl*, that is, that everyone had a social safety net and guaranteed wage whether they worked for it or not, was still very much a part of the Chinese mindset. I remember walking into stores ready to spend money. If I happened into the store around a clerk's lunch break, I was frequently greeted with a sneer. How dare I disrupt them? Many people remained complicit to the fact that their lives were predestined. No matter how hard you worked to excel and no matter what God-given gifts you might employ to achieve, your life resulted in the same drab existence of someone whose only ambition was a lifetime of work in a convenience store. Much like the gray conformity of the physical land- scape at the time—block buildings that had no character from the other block buildings up the street (beauty, character, and individuality were discouraged in Mao's China so that everyone was identified only by the collective proletarian vision)—people's lives were defined within this dullness. If they sold me my goods or not, they would go home with the same paycheck, and so ambition and plurality were effectively nullified, considered evil even. Why strive for anything but the bleak existence that defined Maoist China? Much of that attitude has changed now as China's economy is market-oriented, but this was *equity* in real life (or IRL, as we say on social media these days).

With all that said, I do think that an honest review of history is im- portant, and we should talk about slavery and the other horrors of histo- ry in our correspondence. However, does the constant focus on slavery re-create conditions for its revival in a postmodern slavery of the mind?

I hope in our correspondence you share more insight into your experience at UC San Diego. Do you think that you were ignored because you couldn't relate to the plight of many black Americans who are stuck in a cycle of poverty? Were you seen as an outlier and, therefore, not able to tackle some of these issues with the necessary empathy or understanding? What are your views on the history of slavery in America?

Warmly,

Jen

Letter 5

Dear Jen,

Back in February 2014, a good friend invited me to deliver a presentation as part of a Black History Month panel before a lunchtime gathering at UC San Diego. The general topic was "Fifty years ago, a landmark Civil Rights Act promised to transform America. The UC San Diego Library presents a scholarly panel discussion on the legacy of that act and the state of civil rights today." Three black UC San Diego professors served on the panel, and I was there in my capacity as a former law professor.

I argued that there were obvious gains under the 1964 Civil Rights Act, and we should be thankful for the better world we live in. I even compared the treatment of a black motorist in San Diego in the 1940s with the college road trip we took with our boys in 2013. I had no "Driving While Black" stories. I relayed stories of wonderful road trips to Stanford and Yale.*

---

* It is time for the college road trip. My eldest son is applying to college. I rent a car for the long trip up to the Bay Area and back. We pack snacks because we want to save money, not because of a Jim Crow world. We drive up the 5 through Orange County and Los Angeles. We got a late start, so we are traveling at night through Ventura County and on up the coast to Santa Barbara. I love Santa Barbara, but it is dark when we arrive. We check into this coastal motel and crash. The next morning, we check out the best breakfast place in Santa Barbara. While we are there, my eldest son meets Bruce of the Beach Boys. Bruce shares breakfast with us and urges my eldest son to apply to college in Australia. Very cool moment. We then hit the road and travel a long drive up to San Francisco and the University of San Francisco (USF). A black tour guide attempts to sell my son on USF. It is a beautiful city (spring of

The other black professors piled on me like a ton of bricks. How dare I share my pleasant reality as a black dad on the road with my kids? As my friend put it, she had "never seen a panel get quite so very animated, as generally most of the folks around here agree with one another." And that's the danger of the echo chamber in the Academy nowadays. I literally tried to engage my fellow panelists as they ran away from me in fear and horror.

I face radical politics at home, so I was aware that too many black people major in the minor. There are obvious gains under the 1964 Civil Rights Act, but for some reason, fear pervades black culture and consciousness. Small incidents are always blown out of proportion to scare black kids and adults too. I have no Driving While Black stories. I have several driving while stupid stories.

My friend "Julia" has a Driving While Black story I would like to share. One recent afternoon, I received a frantic text from Julia. She was distraught—"My employer is putting me on a 90 day performance im provement plan and suspending me for the Driving While Black thing."

What Driving While Black thing? A few months earlier, Julia had met with two African American members of the public as part of her job. The meeting was standard and unremarkable until, a few minutes into

---

2013). We then drive across the Golden Gate Bridge, frolic in Sausalito, and spend the night in Danville, one of the most affluent communities in the state. We stay at the Best Western Inn. My eldest son roams around town. He convinces me to have dinner at this vegan place. We do, and he concludes it is too hippie. We then cruise down to UC Berkeley, have lunch at this football-themed restaurant chosen by my son, and then it's off to Stanford. We eat dinner at this upscale restaurant that caters to venture capitalists and Silicon Valley types. The boys love the place. We get a late start going home, and I just can't make it back home to San Diego. We find some motel in the middle of nowhere and crash. We buy gas in Ventura County and eat fast food at McDonald's. Then we head home.

In the summer of 2013, my wife takes our three kids on a college road trip back east. They fly into a small town outside of Princeton, New Jersey, and stay with my wife's cousin, who has three beautiful biracial children. The next day, my wife takes our teenage boys to the Big City, Manhattan, to tour NYU and Columbia. The next day, they drive up to Yale to visit my wife's old college. My son, a Yale legacy, has an admissions committee interview. Then, it is on to suburban Maryland where my wife and the kids stay with my wife's sister, a Harvard College graduate, and her husband in an affluent suburb of D.C. The next day, my wife and kids are off to the University of Virginia in Charlottesville. They do fast food and eat at a nice soul food restaurant in Richmond, Virginia, chosen by my sister.

the conversation, the African American male said he was nervous about driving across the country due to a fear of Driving While Black. Julia thought that having such a fear in 2018 was over the top, and she said so not out of disdain but out of compassion. Julia had known struggle in her life and felt the Driving While Black fears were overblown. The guy should not feel more afraid than someone of any other race. The man was so fragile when confronted with reason that he filed a complaint against Julia with her employer. Now Julia's career is in jeopardy, and all because an irrational person had to be coddled.

You asked whether the panelists ignored and dismissed my experiences because I couldn't relate to the black plight of black Americans who are stuck in a cycle of poverty? I'm not sure I like the word "plight" as it denotes pity. One can have pity on individuals but not groups. Only a minority of black Americans are impoverished—25.1% of native black Americans and 11.8% of naturalized black Americans are stuck in poverty, to use your phrasing. So, we're talking about a minority of black Americans, not "many" black Americans, as that infers or implies a majority.

I don't think I was ignored or dismissed because I was seen as an outlier. We were all black professors, current or former. I was ignored and dismissed because my words did not subscribe to dogma. What is dogma? Any public discussion of the Black Experience is supposed to be about oppression and the downtrodden.* I don't do dogma or performance art. When I present about black history, I lean into authenticity and the things I have personal knowledge of. Why would I deny what I know as plain truth, that we are blessed to not give segregation in public accommodations a second thought? My co-panelists were closed-minded to the blessings of the Civil Rights Act of 1964. And so, they were caricatures—hear no blessing, see no blessing, speak no blessing. Dogma was their problem, not a lack of empathy on my part.†

---

* Public discussions would include, but not be limited to, lectures, panel appearances, public speeches and addresses, opinion pieces, editorial views, podcast utterances, books, diversity training participation, and social media statements. Consider the absence of viewpoint diversity on matters of race at any Ivy League institution.

† For those readers who do not understand my definition, I am defining "dogma" as an incontrovertible viewpoint that Blackness is Oppression. Blackness is being downtrodden. Nothing else matters.

Should I lie and say, "Yes, I have been pulled over for Driving While Black?" Is it better to lie so that one will be heard and embraced by fellow black professors? That is the question I put to you.

As for my views on the history of slavery in America, I tend to follow the evidence, question whether there are lingering effects of slavery today in the year 2019, and urge family and friends to let it go. There is a whole universe out there to engage and conquer that has nothing to do with American slavery from 1660, 1750, or 1860.

For a moment, let's talk about long-ago American slavery.

W. F. Twyman, Jr.

Letter 6

Dear Jen,

One day, six African girls from Africa arrived at the Georgia plantation of a wealthy planter. I know not the year nor the name of the planter or his plantation. The planter immediately placed the six girls under the direction of an overseer. Clear labor tasks were assigned to the overseer for delegation to the girls. The girls were to perform a certain amount of labor each day. If they fell short, they were to be punished with a specific number of lashes, flogged with a whip. In those days, a flogging meant being tied to a tree with your back bare or spread-eagled face down on the ground, with each limb tied to four stakes hammered into the earth. In addition to the flogging, an additional number of tasks would be added to the next day's work tasks. If the girls again fell short in completing tasks on the second day, they would be flogged an increased number of times and an additional number of tasks would be added to the third day's work tasks.

The overseer objected. He argued that the work tasks were unreasonable. The plantation owner swore back at the overseer. Either the girls shall do it, or they shall die.

The six girls were unable to accomplish the work tasks on their first workday. And for this failure, they received lashes from the whip. Their backs were raw from the whipping.

On the second day, the girls now had an increased number of tasks to perform. They had to complete the uncompleted work from the first day plus new work tasks for the second workday. The girls worked diligently, but their hands were unaccustomed to the work and their backs were in pain. They failed to complete their tasks on the second day. As instructed, the overseer flogged them each more than the previous day. The girls limped back to their slave cabins, knowing they had an even greater number of work tasks to perform on the third day.

That night, the girls despaired. They had no hope of completing all the accumulated unfinished tasks from days 1 and 2, plus the new assigned tasks for day 3. And they knew they faced an ever-greater number of lashes if they failed on day 3. Death was certain.

To escape this cruelty, the girls decided to hang themselves from a tree. Plans were made.

The next morning when the horn sounded for work, the six African girls were discovered to be missing. A quick search was made. All six were found hanging from a tree.

The cruel master was enraged.

He tried to bring them back to life. He tried and tried, so that he might lash them even more!

All his efforts were in vain. The girls escaped the cruel master in death.

The master ordered a hole to be dug in the ground. The girls were cut down and thrown into the hole like animal carcasses while the master swore and cursed.

This is one moment from thousands out of American slavery. One can never make these girls whole for what they suffered in this world.

Do we cheapen their memory as we talk about reparations and American slavery in the same breath? These are my visceral views on the history of slavery in America.

Sincerely,

W.F. Twyman, Jr.

Letter 7

Dear W. F. Twyman, Jr.,

Like you, I've read Theodore Weld's *American Slavery as It Is*. Weld doesn't give the history of the six African girls as you do here, but he does share plenty of horrors outlining similar brutality.* As I learned in reading Weld's copious accounts of slavery, African slaves were considered to be not only property but also less than human—even less than animals. Indeed, often slaves were treated worse than the slaveholder's beasts. Rarely do you hear of a slaveholder, or anyone else for that matter, without a serious mental illness who whipped their horses or oxen with the brutality that the slaves endured.

We also know that slavery dates all the way back to biblical times and beyond. By no means did it originate in America in the 1600s; it has a much longer global history. I recently learned that one of the first slave owners in America was a black man by the name of Anthony Johnson. What is particularly interesting is the history of how that came to be.

The African slave trade to the "New World" developed as distinct from previous eras of slavery. Prior to the slavery that mars our country's history, such enforced servitude was typically the result of war and conquests, with the ultimate goal of completely annihilating competing groups. In essence, slavery, especially in Africa, was a form of genocide. It wasn't until the introduction of deep-water navigation, when ships and

---

* For more about the six African girls, see Rev. John Rankin, *Letters on American Slavery* (Boston: Isaac Knap, 1838), 49–51.

navigation were robust enough to conquer the open waters of the oceans and seas, that slavery was introduced as a commercial concept. The Spanish headed west, and the stories of the enslavement of native inhabitants of the New World are barbaric. The Portuguese headed south landing in West Africa, which before deep-water navigation was a no-man's-land (it was called the "Dark Continent" because of its mysteries—not because of the dominant skin color there). There, the Portuguese were able to negotiate with African kings, who engaged in their own wartime slavery, to trade their conquered enemies for European goods. The Portuguese were able to use slave labor to increase their global footprint, and the African kings were able to use European weaponry to similarly fortify and grow their domains. This commercial venture became increasingly attractive, and the slavery of Africans, as we know it, was born.*

The Portuguese dominated the slave trade for about three centuries before England came along and displaced them, redirecting this commercial venture to their own empire, including America. As with the Portuguese, the expanding slave trade was a commercial enterprise and slaves were considered property, promoting their dehumanization. What happened between 1621, when Anthony Johnson, a native of Angola, made his living on English colonial soil first as an indentured servant and later as a free black property owner, and March 8, 1655, when a Virginia colonial court ruled that black indentured servant John Casar was bound to Johnson for life? Why did the colonial courts suddenly decide to use skin color as the determining factor that turned indentured servants into slaves? Why did the English indentured servants not meet a similar fate?

I guess there are several possible reasons. English indentured servants were still protected under the English Crown and eventually given their freedom. African servants were originally given these same rights but ultimately may not have had the same protections as English citizenry. Add to this, the English traditionally thought they had the right to enslave non-Christians, and presumably many Africans fell into this

* There are many reports of African kings involved in the slave trade. For a brief summary, see the section on slavery in "The Story of Africa," BBC, www.bbc.co.uk/worldservice/africa/features/storyofafrica/9chapter2.shtml. See also the story of the wealthy Nigerian slave trader Nwaubani Ogogo in Adaobi Tricia Nwaubani, "My Great Grandfather, the Nigerian Slave Trader," *New Yorker*, July 15, 2018.

category. And then, of course, slavery was simply more profitable than relying on indentured servants who were fed, housed, and typically given "freedom dues" that included land. With the proliferation of the African slave trade and the legalization of slavery, the easy identifiability of Africans over English indentured servants helped to cement a slavery based on immutable characteristics, giving rise to ever-greater levels of prejudice and bigotry.

Earlier forms of slavery, including slavery within Africa, were not based on color but more on conquest. We know that the prejudice and bigotry toward black slaves in America, as witnessed in your story of the six African girls, was so ruthless that death was often preferable to the whip. There is also the story of the pregnant fugitive slave Margaret Gardner, her husband Robert Gardner, and her four children, who were surrounded in a house on the banks of the Ohio River. As slave catchers approached their targets, Margaret killed her two-year-old daughter, Mary, with a butcher's knife and prepared to kill her other children before she was subdued. The light-skinned Mary was the daughter of Margaret's slave owner, who wept inconsolably over the dead body of his daughter.

Abolitionists like Theodore Weld, Rev. John Rankin, and others were often moved by a Christian morality that recoiled at the inhumanity of slavery. As we learn from Weld, so many slaveholders saw themselves as truly Christian (indeed, many slaveholders belonged to or were even leaders in the church), yet they were unable to grasp the immorality of their actions as, over the centuries, they became fully inured to the idea that slaves as property possessed no humanity.* As Weld's wife and fellow abolitionist, Angela Grimké Weld, lamented, "One who is a slaveholder at heart never recognizes a human being in a slave."†And yet, Weld himself does a good job of dismissing the slaveholder's ignorance when he says,

---

* There are many examples of slave owners in the ministry, including notable figures like Jonathan Edwards, Sr., the third president of Princeton. For more on the church and slavery, see James Gillespie Birney, *The American Churches, The Bulwarks of American Slavery* (Newburyport: Charles Whipple 1842), utc.iath.virginia.edu/christn/chesjgbat.html.

† As quoted in Theodore Weld, *American Slavery as It Is: Testimony of a Thousand Witnesses* (New York: American Anti-Slavery Society, 1839), 57.

There is not a man on earth who does not believe that slavery is a curse. . . . Whoever denies this, his lips libel his heart. Try him. . . . Give him an hour to prepare his wife and children for a life of slavery. Bid him make haste and get ready their necks for the yoke, and their wrists for the coffle chains, then look at his pale lips and trembling knees, and you have *nature's* testimony against slavery.*

Despite "nature's testimony," slaveholders remained convinced that slaves were property and could not see the humanity in chattel. The angry reaction of the slaveholder in the story of the six African girls who had the audacity to choose death further illustrates the deep level of dehumanization in American slavery. Their choice to assert their humanity even through death was something incomprehensible to this slaveholder.

You touch on one story in American slavery to illustrate the cruelty. In addition to the whippings, some slaveholders would literally pour salt in the wounds. Salt, pepper, and vinegar, what was called in those days "negro plaster," was frequently used to increase the suffering. Whether arbitrary punishment or punishment for work undone, the physical chastisement was not only administered to break wills but also to induce a lingering suffering.

The most astounding story I found in Weld's accounts, which underlines the cruelty of American slavery, was the slaveholder who took an offending slave named George and gathered the rest of the slaves to witness his punishment. Laying the slave on a plank, the slaveholder built a fire at the base of the plank. With everyone looking on, he chopped off the slave's feet and fed them to the fire. He carried on moving up from the feet until the entire body was fed to the fire, piece by piece, all while the slave begged for mercy. This cruel master was a nephew of President Thomas Jefferson.†

If only this slave could have hanged himself like the six African girls. He was not even allowed that dignity. He never even had a chance to make a horrific choice, like the one Margaret made for her daughter Mary.‡

---

* Ibid., vii.

† Rankin, *Letters on American Slavery*, 62–64.

‡ In addition to killing her daughter Mary, Margaret Gardner at a later point threw another daughter into the river and rejoiced upon learning her daughter had drowned. Her daughter

I think what may amaze me more than the cruelty itself is how the slaves found ways to survive and even push back in small ways that slowly became revolutionary. As Eugene D. Genovese writes in *Roll, Jordan, Roll: The World the Slaves Made,*

> Many years of studying the astonishing effort of black people to live decently as human beings even in slavery has convinced me that no theoretical advance suggested in their experience could ever deserve as much attention as that demanded by their demonstration of the beauty and power of the human spirit under conditions of extreme oppression.*

So, you ask, "Do we cheapen the memory of six African girls as we talk about reparations and American slavery in the same breath?" What an interesting question. I'm not sure I'm fully grasping the thrust of your question, but I will try to give you some thoughts in an attempt at an answer.

These six girls and the countless others who suffered from slavery still live on in the communal history and mindset of Americans today. Almost all black Americans who have not newly immigrated will be able to tell stories of great-great-grandparents who suffered the dehumanizing cruelty of slavery's past. Some families remain crippled from these stories and still carry with them these lessons of inequality. Others have refused to accept the history of inequality and have fought tooth and nail to recapture the deserved dignity of the human spirit. I see in your question two truths.

First, we must never forget the past. Unlike the slaveholders who were able to find immunity from their sins secure in the idea that slaves were not human but chattel, we must never allow such complicity to erase the crimes of our history. We should not ignore or erase history, lest we forget.

Second, we must also remember and exalt the power of the human spirit to overcome. Of course, this is not to dismiss inequalities that continue into the present, but to say that we should simultaneously fight them while also encouraging a strength that lifts not only the black com-

---

was free at last from American slavery.

* From the preface of Eugene D. Genovese, *Roll, Jordan, Roll: The World the Slaves Made* (New York: Vintage Books, 1974).

munity but also an overall American identity. The beauty and strength in our American identity come not only from our diversity but also in the stories of those, especially black Americans, who encapsulate the human spirit in the face of brutality.

So, in sum, I guess what I'm saying is that these two truths need to be the foundation of reparations. The financial reparations that dominate the current political discourse discredit our history. They are sloppy and threaten the rise of new inequalities and divisions. The necessary reparations are an acknowledgment of a painful past with the introduction of a variety of lessons that explore all dimensions of American history from different perspectives, encouraging critical thinking. This is not to promote the indoctrination that now dominates a lot of the *diversity, equity, and inclusion* ideology and pedagogy. It certainly doesn't include the racial essentialism that has led to a neo-segregation in the classroom.[*] It does, however, include reading books like Isabel Wilkerson's *Caste*, perhaps alongside Wilfred Reilly's *Taboo* (of course in an age-appropriate classroom), and encouraging good-faith discussion and open inquiry in a space that allows discourse and constructive disagreement.

It is this juxtaposition of resources that will give our kids the necessary skills to address our checkered past with a healthy dose of inspiration to guide them into the future—and, ultimately, allow us to create a new American identity, together.

Warmly,

Jen

P.S. Would you like for me to call you W. F. Twyman, Jr., or do you prefer another name?

---

* See Antonio Planas, "Atlanta Mom Files Complaint Alleging Daughter's Grade School Segregated Black Students," *NBC News,* August 11, 2021, www.nbcnews.com/news/us-news/atlanta-mom-files-complaint-alleging-daughter-s-grade-school-segregated-n1276584; April Corbin Girnus, "Las Vegas Charter School Sued for Curriculum Covering Race, Identity," *Nevada Current,* January 21, 2021, www.nevadacurrent.com/2021/01/21/las-vegas-charter-school-sued-for-curriculum-covering-race-identity/; and the *Hold my Drink Podcast* (now called the *Counterweight Podcast*), especially episode 47 with Bonnie Snyder, episode 46 with Jon O'Brien, episode 42 with Lyell Asher, and episode 38 with Gabs Clark, podcasts.apple.com/us/podcast/hold-my-drink/id1537516628.

Letter 8

Hi Jen,

You can call me "Wink." I tried to imagine continuing this series of letters as "W. F. Twyman, Jr.," but that seemed too stilted over the long haul. So, Wink is fine.

Like William Leftwich, a fellow native of Virginia who wrote an account in *American Slavery as It Is,* despaired, "my soul sickens at the remembrance of these things." Remembrance is the only way, however, to acknowledge unspeakable horrors and brutality. Past suffering must be used for the benefit of others, a way station on the way to healing and a better tomorrow. I suspect many who beat the drums the loudest about reparations for American slavery and "Blaming the Man" have never read *American Slavery as It Is* from cover to cover. Unprocessed pain festers and corrupts quality interaction across the color line.

I'm not sure you have answered my question to my satisfaction. Life is priceless. One cannot set a price on its worth. Similarly, some deaths are gentle ripples, like the ninety-year-old great-grandmother who passed away after a long, good life. Other deaths so offend the human spirit that they continue to jar the conscience centuries later, such as the horrific murder of George the slave at the hand of Thomas Jefferson's nephew or the despair of six African girls on the morning of their third day in America.

One can never set a price on what was done to George and the six African girls and how their horror rippled through the slave cabins. So, shouldn't it be made clear and understood that some things are beyond the healing balm of reparations, financial or nonfinancial? It seems like some acts are beyond the human capacity to make right. We are just stuck with the past and must make our peace with George and the six African girls for our own mental health in the here and now.

Do you really think *"almost all black Americans . . . will be able to tell stories of great-great-grandparents who suffered the dehumanizing cruelty of slavery's past?"* How many black Americans have shared with you stories of great-great-grandparents and cruelties from the slave past? I would wager the number is low. I don't know any oral stories of cruelties from the slave past. Here is the only slave story I know from a member of my family: I once asked my grandmother, Rosa Nell Brown Twyman Jackson (1897–1983), about her paternal grandfather, Daniel Brown (1833–1885). The only story grandma could tell me was that her grandfather would open and close the gate and sweep flies away from the master's plate. That's it. No floggings. No extracted front teeth. No malnutrition or starvation or inadequate clothing in the wintertime. Now, there was a written family history that expanded upon his slave history. It included a detailed account of a poker game in which Daniel Brown's slave mother was acquired as a "bed warmer" and related that she never married. But that's it.

I think our family is typical. Do you have proof or evidence to show almost all black Americans can tell stories of cruelty from the slave past? I suspect those stories are not always there or remembered, but I could be wrong.

Ninety-nine percent of my knowledge about American slavery has come from reading books, the same way you have acquired knowledge about it.

Exactly how are some families crippled by these stories of slave cruelty? In what way? Which families? I'm curious since if the family oral history isn't there, why would families be crippled?

Isn't it possible to both accept the history of inequality *and* fight tooth and nail to recapture the deserved dignity of the human spirit? One doesn't negate the other, you know. Life is nuanced and complex.

Can you expand upon your thought on nonfinancial reparations for American slavery? What do you have in mind? I think this is probably a good idea, but I'm not sure reparations is the right word. Nor does *diversity, inclusion, and equity* fit the bill. Maybe the idea is that we're all one—that there's a unity in the American Experience which we possess. Eugene Genovese talks about this unity when he argues that one shouldn't understand the slave without understanding the slave owner—and vice versa.

Warmly,

Wink

Letter 9

Dear Jen,

It is a blessing to be free of a burdensome legacy!

In my last letter, I pressed back on the idea that the legacy of American slavery has trickled down as a shibboleth crippling the soul and spirit of black Americans from birth. That didn't ring true to me in this sense—I first learned about American slavery in my Virginia History class in the fourth grade. Before the fourth grade, I was unaware of American slavery. Neither my parents nor grandma nor uncles nor aunts talked about American slavery. They talked about other things, such as desegregation, busing, and black flight but not bondage from a century or more ago. If something could have crippled my spirit, it would have been treatment at the hands of prejudiced white students in 1969, not American slavery from 1655 or 1769 or 1865. This was my lived experience. As always, I can't speak for over 40 million black Americans.

I often wonder if learning about American slavery sets the young psyche on a bad path. Do constant reminders of American slavery sever black culture and consciousness from the rest of American culture and consciousness?

Because hard questions demand hard answers, this is my best way of thinking about the problem of remembering slavery. I don't claim my thought is perfect since we're dealing with human motivations and drives, not robots.

Some say we should never forget American slavery. We should return to the well of pain and torture generation after generation. Never forget. Others might suggest that it is best to not think or dwell on such things. What is in the past should remain in the past.

As with all things, Jen, the truth lies in between.

Why can't the past of American slavery serve as rocket fuel for black achievement going forward? As I write these words, I'm listening to an old gospel singer, Rev. James Cleveland. My mom loved Rev. Cleveland because he sang with a stirring soul, unforgettable emotion, and passion rooted in the black experience. He sings about pitfalls in life and how our ancestors never felt tired in the face of adversity. To paraphrase: "We have all come too far from where we started. (And we all started from the slave cabins.) No one told us the road would be easy. And we don't believe the Lord would bring us this far to leave us." These are the spirituals and messages that caused my mom to burst out in song around the house.

Why couldn't American slavery be perceived as fuel, motivation for a drive to overachieve as a way of honoring our slave ancestors? I suggest that, if we are going to talk about American slavery today, let's talk about American slavery as a reason for having something to prove, a drive to succeed. Drive caused former slaves to acquire hundreds of acres of land for their families after the Civil War. Drive caused a former slave to run for Congress one day and another former slave to write fourteen books and create the Tuskegee Institute. I say the insult of American slavery should be weaponized into a drive to succeed.

Consider that the black descendants of American slavery live psychologically apart from their fellow countrymen. The struggle for acceptance coexists uneasily with avoidance of the mainstream. How else can Historically Black Colleges and Universities make sense today? Black Americans are always aware of a desire to prove themselves, more so if they know their credentials might not be as strong as those of white colleagues in the academy and the workplace. To borrow from something I once heard in the Jewish context, people don't dislike being black. Rather, they dislike being disliked for being black. If we assume a long history of oppression, why shouldn't that oppression coupled with an enduring ability to survive translate into a "restless optimism." Logically, shouldn't blacks have the greatest need for achievement on the planet like other descendants of slaves from long ago, the Jews?*

If American slavery can be perceived as rocket fuel for a burning hunger for achievement, then remembrance of slavery in 2023 can be turned into a positive good. Let's remember slavery. But let's also teach that black Americans have a duty to achieve because they have infinitely more opportunities than their slave ancestors. Let's remember the slave children sold away from slave mothers, internalize that image, and set the world on fire with long-range plans. Work harder than the guy next to us in college, and work harder than the woman in the workplace for tangible and intangible rewards. Celebrate Juneteenth if one must but be the first one to arrive at the library in the morning and the last one to leave the library at night. Be driven! Believe in one's self-determination! Make these the legacies of American slavery.

Mindset is all important, especially for a person driven to prove something. Shouldn't black people be more driven to prove their mettle than any other group in this country?

You write, "we must never forget the past." Who wants to forget the past? Who can forget the past? It is impossible to forget the past in a place like Richmond, Virginia. Are the United Daughters of the Confederacy a force for good in your view? They do not forget the past, right? If we remove Confederate statues from Monument Avenue in Richmond, aren't we forgetting the past? Is the removal of the Confederate general atop a horse forgetting the past? Why or why not?

Life goes on,

Wink

---

* See Steven Silbiger, *The Jewish Phenomenon: Seven Keys to the Enduring Wealth of a People* (Atlanta: Longstreet Press, 2000), 192–195.

Letter 10

Dear Wink,

Let me first respond to your question on reparations. I think we are of the same mind here—some things are beyond repair insofar as you cannot put a price tag on a life. Reparations, instead, would be whatever structures or resources, namely, better resources in educational institutions, are needed to fulfill your dream of slavery being fuel for achievement. Of course, as already noted, the majority of black Americans aren't living in poverty and may already have access to adequate resources. Where there is disparity, such as between suburban schools and inner-city schools, I am in favor of introducing programs that give children from lower-income households and communities better resources, be it more books or more extracurricular and after-school programs. Even when such resources are available, we need parents who push their kids toward these opportunities, and perhaps that would mean additional programs that provide parents with the means to get involved, especially those whose employment situation restricts their ability to consistently engage. I'm not exactly sure what this would entail. I think it would have to be assessed on a community-by-community basis, but perhaps more frequent school transportation for their children so that the children can be involved in a variety of programs without relying on their parents to take off work to taxi them here and there. I interviewed David Ben Moshe, who told me that his parents used to rent tapes from the public library so when they couldn't be at home, he could listen to someone reading to him. He credits his parents' determination as a primary influence in his drive to succeed, even when he found himself making poor decisions on the street.* We can't re-create this determination, but with more access to similar resources, perhaps we can encourage it.

There are many instances of black excellence, even during times of sanctioned bigotry and few resources. I recently read about the Rosenwald schools, which were the brainchild of Booker T. Washington and Jewish philanthropist Julius Rosenwald. While Rosenwald provided some of the financial backing, these were community schools that received a majority of their funding from within the community and where teachers were part of the community.† Both the late civil rights fighter and Congressman John Lewis and the beloved late poet Maya Angelou went to Rosenwald schools. Re-creating these community initiatives throughout the country, not just in majority black communities, would not only provide a form of reparations, but also initiate a much-needed renaissance of our educational institutions.

In many ways, reparations culminated in the Civil Rights Movement, which began to dismantle the institutions and infrastructures that were designed to keep black Americans confined to a second-class citizenship. To the extent that there remain discriminatory policies, further reparations would be necessary. Interestingly, the new insistence on ideological indoctrination in many K–12 institutions, despite people's best intentions, is the antithesis of reparations and has created a victim mindset that supports rather than breaks the cycle of poverty. This fuels the flames of resentment and not the fire to succeed that you mention. One may say this is the new discrimination.

So, what would reparations look like? We are so focused on *equity* and *affirmative action* that in today's institutions of education and in the workplace, if two people—one black and one white—with similar skills and background were vying for the same position, I think it would be a hard case to prove discrimination against black Americans. In fact,

* You can hear more of David Ben Moshe's story in the *Hold my Drink Podcast,* episode 39, "From Incarceration to Emancipation," podcasts.apple.com/us/podcast/episode-39-from-incarceration-to-emancipation-david/id1537516628?i=1000529659638.

† Robert Woodson, "The Lessons We Still Haven't Learned from the Rosenwald Schools," *Hill,* October 4, 2021, thehill.com/opinion/civil-rights/574579-the-lessons-we-still-havent-learned-from-the-rosenwald-schools/.

in some cases, in the effort to "level the playing field," black candidates will receive preference. However, I go back to resources in lower-income schools to ensure that everyone has the same starting place. Whether or not they choose to line up, or parents even bring them to the race, is an individual matter. Is this reparation? Maybe, but not necessarily. Resources are not racial but economic. And even were we to find the solution to educational resources, would it change the landscape? Yes, if there was a correlation between resources and personal ambition. Do you know of any such study? Is there a correlation between slavery and the fuel for achievement you mention?

I like your own personal mindset and drive for achievement. I see so much strength and resilience in the black American experience. That is my America. That is why I fly the flag—to represent all the struggles—from the American Revolution to the Civil War to the Civil Rights Movement and beyond—and to expand the ideas of equality, liberty, and freedom *for all*. And so, perhaps, reparations would include promoting these stories of strength, especially for young children who need positive role models.

Instead, it seems that the entire conversation around reparations has stalled meaningful progress due to the conversation's focus on blame.* Instead of *black strength*, we've focused on *white fragility*. We've opted for segregation and division. We've exchanged the opportunity to lift up black achievement for the chance to devalue anything perceived to be the domain of white people or Enlightenment values, including math, science, grammar, and even time, which apparently are all "white" (scratching my head here . . .). Meanwhile, black children continue to score lower than their white counterparts in tests on fundamental subjects. Figuring out how to change these statistics has lost its importance in the cacophony. These symbolic battles may provide a salve in a temporary comeuppance, but we are losing the war. We collect our social media medals in our virtue-signaling skirmishes, and our children are the collateral damage.

You disagreed with my idea that families have been crippled from slavery. And, I must admit I don't have any black friends who have shared

---

* Shelby Steele makes a similar point. For more, see Tunku Varadarjan, "How Equality Lost to 'Equity,'" *Wall Street Journal*, February 12, 2021, www.wsj.com/articles/how-equality-lost-to-equity-11613155938.

stories of slavery, save one, and that story is one of strength and pride. My father's best friend was one of the first black cadets in the Air Force Academy—Ike Payne. They called him one of the "Trailblazers." Ike told my father the story of how his family escaped slavery to live with the Seminole Indians. That's it. It is a story that my father says Ike would tell with honor. Perhaps it is this story that served as one of the reasons that he was personally compelled to follow the prescription you propose. Perhaps he took that strength and resilience passed down to him through this story to become one of the first black Air Force test pilots.

As I think on this and digest your proposal, I wonder if what is "crippling" black America is not the legacy of slavery but these new ideologies that have consumed our public dialogue. When we discuss reparations, are we saying—we can put a price on your life? Are we saying, similar to the days when slavery was "real," that you are merely property, and property can be bought and sold? Maybe in this new discourse, we have re-created a slavery of sorts. *American Slavery as It Is*, version 2.0.

None of this is to say that where discrimination exists, we shouldn't stand against it. Prejudice and bigotry are the mainstays of all cultures across the world. It is human nature, regardless of skin color. Dreams of a Marxist utopia are what bolster much of the new ideology we are discussing, stripping us of our individuality and resigning us to group labels and a new form of segregation. We must examine the ways we are fighting discrimination. Good intentions with unintended consequences can sometimes do more harm than good.

Hope, which I think is related to upward mobility, is very evident in the black immigrant experience. By most statistics, black immigrants fare better in the United States than native-born black Americans. For example, a 2015 wealth survey in Boston showed that the median black American household there had only $8 of wealth, whereas the median black immigrant family from the Caribbean had $12,000 in wealth.[*] Thomas Sowell has cited similar numbers, highlighting how black West Indian families earn over 58 percent more than native black American families.

Even though slavery underlines the history of both groups, we could argue that cultural differences or other local sociological factors may ac-

[*] Coleman Hughes, "Black American Culture and the Racial Wealth Gap," *Quillette,* July 19, 2018, quillette.com/2018/07/19/black-american-culture-and-the-racial-wealth-gap/.

count for some of this gap, but I think it has more to do with the fact that immigrants are a self-selected group who positively elect to undergo a transformational process. When a black immigrant comes to America, even if they have experienced prejudice and faced discrimination based on color, there is likely something in the immigration process itself that changes their outlook and, therefore, their futures. This may be as simple as a sense of hope. Hope fuels achievement. Most immigrants come here with hope—whether it's simply hope for a better job, or the hope to escape violent oppression. This attitude of hope is perhaps the distinguishing factor between the life experiences of black and other immigrants and native black Americans. However, stories of hope and strength and resilience in black America abound. We bury them with stories of disempowerment and learned helplessness.

Speaking of learned helplessness, is *affirmative action* an appropriate vehicle for reparations? I'm not sure that it is. Perhaps it made sense at the height of the Civil Rights Movement when institutions still actively held black Americans down. However, policies today that attempt to atone for past sins by helping black people get a leg up suggest that black people cannot achieve without help. I don't believe that is true, and it smacks of pretension. It is perhaps even the most insidious form of *racism*. Authors like John McWhorter have said as much: "I know of no more vivid hypocrisy on part of those who style themselves black people's fellow travelers than to earnestly dismiss claims that black people's average IQ is lower than other peoples' while in the same breath nodding vigorously that a humane society must not subject the same people to challenging tests."[*]

We need to empower, not emasculate.

Jen

---

[*] John McWhorter, "Affirming Disadvantage," *American Interest,* June 28, 2018, www.the-american-interest.com/2018/06/28/affirming-disadvantage/.

Letter 11

Dear Jen,

I view IQ through the lens of the individual, not some collective group average. We live our lives within five to ten family members, not tens or hundreds or millions of random people. My Aunt Amy was recognized as a math genius in grade school. My wife's cousin David corresponded with Albert Einstein and entered Harvard in the pre–Civil Rights days. One of my sons scored one of the top 20 math scores in California on a national/international math test while in elementary school. So, references to IQ scores and group averages leave me flat. How do exceptionally gifted and talented/genius black people feel when they read about their racial group bringing up the rear on IQ test scores? Just more alienation from the racial discourse. Monstrous alienation.

Moving on . . . You wrote, "When a black immigrant comes to America, even if they have experienced prejudice and faced discrimination based on color, there is likely something in the immigration process itself that changes their outlook and, therefore, their futures. This may be as simple as a sense of hope." Let me tell you some stories of hope.

The first black lawyer in the United States, Macon B. Allen, was born in Indiana but made his professional mark in Maine, Massachusetts, South Carolina, and Washington, D.C. The second black lawyer, Robert Morris, Sr., was born in Salem, Massachusetts, but made his career mark in Boston. The third black lawyer, George Boyer Vashon, was born in Pittsburgh but made his mark in Washington, D.C. The fourth black lawyer, John Mercer Langston, was born in Louisa County, Virginia, but made his mark in Oberlin, Ohio, and Washington, D.C. Attorney and Doctor John S. Rock was born in Salem, New Jersey, but made his mark in Boston.

It seems that your argument about immigrant hope equally applies to native black Americans who move in search of greater opportunity. You should recognize the long tradition of native-born black Americans who moved with hope in search of greater opportunity. Hope is not limited to immigrant black people!

You should know about Rev. Lemuel Haynes, who was born in West Hartford, Connecticut, but who moved in hope to Rutland, Vermont, where he left his career mark. You should be aware of Alexander Twilight, who was born in Bradford, Vermont, but who made a name for himself in Brownington, Vermont. Surely, you must have known that Booker T. Washington entered this world near Hale's Ford, Virginia, but that he rose to the pinnacle of success in Tuskegee, Alabama. Washington's archrival, W. E. B. DuBois, was born in Great Barrington, Massachusetts, but he moved in hope to Cambridge, Massachusetts, for his higher education and then to Germany for further advanced studies before finally settling in at Atlanta University, where he left his legacy as a professor.

To paraphrase the 1619 Project, why can't we teach the black American search for greater opportunity in our schools and classrooms?

Wink

Letter 12

Dear Jen,

When I think of my ancestral connection to American slavery, I think of my family's founding father, Daniel Brown. Daniel Brown was born in 1833 in Charlotte County, Virginia. He died on March 4, 1885, in Manchester, Chesterfield County, Virginia, at the age of fifty-two.

In the courthouse in Charlotte County, Virginia, there is a bill of sale stating that in August 1813, a farmer named John Hamblin sold all his possessions to a set of (white) brothers named Herbert and Daniel Brown (1783–after 1860). This was done to settle a gambling debt of $3,000. The goods were divided among the brothers. Daniel received the slaves and furniture, and Herbert received everything else. One of the slaves was a mother named Phyllis.* She never married, but five of the slaves were her children: Permelia, Delila, Ebony, Bolling, and Robert. Phyllis was very pretty and light in complexion, and as a result of this, she was often used as a "bed warmer." Daniel, the slave owner and recipient of Phyllis, wasn't any different from Hamblin. Daniel, too, found favor in Phyllis and infringed on her body at his convenience.

Phyllis became pregnant by her new slave owner and bore a son. She named him Daniel Brown after his father/slave owner. He was called "Little Daniel Brown." Daniel was even lighter in complexion than his mother and could have passed for white. At a very early age, Little Daniel

---

* Although the indenture from 1813 granting a property interest to Daniel Brown names the mother as "Phillis," family lore and memory tell us her name was "Phyllis."

was moved into the "Big House." One of the chores that he performed as a young boy was to fan flies off his father/slave owner's family while they had their meals. At the age of twelve, Little Daniel was appointed overseer of the other slaves. A few years later, Little Daniel took on a full-blooded Cherokee woman as his bride. Her name was Sally Anne Giles. They both were very young. According to family oral history and more recent genealogical research, this union produced seventeen children, five of whom were born in Charlotte County, Virginia: Benjamin, Eliza, Emma J., Goodrich R., and Hatty.

All of this was around the time Black Moses (Harriet Tubman) was making a name for herself, helping slaves escape all over the South. The elder Daniel heard the whispers and the slave songs in the fields. To eliminate the possibility of losing his son, he called Little Daniel into the Big House and made him an offer of a large tract of land and a large sum of money if he stayed on the plantation. The same tract of land today would be equivalent in size to an entire town. Daniel accepted this offer from his father/slave owner.

Shortly after Little Daniel's decision to take the offer, Big Daniel died.

Little Daniel and his family took the money and left, abandoning the land knowing the town would never accept him owning the plantation. They boarded a train and headed for Richmond, Virginia. He ran into many obstacles and had to try several locations before finding a place where they could settle down along the waterfront. He started farming, knowing that in order to be recognized, he had to own land. That grubstake was his collateral as he started buying property. When he stopped purchasing property, he owned over four hundred acres of land. This development included a church, school, and a couple hundred acres of farmland.

The names of his other children were Anna, Cora, Daniel Webster, Edward, Harriet, Joseph, Martha Jane, Mason, Richard, Robert Daniel, Theodore, and William Issac. Four of his children are known to have passed for white, thus possibly giving birth to branches of the family unaware of their high-achieving ancestor. At least two of his children died in infancy.[*]

Only pneumonia at the age of fifty-two would lay to eternal rest this

---

[*] See appendix V.

great spirit. "And one day, they will come back here, on the railroad and the steamboat, and say, 'This one little spot shall not be touched—this hovel shall be sacred—for here our father and our mother suffered for us, thought for us, laid the foundations of our future as solid as the hills!'"*

Sincerely,

Wink

---

* Mark Twain, *The Gilded Age* (Hartford: American Publishing Co., 1873).

Letter 13

Wink,

Do you think Daniel Brown's experience with slavery shaped a certain mindset for you in particular? As you've already noted, there are over 40,000,000 black Americans and over 40,000,000 distinct histories. How did your history shape you?

I think the problem I am having right now is that many are trying to group these histories into a singular story, and too often, it is one of *oppression*. Rarely do you hear the stories of Daniel Brown. Rather, we are consumed with stories from writers like Ta-Nehisi Coates who exclaim that the whole of America is set out to destroy "black bodies."[*]

The *New York Times'* 1619 Project, which has been made into a curriculum by the Pulitzer Center, offers a deep dive into the history of slavery in America. I appreciate a quote that buttresses the series: "Our democracy's founding ideals were false when they were written. Black Americans have fought to make them true."

But I would argue that the ideals weren't false; they just weren't applied to all. Working toward equality and enforcing that equality through these ideals is an important goal for me. I believe in the ideals of our Founding Fathers—for everyone.

The problem with such initiatives is that everything is boiled down to race. We review and lament our history. We pull our hair and scream at the injustices. But we are more divided. How have these noble projects

---

[*] Ta-Nehisi Coates, *Between the World and Me* (New York: Spiegel & Grau, 2015).

offered solutions? Perhaps that is not their aim.

For example, one of the essays in the 1619 Project, which launched in August 2019, presents the argument that NBA team owners should not be called "owners" because 80 percent of the players in the NBA are black, and this word has a connotation to slavery. I really don't know one person who would've made that connection in 2010, or even in 2015 or later. If they own a team, they are owners. If I own a business, I am the owner. If I hire people of color, my title doesn't change. I mean, of course, we can change the title to make people comfortable, but I still own the company legally speaking. And really, more importantly, does any of this make any kind of meaningful difference? Is it helpful in any way? If so, how? The language police cause us to have LESS authentic discussions and lead us further and further away from finding REAL solutions. This kind of thing comes close to George Orwell's "thought crimes."

Do we not refer to MLB team owners as "owners" either, even though the majority of players in the league are white?

Let me tell you a funny story about language.

Contrary to what some may think, China's biggest fear isn't the United States with its aircraft carriers and nuclear weapons. Its biggest fear is its own citizens rising in revolt. China's economy, since opening up to the world, has been built on trade. Trade is what lifted post-Mao China to become the world juggernaut it is today.

Since Mao, the legitimacy of the Chinese Communist Party has been predicated on economic growth, not ideology. If that growth falters, fears of internal revolution rise. China's state-run media plays a crucial role in creating cohesion and promoting nationalism, blocking any sentiment that may jeopardize state control. This is one way to minimize internal political dissonance. The censors are always alert to any words or phrases that may in any way threaten the government, and they quickly scrub them from the Internet. For example, "1989"—the year of the Tian'anmen Massacre—is on the censorship list. The censors go on overdrive every year near the anniversary.

However, the Chinese have found unique ways to get around censorship. My favorite is "grass mud horse." In Chinese, the word "grass mud horse" (*caonima*) sounds very similar to quite a nasty obscenity *cào nǐ mā* (F your mother). In 2009, a little ditty on the grass mud horse popped up all over Chinese websites before censors realized the song was directed toward them.

This seems to be the way that we are heading in the United States. We have censored and sanitized some language or words, for example, "melting pot" or "master bedroom" or "mother," and created a bevy of banal words to erase any perceived offense. A "melting pot" is now a "salad." A "master bedroom" is the "primary bedroom," and a "mother" is a "birthing person." Like the year 1989 in China, might any mention of the year 1776 be censored for wrong-think in the future?

As for the 1619 Project lesson plan for schools, I applaud efforts to teach black history in schools, but the stories captured in the 1619 Project are incomplete and biased. First, it focuses primarily on oppression and helplessness and fails to capture a global history of slavery. If we're going to study slavery, the lesson should start much earlier than 1619 America. While there is nothing wrong with focusing on American slavery as we study our own history, not taking the time to review slavery as a global phenomenon fails to put our country's history in context. The single-minded focus is meant to undermine American history, and many students are left with the impression that our history is singular and unique in the world of slavery.

It's not.

It makes me wonder, do we even want to find unity or, if not unity, at least some common humanity? Are we all caught up in the dopamine of social media addictions fed through fury and rage? Does it bring a necessary stimulation to a relatively mundane life? If we found ways to unify across our differences, then the ideological battles that fund our media and fuel colorful political rivalries would disappear and leave us with the monotony of daily life. Boring.

The victimhood culture that has coincided with our social media culture is no accident. Bradley Campbell and Jason Manning describe victimhood culture in their paper "Microaggression and Moral Cultures" this way:

> A culture of victimhood is characterized by concern with status and sensitivity to slight combined with a heavy reliance on third parties. People are intolerant of insults, even if unintentional, and react by bringing them to the attention of authorities or to the public at large. Domination is the main form of deviance, and victimization a way of attracting sympathy, so rather than emphasize either their strength or

inner worth, the aggrieved emphasize their oppression and social marginalization.*

In a victimhood culture, we identify more and more with stories of marginalization instead of strength and resilience—a strength and resilience that is especially apparent in much of black history. Today some people claim that there is a syndrome that negatively affects black Americans—post-traumatic slave syndrome (PTSS), a concept popularized by social worker Joy DeGruy.† The psychotherapist Brandon Jones goes further, claiming the trauma of slavery has been passed down biologically over generations.‡ His research centers mostly on epigenetics, which looks at how certain experiences can change how a gene is expressed, ultimately having an effect not only on our own well-being but also on the well-being of our descendants.

And yet, we've seen plenty of black Americans make great strides. Lawrence Otis Graham, in his book *Our Kind of People: Inside America's Black Upper Class,* highlights black elites and numerous black elite societies that do not seem to suffer from the epigenetic phenomenon that Jones proffers. I'm going to go out on a limb here and say that you don't suffer from PTSS. I can't help but wonder if PTSS is less a disorder that ties back to 1619 and more a modern malady. An affliction resulting from the public insistence that we re-create a kind of modern slavery that binds people to their past, wrapping them in a victimhood mentality and casting a shadow on their future.

What are your thoughts on the current review of slavery? Are we doing justice to black history?

Jen

---

* Bradley Campbell and Jason Manning, "Microaggression and Moral Cultures," *Comparative Sociology* 13, no. 6 (January 30, 2014): 692–726, brill.com/view/journals/coso/13/6/article-p692_2.xml.

† Joy DeGruy, *Post Traumatic Slave Syndrome* (Joy DeGruy Publications, Inc., 2017).

‡ Brandon Jones, "Legacy of Trauma: Context of the African American Experience," Jegna Institute, available at Minnesota Department of Health, www.health.state.mn.us/communities/equity/projects/infantmortality/session2.2.pdf.

Letter 14

"One who is a slaveholder at heart never recognizes
a human being in a slave."

American Slavery as It Is, pg. 57

Hi Jen,

Thank you for asking me questions born out of humanity. At its root, much ancestral resentment and grudge-holding derive from the denial of humanity in American slavery. We are at our best when we are "anti-slave" in our discourse, not "antiracism" so much. Mental slavery comes out in the little asides we sometimes hear from otherwise intelligent, well-educated black people—for example, a quip from a black mom to her black kids that they might need their freedom papers when visiting a certain part of town lest someone question their presence. Why would a black person recycle ticks of mental slavery? In this case, perhaps the mom was trained by her mom (out of love) to distrust the larger world of whites? And, in turn, the great-grandfather taught the grandma to be wary of whites since the family had been chased out of Charleston, South Carolina, in the early 1900s? Perhaps the mom learned in Jack and Jill* that whites were not to be trusted like fellow blacks? Perhaps the

---

* Jack and Jill of America, Inc. is a national association of black mothers dedicated to centering children in black heritage, culture, and consciousness as children develop into future leaders. Founded on January 24, 1938, in Philadelphia, Pennsylvania, by Marion Stubbs Thomas, Jack and Jill membership is based on legacy and by invitation only. The reader

mom has internalized blackness as oppression and not mental strength. The slaver is long gone, but the echoes resound.

This isn't genetic.

You raise the question of post-traumatic slave syndrome. I appreciate the whole epigenetics thing, but that doesn't ring true for me. My grandma's grandfather, Daniel Brown (1833–1885), was born and lived as a slave. Nothing in family lore suggests his genes were afflicted with the trauma of slavery. The man was our ancestral John D. Rockefeller, Sr., as he plowed through obstacle after obstacle and acquired acre after acre after everlasting acre. Lord, he was appointed overseer at the age of twelve by his father/slave owner. He was probably inflicting trauma on his fellow slaves but put that point aside for the moment. Nothing in family history or the land records suggests a damaged, traumatized ancestor. Daniel Brown comes across as a Titan. If an ancestor born a slave in 1833 left no trace of trauma from slavery, why would his grandchildren's grandchildren come down with a bout of post-traumatic slave syndrome in their genes? It is laughable to me. And my uncles and grandma would have joined in the laughter, too!*

Next example—Congressman Joseph Hayne Rainey (1832–1887). Congressman Rainey's father, Edward Rainey (1807–1883), was born a slave. If the post-traumatic slave syndrome holds up, Edward and his descendants would have been traumatized at the level of their genes. And we should expect to see biological disorders in Edward's descendants, presumably scarred by underachievement and dysfunction and higher mortality rates. What does the evidence show? Edward Rainey was like some crazy dynamo of nature in antebellum Georgetown, South Carolina. He purchased the freedom of his family in 1846 and immediately set forth on a path of civic and economic triumph. Slavery was all around Edward as he became a leader in the local white Episcopal Church, a prosperous barbershop owner, a slave owner in his own right

---

should note that any and all references to Jack and Jill in this book are unauthorized. The opinions expressed are mine and Jen's alone. Our opinions may or may not reflect the facts on the ground within Jack and Jill. Further, I have never been a member of Jack and Jill. As a mother, my wife held the membership. These standard disclaimers are offered out of respect for all of the good Jack and Jill brings into the world.

* For historical and family records related to Daniel Brown's estate and descendants, see appendices II–V.

(three slaves), an owner of several rental properties, and the wealthiest black man in town before the Civil War. His son would become the first black congressman. One granddaughter would become the first black school teacher in Springfield, Massachusetts. One great-grandson would become one of the first black judicial officers in the state of Pennsylvania. And his great-great-great-grandchildren are living lives of leisure and comfort on Martha's Vineyard and in Montgomery County, Maryland.

Just this slave family alone suggests to me the epigenetics idea about post-traumatic slave syndrome tries too hard to explain too much. Nothing about American slavery damaged genes over the generations. To the contrary and for some families, American slavery turbocharged high aim and aspiration over the generations.

Another example—U.S. Senator Blanche Kelso Bruce (1841–1898). This man was born a slave. Were his genes damaged, thus crippling future descendants with post-traumatic slavery syndrome? Hardly. Bruce became a wealthy Sheriff and property owner in Mississippi (of all places), a U.S. Senator from Mississippi, and married up into the Dr. Joseph Willson family. His son would graduate from Phillips Academy and Harvard College before serving as a colored school principal in West Virginia. His two sons would follow their dad's lead and, I believe, both graduate from Harvard Law School. Bruce's daughter-in-law would be the first black woman to serve on the law review at Boston University, the first black person to serve as Editor-in-Chief of a law review in American history, and the mother of two Harvard Law School graduates. These descendants are all descendants of the cruelties of American slavery, and yet they are knocking it out of the ballpark between 1900 and 1940!

In a review of American slavery, one may hear about Frederick Douglass and Harriet Tubman, but stories of those like Daniel Brown, Edward Rainey, and Blanche K. Bruce are missing. Outside of a few notables, black agency is silent in many of these stories. Where is the story of Alexander Twilight, the first black college graduate and member of the Vermont State House of Representatives who built a boarding house for a school when the board of trustees denied him funds? How about the first black president of Howard University, Mordecai Johnson, who transformed Howard into a first-class institution? Or Sadie Tanner Mossell Alexander, who became the first black woman in the United States to earn a PhD in economics and one of the first two black students to serve on the University of Pennsylvania's Law Review, and who later became the school's first black female graduate and first black woman admitted to the Pennsylvania Bar? American slavery is an important addition to any history curriculum. The truth is slavery existed alongside black American triumph over adversity. Slavery without the proper context seems more and more to be an exercise in division, while the unsung heroes of black achievement are ignored and erased.

Teaching black American history as horrific slavery and never a mention of black American triumph over adversity is like a mom loving two legitimate sisters and never a mention of three illegitimate siblings. The power of the single story means blood aunts and uncles are invisible to nieces and nephews, and black achievement is scrubbed from the memory of all Americans.

(Taking a short breath)

Maybe genetics is at work in families. But the genetic inheritance is producing achievement and accomplishment and *Our Kind of People*, not dysfunctional well-being or higher mortality rates so much. Did you know that, in 1964, a disproportionate percentage of all black American PhD holders came from a small number of families?[*] I would wager most of their families were descended from slaves. So, why were these families cranking out PhDs generation after generation, as well as JDs and MDs? I'm not sure post-traumatic slave syndrome is the answer.

Now, this is a lovely segue to your ancestral connection to American slavery. One of the wonderful insights from *Roll, Jordan, Roll: The World the Slaves Made* is that one could not understand slaves without understanding slave owners. One could not understand slave owners without understanding slaves. Does there exist a counterpart to the post-traumatic slave syndrome for the descendants of slave owners? Can it be [adopting the tone and inflection of the narrator in *Ancient Aliens*] that a condition we might term post-traumatic slave-owner syndrome continues to play a role in our present-day society? Can you share what it was like to grow up with slave owners in your family line?

I would like to know how you think of yourself as a descendant of a slave owner? How do you discern the good from the deplorable in your ancestry? Maybe there's no good to be discerned, and that's fine. Were

---

* Horace Mann Bond, *Black American Scholars: A Study of their Beginnings* (Detroit: Balamp Publishers, 1972).

there any stories in your family passed down the line about the horrors of American slavery? And, if no stories were passed down, how does being the descendant of a slave owner inform your identity? I have a white fifth cousin who did not reply to an e-mail welcome from me on 23andMe. After TWO YEARS, said cousin wrote me a furtive response where she said (1) her (our) ancestor had sexed up slaves on his farm and (2) she hoped he burned in hell. Doesn't my distant cousin suffer from post-traumatic slave-owner syndrome as it took this cousin two years to build up the courage to respond and damn to hell our most recent common ancestor? What am I to make out of that?

These are questions I grapple with. My desire is to embrace my full and complete genetic ancestry, warts and all. It is something I think about and mull over. On the one hand, I have done a good thing to document for my family a family past dating back to the first Twyman in the New World, George Twyman (1661–1703). This is a lasting good for my family.* Many black families have no clue about their ancestors from the 1600s, and that creates a sense of no roots.

On the other hand, how would my white ancestors have treated me and my family? Perhaps that is the psychological dilemma for all black descendants of American slave owners. How does one resolve that tension? How do I embrace General Robert E. Lee as a distant fourth cousin?† I found myself researching the black granddaughter of a German Nazi Commandant at Auschwitz. I started this research after the discovery of a Lee family relationship. Is this the way I should go? Do I conceive of General Lee as Adolf Hitler? Was Robert E. Lee the most horrible man who ever lived? Was Lee evil like Amon Göth, the notorious Nazi concentration camp commander depicted in the movie *Schindler's List*? So much for pride in a deep family past. I didn't choose the genetic family I was born into, but I am searching for coherent integration of all the genes

---

* On my mother's side of the family, I recently discovered an ancestor, Bishop Lawrence Womack (1550–1642), a bishop in the Church of England at St. Mary's Cathedral. Notably, several of my Mom's brothers were pastors and ministers.

† Cousin Nathan Twyman claims that the documentary evidence from George Twyman III doesn't support a blood relation, but genetic research from cousin James Edwin Smith III supports a genetic match along two separate lines of descent from Col. Richard Lee I (1613–1664). See J. E. Smith III, *Migrations: Our Family's Immigrations to America, From All Over the World* (CreateSpace Independent Publishing Platform, 2016).

that make me who I am. What are your thoughts?

We're both descendants of American slave owners. Maybe we can wade through this thicket together.

You ask, what are my thoughts on the current review of slavery? If the comeback of talking about American slavery today can be fuel for more black achievement, sign me up. That is a positive and constructive outcome. If renewed interest in American slavery is just a Trojan Horse for Blaming the Man and fueling resentments and grudges, I have no use for it.

Are we doing justice to black history? Far from it, but we can talk about that more in due course.

Another sunny day in San Diego,

Wink

Letter 15

Wink,

First off, I forgot to say in my last letter that I'm so glad I can call you "Wink." It is pretty much the happiest name I've ever heard. Jennifer— not so much. Have you ever read *Freakonomics?*[*] Brilliant book. At any rate, the authors basically say that the name "Jennifer" is about as white middle class as you can get.

You ask whether or not I have post-traumatic slave-owner syndrome. Way to turn this question and issue on its head! Do names and histories matter? Are genes "expressed" due to a name or family history? And even if there is some truth in this, is simple awareness enough to change our genes in another direction?

Before I get to my slaveholder history, I want to explore this just a few lines more. An acquaintance of mine has been training as an epigenetics practitioner (yes, it's a thing now!). He enthusiastically argues that we have the power to turn genes "on or off" with the right mindset and training. Well, perhaps not a gene that ascribes certain immutable characteristics, but genes that determine behavior. With this in mind, I would argue that my name doesn't matter. I mean, I don't think my parents were being particularly creative in naming me—they tell me I was named after the character in the 1970 flick *Love Story*, which I guess is kinda sweet—but despite having a common and arguably boring name, I

---

* Steven D. Levitt and Stephen J. Dubner, *Freakonomics: A Rogue Economist Explores the Hidden Side of Everything* (New York: William Morrow, 2005), 175.

never identified so much with my name that it held me back in any way. My name never affected my behavior or choices. (Although I will admit that while at university I changed my middle name from Sue—another yawn—to Savannah. My parents found no amusement in this.)

So, I guess I'm agreeing with you that post-traumatic slave syndrome rests on shaky ground, at best. I agree that we—through the way we process our experiences—have the ability, to a certain extent, to determine our trajectory. The caveat is that we need to know we have this power. I think the current discourse in the public space is that we are powerless against the forces around us. I reject this premise. Of course, while there may be many things we cannot control in life, including the color of our skin, we can control our mindset and our reactions. And often, this makes all the difference in the world.

Clearly, even being treated by their slave owners as "less than" couldn't tarnish the mindset of the likes of Edward Rainey or your ancestor Daniel Brown. They weren't having any of that baloney. And these are just two examples out of hundreds of thousands of examples.

After having done a bit of historical research, I have so far been able to find one documented slave owner in my family, my 4x great grandfather William Richmond (whose father, John Richmond, immigrated from Scotland). I know this as I discovered a deed in which he bequeathed a number of slaves to his son Adam Richmond (so I guess that makes two slave owners, as I assume Adam came into possession of the slaves).* William and his son were landowners in North Carolina.

Prior to this discovery, I knew my family had had some association with slavery based on oral history. I have heard that the freed slaves of one of my ancestors, who I now believe was Macon Richmond, grandson of Adam, emigrated with them to Texas. I had always figured that, as my family had long been involved with ranching and farming, they likely had had slaves at some point. Now that I have actual documented proof, has it changed anything?

Before I answer this question, let me say that while I don't believe that my slave owner ancestry has necessarily affected me genetically, I do believe that some "genes" have been passed down.

Let me explain.

---

* To read the deed, see appendix VI.

I have worked most of my life in geopolitics. One of the premises of geopolitics, and one to which I ardently subscribe, is that our geographies shape our personalities. Malcolm Gladwell, in his book *Outliers*,* also notes this phenomenon. He emphasizes how certain terrain, for example, the hilly, forested areas of Kentucky, attracted settlers from regions with similar terrain (namely, Northern England). This was an area that was not suitable for farming, but it was good for raising livestock. It makes sense that early settlers would have gravitated to areas in the New World where they could participate in the livelihood and professions they recognized.

The culture that was born from agricultural societies was different from the culture of herders. For example, as Gladwell notes, crop theft is not a major concern in agricultural societies, but for those dependent on livestock, the threat of "cattle-rustling" is very real, and harsh retribution was necessary to deter theft (the television series *Yellowstone* illustrates this nicely, IMHO). Different regions breed different industries and pursuits, and these, in turn, shape not only our individual experiences but also our culture (and perhaps our genes?). Those growing up in this hillier terrain were typically much more territorial, and they developed a "code of honor" system that has permeated through the centuries. It is something still very evident today. J. D. Vance's book *Hillbilly Elegy* does an amazing job elaborating on the preservation of this "code of honor" culture, even for those "hillbillies" who are generations removed from the land.

Of course, the American South is not necessarily hilly, but perhaps to the extent that livestock often went side-by-side with agriculture here, the theory still holds, accounting for evidence of violence in the South. *Roll, Jordan, Roll* also mentions this Southern honor culture:

> They were tough, proud, and arrogant; liberal-spirited in all that did not touch their honor; gracious and courteous; generous and kind; quick to anger and extraordinarily cruel; attentive to duty and careless of any time and effort that did not control their direct interests. They had been molded by their slaves as much as their slaves had been molded by them. They were not men to be taken lightly, not men frivolously to be made enemies of. And they wallowed in those deformities

---

* Malcolm Gladwell, *Outliers: The Story of Success* (New York: Little, Brown and Co., 2008).

which their slaves had thrust upon them in the revenge of historical silence—deformities which would eventually lead them to destruction as a class.[*]

Does this culture shape me? Yes.

The fierce independence of the "cowboy culture" has shaped my family, even though I did not grow up on our family's ranch. The "rugged individualism" motto is very much imprinted on the psyches of those in these environs. Although ranching communities are often close-knit, the distance between ranches typically instills a necessary "personal responsibility" and "individual grit" ethos. If you're caught in a storm in a distant field with a cow giving birth, typically you're on your own. You're responsible if the cow and her offspring live or die, which subsequently determines your own livelihood.

Now, let me get back to the question on slaveholding.

While I do believe that my environment has shaped me, my awareness of the cruelty and inhumanity of slavery has also shaped me. I do not like that I can trace my ancestry to slaveholders. A slave owner's blindness to humanity literally hurts my soul. And yet, I believe all of us, in some way or another, have had ancestors that make us cringe. As you note, even some black Americans have slave owners in their family histories, and if some could trace their families back to Africa, they may find a few more disappointing revelations. As a side note, I think the fact that most black Americans cannot trace their roots past American soil is one of the worst lingering effects of slavery and something that most white Americans do not face. This inability, I would imagine, may leave one with a sense of displacement. I honestly cannot say that knowledge of my ancestry gives me any greater sense of rootedness, but the fact of the matter is that I can trace it. My ancestors weren't erased on their passage to America, and we get to visit the Old World haunts of our forefathers and collect various "coats of arms" and other trinkets that point to our history. Add to this that I know my ancestors came over willingly, which perhaps in some sense provides a feeling of "belonging," if you will.

Of course, given that the average black American has 24 percent Eu-

---

[*] Genovese, *Roll, Jordan, Roll*, 96.

ropean ancestry,* I'm sure that some may be able to trace their roots all the way back to the likes of Holy Roman Emperor Charlemagne or even the infamous, murdering King Henry VIII. Is this enough to create a sense of belonging as Old Americans? On this note, I find it interesting that many black American descendants of slavery refer to themselves as African Americans. I sense the need for connection and belonging. White Americans don't refer to themselves as European Americans. Can we create that connection we seek in a common "Old American" identity?

We all have sinners and saints in our family tree, and I recognize my past, but I embrace the future. I have things to do in this life, and compensating for ancestors I don't even know matters not to me. Family is so important to me, and yet going back and lamenting my ancestors is of no interest. You mention your connection to Robert E. Lee. As we've spent the past few years removing his statues across the South, so many would place him in the sinner bucket. Clearly, he was on the "wrong" side, but it is too simple to say he was purely evil. We can embrace our complicated and complex histories together; we are not evil. Robert E. Lee may have been on the wrong side of history, but to say he was purely evil belies the complexity of his and our humanity. We are not stamped from birth.

The other day my family got into a heated debate about our own ancestors who fought for the Confederacy. (We can trace ancestors back to both sides of the Civil War.) My son was disgusted. They were bad people, he said with a grimace. My dad came unglued. Wrong and evil are not synonymous. In the instance of our family member in the Confederacy, he actually started out in the Union Army, but when the lines were drawn and his hometown fell on the "wrong" side, this ancestor, who never owned a slave, switched sides in what we assume was a sense of duty to protect his home.

A few days ago, I found myself in the car more than usual as my dad and I sought a miracle for his cancer "up the road" at MD Anderson in Houston ("up the road" is Texan for "not too close," while "yonder pasture" indicates proximity). On our drive, we spent a lot of the time listening to the news on CNN. Remembrance of 9/11 dominated the airwaves. In one segment, they were interviewing the family of someone

---

* Lizzie Wade, "Genetic Study Reveals Surprising Ancestry of Many Americans," *Science*, December 18, 2014, www.science.org/content/article/genetic-study-reveals-surprising-ancestry-many-americans.

who died that day, and it was mentioned that this woman's family had proudly served in the U.S. military all the way back to the Civil War. The commentator responded, "I hope for the right side."

It goes without saying that the "right side" won, thankfully. But I couldn't help but wonder if we will now be castigated and shamed in the public square if we are found to have a drop of Confederate blood in our veins. Is this a new rendition of the "one-drop" rule? Does it help move us toward equality? Perhaps a true reconciliation comes when we recognize the sinners and saints in all our family trees and absolve each other of the "sins of our fathers."

And so, I would argue that I am not blind to the past, but I reject a post-traumatic slave-owner syndrome. I can acknowledge the past, but bringing the trauma into my daily life would not help me—nor others—as I try to forge a new future. Clearly, from the account of your white cousin, not everyone does. To the extent that post-traumatic slave and slave-owner syndrome can even be discussed seriously, here is the distinction I would draw: post-traumatic slave syndrome suggests something that cannot be controlled. It is something that is genetically passed down, which you dismiss and even recoil at the suggestion.

Conversely, post-traumatic slave-owner syndrome is a by-product of a culture of resentments and grudges. Could it be that white Americans with black cousins automatically assume their connection is a result of white-on-black rape? Is that how black Americans see their white cousins, and why they won't acknowledge a shared family lineage? It would seem to me a plausible explanation that anxiety about having "rapist genes" is the genesis of post-traumatic slave-owner syndrome. Although this undermines the complexity of many antebellum relationships, we do know that rape was common (sadly, the last time I checked, it is still a criminal activity with miscreants that span the color spectrum). Do rapists run in families? If we look at our cousins and see only rape, we may suffer from a syndrome. But I can't help but to wonder how much of this is just performative art and power plays that rely on both the demonization and weaponization of race. This is not to say that one shouldn't be saddened by the sins of an ancestral past—we all want to unearth our saints and bury the sinners.

If it weren't for the cultural cacophony that dominates our airwaves, I wonder if your cousin would've taken so long to respond. I imagine that she may have thought you were writing to her with an agenda to expose and shame her. I know you weren't, but shame and blame is the name of the game, at least lately. Retreating from shame is a normal human reaction. When faced with shame, if we can't hide, we often crumble and beg for repentance. If everyone could embrace their full ancestral past as you have done, we would quickly debunk PTSS in all its forms, but it appears we aren't there yet.

As for me, am I genetically predisposed to look to the future instead of the past? Maybe so. Like you, I accept my ancestry, warts and all. But it doesn't constrict my future. To the extent that I have power over my genes, if we do have such power, I'm turning the "oppression gene" off.

To the future,

Jen

P.S. I like to go by Jen for several reasons, but as someone who has studied Chinese culture, I have chosen to not identify the name with ordinariness but with the virtue of "Jen" (also spelled Ren) in Confucianism—the "bearing and behavior that a paradigmatic human being exhibits in order to promote a flourishing human community."* Yea, okay, I can at least aspire to that!

---

* To read more on the Confucian value of *Ren*, see Matt Stefon, "Ren," Britannica, www.britannica.com/topic/ren.

Letter 16

Hi Jen,

You ask if Daniel Brown's experience with slavery shaped a certain mindset for me in particular. I think so. The faint echoes of my grandma's grandfather were felt in a sense of rootedness in the land, that first and second and third cousins all around were family, that we were all related to the world of Hickory Hill and that Hickory Hill from Ebenezer AME Church on Terminal Avenue to the James River had been a family farm, *our family's farm*. I was a Twyman on Twyman Road, but, through grandma, I was also an extension of a giant of a man long gone.

On second thought, it wasn't Daniel's experience with American slavery that shaped my mindset. It was all that my ancestor achieved as a free man that created my pathos.

One of the reasons I'm attracted to *Old Money: The Mythology of America's Upper Class* by Nelson Aldrich, Jr., and not *Between the World and Me* by Ta-Nehisi Coates is family memory—I know what it feels like to have the uplift of a Dead Hand reflected in family roads, ancestral white frame homes from the 1800s beyond the railroad tracks, a photograph of a founding father on the hallway of the family church, tombstones of great-grandparents lovingly cared for, acres passed along through the generations with a sense of love and reverence.*

---

* "Men in traditional societies possessed little but did not consider themselves poor, insofar as they were all bound in a network of social relations, organic communities, and extended families structured as clans." —Piero San Giorgio

I do not feel my family memory in the evils of *Between the World and Me*, so I tune out the New Fatalism as unattached to my lived experiences picking blackberries in the shadow of great-grandfather's home or driving down Castlewood Road and my dad pointing out a second Brown cousin here, a third Brown cousin there. And so, yes, this mindset that the world was related to me armored me well for the larger world of public school desegregation in the fall of 1969.

The most important things in life are family and a sense of self.

I have not felt empathy for cosmetic disputes like the use of the word "owner" for NBA owners. Let me first say that I am not into sports at all. I enjoy watching *Star Trek* and *The Twilight Zone* reruns. The NBA does not occupy my time. Nonetheless, this tempest in a teapot is even more reason for me to ignore professional basketball. Jen, it doesn't matter to my life what one calls owners. It just doesn't. The term "owner" is a legal term. It is devoid of race unless one is driven to see race in everything in life. I feel pity for those who are consumed by this non-issue. Life is too short.

So, no, we should not change the name of team owners. That's a legal term. If you can't deal with it, take a pill and chill out.

Many of these micro-calamities are rooted in Black Fragility, an inability to see beyond slaveholding. I see Black Fragility as the greatest threat to a healthy black culture and consciousness. If we engage in a program of therapy for Black Fragility, would that include a mandatory read of *American Slavery as It Is* (1839) for every living black American? Would coming face to face with the God-honest reality of slavery force a radical readjustment in black culture and consciousness? Would black Americans keep things in better perspective if they knew of the runaway George and the six African girls and the beautiful mulatto teenager disfigured as punishment for running away in Charleston, South Carolina, and the man of God flogged to death on a dare as he refused to deny Jesus Christ? I wonder . . . I wonder if we could address this cancer of Black Fragility with a direct infusion of truth about slavery? Or would we turbocharge ancestral resentments and grudges?

What do you think?

Long ago, my family removed the virus of victimhood from my soul. All praise to grandma and mom! I often have difficulty looking at life as a victim. It feels unnatural, untrue to my ancestors. And if given a choice,

I will honor my ancestors over *Between the World and Me.* Every day and every night of my life.

And so, I leave you with this simple reflection—the mindset of Daniel Brown is now added to the conflicted character of Robert E. Lee as ancestors. As always, I draw the great from these men in how I place myself in the universe. I bemoan their connection to American slavery. I infuse my spirit with greatness from these characters, and I pack away their imperfections as they do not serve me in my wonderful life as Lourine Twyman's son and my daughter's dad.

Regards,

Wink

P.S. When I think of the name "Jennifer," I think of Aunt Jennifer, a black doctor who graduated from Harvard College and Howard Medical School. Jennifer is not as white middle class as you can get in my family experience.

Letter 17

Dear Wink,

Black fragility. That's a concept that may not get a lot of applause in the current polemical climate! What does get a lot of currency is the concept of *white fragility.* I can't say I really understand it all, but I read about it a lot. From what I'm able to gather (it seems that everyone has their own terminology or manipulates it for a particular agenda), it is the sensitivity white people exhibit in talking about racism. *White privilege* is the foundation of white fragility.

Are our various emotional fragilities now segregated into racial enclaves? This is not to deny that racism exists, but it feels like instead of searching for ways to resolve any vestiges of racism, its purpose is further division, and it is seeded in animosity and anger. Diversity training modeled on Robin DiAngelo's *White Fragility* or Ibram X. Kendi's vision of "antiracism" has become ubiquitous. An "us vs. them" ethos has pervaded our society, all based around qualitative research that, while not entirely fallacious, lacks a lot of empirical backing.

Of course, the first objection to my statement would be that *lived experiences* matter, and one cannot quantify lived experiences in a petri dish. But indeed, this criticism is telling. Just as one cannot throw whites into one group, we also cannot put individuals of any race, ethnicity, gender (whatever) into one group. To do so is to negate the premise of lived experiences. More importantly, it automatically shuts down authentic discussion—and, ultimately, discussion is the only way we can move forward with empathy and understanding.

As a result of pervasive diversity classes and training, race has become a hot topic and has found its way into our public discourse and even education. Everything now seems colored—literally and figuratively—with racial underpinnings, with a new emphasis on *implicit bias* and the *deconstruction* of white identity. I'm unable to generate the necessary empathy to understand a lived experience marred with racism in the constant deconstruction of my whiteness and dismissal of any of my own experiences, which must be tainted with an unholy alabaster stain.

The ideas of white fragility and white privilege are, in some ways, a result of the postmodern movement, which "eschews objectivity, perceiving knowledge as a construct of power differentials rather than anything that could possibly be mutually agreed upon."[*] The postmodern urge to deconstruct all discourse to a power struggle leaves us with few options to craft real solutions to many of our problems, including, most importantly, discrimination. There will always be a struggle. Societies the world over are unequal in innumerable ways. And struggle on we must. But when the struggle becomes the goal, we miss real opportunities for change, let alone understanding.

I'm sorry, I am a bit off topic here and have not yet really replied to your letter, but this idea of fragility I find so confusing. In our new digital world, we like to simplify everything at the expense of real meaning. We are so overwhelmed with the "noise" that if someone comes up with a catchy phrase, as DiAngelo has done with white fragility, it is easy to attract those overwhelmed with information overload who don't want to think too hard but are eager to find solidarity in a misguided cause. As we become more digitally addicted and simultaneously more isolated, we are in search of lost human connections, and the need to belong becomes entrenched in groups that are able to define "the Other." Fears that emanate from not belonging and digital distance, as opposed to genuine interpersonal interaction, are the tools waged in these tribal bubbles to ensure solidarity and give meaning to an identity.

To the extent that black fragility is a thing, I would wager that, like white fragility, it is a new construction of the postmodern era. Do you think in 2010, or even 2015, that this defining focus on slaveholding was

---

* Michael Aaron, "Evergreen State and the Battle for Modernity," *Quillette*, June 8, 2017, quillette.com/2017/06/08/evergreen-state-battle-modernity/.

a prevalent concept in the mindset of average black Americans? This was never even intimated in the interracial discussions I've had until recently.

It would never have occurred to me to assume that my middle-class black friends were in any way held back because of slavery, and honestly, if I were to have suggested as much ten years ago, they would've been offended. One of my father's best friends, Ike Payne, who I've mentioned in earlier letters, found pride in his family's escape from slavery to live among the Seminole Indians. They took pride in their family's resilience, a pride that landed him as one of our nation's first black test pilots. If he were alive today and I suggested that he couldn't get past slavery, he probably would've either laughed himself silly or swatted me. Perhaps both.

What I think is the worst injustice in this dialogue is that it has introduced a new and misleading concept for lower-income populations to use in power negotiations, perhaps adding to its allure. There is truth in the reality that redlining and the other injustices of the Jim Crow era made it more difficult for black families to get ahead, and this is still evident in the persistent wealth gap. Although again, the families outlined in the book *Our Kind of People*, and the recent statistics that note that more than half of black Americans have made it to upper- or middle-class status, despite any lingering racism, show a side to the story that is curiously absent in these racial narratives.[*]

Black achievement and success are erased. The full story is not being told. Perhaps these stories undermine the story of oppression that has been a cornerstone in our recent emphasis on reparations. According to one study of U.S. census data, the percentage of black men who are in the upper-income bracket rose from 13 percent in 1960 to 23 percent in 2016. Similarly, the poverty rate for the same demographic has fallen from 41 percent to 18 percent since 1960.[†] Does increasing status and

---

[*] See, for example, Christopher Pulliam et al., "The Middle Class Is Already Racially Diverse," Brookings, *Up Front* blog, October 30, 2020, www.brookings.edu/blog/up-front/2020/10/30/the-middle-class-is-already-racially-diverse/; and Andre M. Perry and Carl Romer, "The Black Middle Class Needs Political Attention, Too," Brookings, report, February 27, 2020, www.brookings.edu/research/the-black-middle-class-needs-political-attention-too/.

[†] See W. Bradford Wilcox et al., "2.5 Million African-American Men Are in the Upper Middle Class," Institute for Family Studies, July 23, 2018, ifstudies.org/blog/2-5-million-black-

success compromise a movement that centers on resentment? None of this is to say that more progress is not needed. Indeed, more progress certainly is needed, but to deny the progress made thus far and other intervening factors is to peddle falsehoods. (I feel like I keep making this argument—"none of this is to say that . . ." yadda yadda yadda—but honestly, this is the defensive crouch I find myself in when engaging in this conversation with people who deny progress. It has become my own tick of sorts!)

So, we dismiss these accomplishments and point at the (dwindling) low-income bracket to make fallacious claims of disempowerment, which, in reality, disempowers. We infuse a whole group of people with a victim narrative that serves to dispirit rather than uplift. Am I missing anything, Wink? Does my *whiteness* blind me to a reality that I cannot grasp? Even if it did, the truth remains that the significant progress of black Americans continues to be hidden under a growing (and well-funded) story that ghettoizes a whole category of people.

You ask me if every black American were to read *American Slavery as It Is* would it change anything? I think it would depend on the filter with which it was consumed. Would it highlight the progression of black Americans and the amazing ability to overcome, or would it entrench grudges? Who narrates the story? That is what matters.

Jen

---

men-are-in-the-upper-class.

Letter 18

Dear Jen,

"To the extent that black fragility is a thing, I would wager that, like white fragility, it is a new construction of the postmodern era." Yes, my friend, you would win that wager. I made the term up five minutes ago.

Regardless of the prevailing winds, I believe an inability to see beyond slaveholding is the greatest threat to a healthy black culture and consciousness. What does seeing beyond slaveholding look like? One would see people living in humanity looking forward. Spirits would be uplifted with goals sought after and long-range plans executed. If one is running a race for the finish line, one looks ahead into the future, not backward over one's shoulder.

Your very details to me about how this focus is a recent *cause célèbre* among your middle-class black friends tell me black Americans are being manipulated and controlled to focus on the inconsequential, not the material. Of course your father's best friend would have laughed. It is all laughable. We should laugh more about the comeback of American slavery as a thing. My grandma, born in 1897, moved on from American slavery, but my privileged daughter born in 2002 should be thinking about reparations for American slavery? Crack some jokes about this, Jen. Make some quips and snarks.

Channel your inner Dave Chappelle. You've got the humor gene. I'm too serious. Make some merriment about the absurdity of it all.

Could it be that I feel free to be real here because I am the descendant of American slaves? Does that bloodline give me the freedom to call a spade a spade? It shouldn't. And besides, you are equally a descendant of American slavery as well, just on the slave-owner side.

I oftentimes wonder if descendants of slave owners feel they have no right to voice their genuine opinions and thoughts about reparations for American slavery. I am the descendant of at least three slave owners (Daniel Brown [1783–after 1860], George Twyman III [1731–1818], Col. Richard Lee I [1617–1664]), and I feel no sense of shame or guilt in voicing my opinion about these matters. Could it be that part of Black Fragility is racial innocence? A mind-blindness to one's full genetic past? I have never read about Ta-Nehisi Coates perceiving himself as the descendant of a slave owner. Why is this? Could it be Black Fragility renders full acknowledgment of his full self too painful? Is there too much cognitive dissonance for the reparations-Spartacus to handle?

I wonder.

One of the best things for my self-acceptance was to discover, and embrace, my distant Twyman cousins. I felt more complete as a person. I was more than a descendant of American slaves. I was a descendant of men of learning and real property and colonial bravery. I'm not a poet or psychologist, but, as best I can tell, tracing my roots back to indentured servant George Twyman (1661–1703) centered me in a larger truth. Am I who I am because of this ancestral self-knowledge? I'm part of a name that originated in Birchington, Kent, England. That's a wonderful bit of self-knowledge to have. And it is uncommon for black Americans.

Despite her impressive pedigree, my wife has no earthly idea where her family name, Rainey, came from. Was it a bastardization of Raney or some other name? I've uncovered no treasure trove of distant Raineys whose DNA matches my wife. She came into being as a Rainey when slave Edward Rainey was born in 1807, and that's not a bad origin at all. But she was an "orphan" before 1807. What might the unconscious impact of this be on her and her family, of having no knowledge of Edward's ancestors? I don't want to overstate the point. My wife can trace her Hudnall ancestors back to England in the 1500s if she chooses to. She has traceable roots, but she chooses to ignore her white lineage. She lives in a voluntary rootlessness traceable to ancestral resentments and grudges.*

---

* Although the family name was spelled "Hudnall" in England, colonial Virginia, and antebellum Virginia, the black family members would change the spelling of the name to "Hudnell"

Let's tackle this idea I have about *American Slavery as It Is* as required reading for every black American. Does the idea make sense for all blacks in the United States or just the descendants of American slavery? Surely, African immigrants should learn about the slave roots of black American culture.

You ask, who should narrate the story? Why should anyone have to narrate the story? Why couldn't the book be self-directed reading? I gained the most knowledge in junior high school by going to the library every day after school, selecting a history book, and reading my selected book at home that evening. No one narrated these books for me. I had the reading skills to read these books myself and draw my own conclusions.

Some might say black American students don't read. The reading skills are below grade level in too many schools, so my idea is more suitable for the top 1 or 2 percent most likely to be self-directed and not need a narrator.[*]

I don't have a good answer to this critique. When I draw upon my own lived experiences for policy prescriptions, I make middle-American assumptions about standards and curiosity and achievement. Would the required reading of a 200-page tract on slavery be foolhardy and a waste of everyone's time like some Great Society programs?

I think these are genetic and environmental causes and effects. American slavery plays no role.

What does play a role? Did one have a smart mom? Did one have a wise grandma? Did one grow up loved and cherished as the blessed

---

around the time of the Civil War.

[*] Eighty-five percent of black students in the eighth grade in Virginia are functionally illiterate. Armstrong Williams, "Many of America's Black Youths Cannot Read or Do Math—and That Imperils Us All," *Hill,* November 4, 2021, thehill.com/opinion/education/579750-many-of-americas-black-youths-cannot-read-or-do-math-and-that-imperils-us/. Just 15 percent of black eighth graders are at or above reading "proficiency." Colette Coleman, "How Do We Get Black Kids' Literacy to Matter? Have More Journalists Cover It," *Phi Delta Kappan,* November 3, 2020, kappanonline.org/black-kids-literacy-matter-have-more-journalists-cover-it-russo-coleman/. Three out of four black male students in California do not meet basic reading standards. Mike Szymanski, "'Terrible Data' on Black Boys in California Show the Need to Break Down State Test Scores by Gender, Advocate Says," *LA School Report,* June 2, 2017, www.laschoolreport.com/terrible-data-on-black-boys-in-california-show-the-need-to-break-down-state-test-scores-by-gender-advocate-says/.

future? Was one expected to be someone in life? Did one grow up in a predominantly white, small-town, suburban conservative school? Was one ambitious? Did one seize opportunity at every turn? Did one have a genetic disposition for optimism? Did one have a genetic bent for worry and anxiety? Did one have a genetic predisposition for in-group tribalism or out-group empathy?

I think these are the causative elements that leave the slave past in the past for me. If you think about it, my life began in 1961. My life didn't begin in 1619 or 1790 or 1865. My life began in 1961 in Richmond, Virginia. Doesn't it stand to reason that the most important psychological dimensions for me would be moments I lived and the purpose and meaning of my lived moments, not moments a 5x great-grandparent lived?

Not to beat a dead horse, but I do urge you to laugh at the concept of post-traumatic slave and slave-owner syndrome. I'm pretty sure my deceased ancestors are laughing in their graves too.

Laughing hard this evening,

Wink

P.S. Similarly, redlining has become a clumsy and imprecise tool for understanding the past. Although Coates popularized the shibboleth of "redlining" in his iconic Atlantic magazine article calling for reparations, the truth is some black families were always buying properties and building homes and accumulating wealth since well before the Civil War. Curiosity drove me to know if redlining held back the descendants of Daniel Brown. I obtained a copy of a redlining map for South Richmond/Northern Chesterfield County and found no evidence of redlining in the Hickory Hill neighborhood. Did redlining matter for descendants of Daniel Brown in the 1930s, 1940s, and 1950s on land acquired by the founding father in the 1870s? I welcome any documentation of redlining on Brown legacy land in Hickory Hill.

Letter 19

Dear Wink,

Let me first answer your question about narration. I'm not concerned about who narrates the book *per se* but rather about what "narration"—i.e., what filter—informs any given reading of the book? That is to say, if someone from a family that stresses the tenacity and strength of black America reads the book, then they will likely internalize the resilience found in the book. They would see the horror of slavery and trace the trajectory of black Americans from having nothing, from being considered mere chattel, to becoming a dynamic force that has increasingly asserted their power and humanity against all odds. Indeed, it is a feat of humanity that needs to be embraced and celebrated. If, however, someone is immersed in the slogans of *white privilege*, *reparations*, and *white fragility*, perhaps they will read the book in a different way. With those types of filters, the book might only further fuel anger, resentment, and grudges.

Through my ancestry research, I've been able to trace my family back to slaveholders and find black relatives who are also descended from them. This has been such a fascinating journey for me. I've so far connected with several of my black cousins. I haven't asked any of them if they feel the lingering effects of slavery, but none have intimated as much. Let me tell you a little story about an elderly black woman named "Jane," who is estimated to be my fourth cousin based on our shared genes. Jane is eighty-eight years old and lives in the Midwest. We write frequently, trying to discover our common ancestor and swapping stories.

Did you know that back in the early 1900s, the Canadian govern-ment advertised free land in their western provinces for U.S. settlers? What the Canadian government didn't anticipate was the number of black Americans who would respond to this invitation. With this influx, they started to turn a lot of black Americans away, including Jane's fam-ily. As a result, Jane's family turned back to settle in the Midwest, which she now calls home.

Jane was a professional singer and an artist. One of her ancestors was a famous black sculptor in New York City. Jane herself received several scholarships to study art, including one in Alaska.

She has shared some memories of the racism she has experienced in her life. For example, she recalls that a few restaurants intentional-ly over-salted her food when she was younger. She never graced those establishments again with her presence. From what I can tell in our ex-changes, she never let her family's history of slavery dictate her circum-stances, although she clearly has not been immune to prejudice.

Another cousin is the author of children's books. She has even been recognized as one of the "50 Great Writers You Should Be Reading," and her books have received support from Hillary Rodham Clinton, Laura Bush, and Sarah Ferguson, Duchess of York. Her books focus on chil-dren making positive choices, family unity, and staying in school.

I don't want to speak for my cousins. As our conversations continue, I may learn more about their perspectives on slavery. However, what I can say from our current conversations is that neither of these cousins allowed slavery to create what you call a mindset of *black fragility* or to preset grievances that kept them from excelling.

When we watch mainstream media, many stories are replete with crime and poverty that are claimed as holdovers from slavery. I don't know if they are holdovers from slavery *per se*, but more the result of a poverty mindset. A broken spirit can be passed down from parent to par-ent. A poverty mindset can continue to whisper, "You're worthless." Fur-ther, I believe that many lower-income and inner-city schools do little to help overcome this mindset, which may be due to a lack of resources. Some of this mindset may also be propagated by internal group dynamics, such as the slur of "acting white" hurled by family and friends.*

Of course, you don't need to be poor to have a poverty mindset. However, put yourself in that position. Assume that your parents are poor and have a poverty mindset. They don't even know how to get a leg up. Their parents didn't help them, and schools haven't helped, and maybe their environment has even encouraged a poverty mindset as an effect of slavery and its legacy. Mentors are few and far between, except for the mentors they find on the street. They take you in and show you "how to make it." Can we, as fellow humans and travelers, do something to help uplift those who don't have the type of grandmas and mothers you and others had?

Ultimately, I think it really does start at home, though, as it seems to have with your parents who grew up with a middle-class mindset no matter their financial circumstances. And when it comes to schools, Thomas Sowell does a great job of highlighting schools that excelled against the odds prior to the dismantling of segregation, when overt racism was ubiquitous. For example, Dunbar High School in Washington, D.C., "sent a higher percentage of its graduates on to college than any white public high school."[†] Why is this? Is it possible that the poverty mindset, or perhaps the spread of the poverty mindset, is a rather new phenomenon? Where was the lingering effect of slavery on these children at Dunbar?

I think there is a growing culture of fragility and victimhood that has stalled any meaningful uplift. It has allowed people—of all colors—to look for blame, dismissing any responsibility. This is not to say that racial biases have been wiped out, but it is to say that if you have grit and determination, in this day and age, there are more opportunities for black Americans than ever before.

Can schools and family organizations do a better job of underlining these opportunities so that kids don't fall prey to a mindset of hopeless helplessness? My favorite organization that empowers young children, especially young black boys, is called The Cave.[‡] Through after-school

---

* See, for example, Stuart Buck, *Acting White: The Ironic Legacy of De-segregation* (New Haven: Yale University Press, 2010).

† Thomas Sowell, *Discrimination and Disparities* (New York: Basic Books, 2018), 64.

‡ To see more about The Cave's activities, see theyunion.org/catta/.

martial arts, they teach children real power—as in kung-fu fighting power—self-worth, and discipline. And as a result, guess what? Their academics also get a generous boost. In fact, 78 percent of the kids in the program see their GPA rise, according to one of their reports. Victimhood, fragility, and a poverty mindset are not something you find in their dojo.

And then, I exchanged letters with a professor in Florida who is black, and her mother insisted that she and her brother attend the Boys and Girls Club of America. She is very much in support of this organization and what it offers. And, of course, there are also Jack and Jill chapters nationwide. Aren't they about empowerment? You would know better than me, but from what I have gleaned, it is an important stepping stone into elite black society. Are these types of opportunities available only in select communities? Could we perhaps include these opportunities as part of an after-school educational curriculum so that all children had exposure to them?

There will always be children and families who do not choose these options, even when they are free and accessible. The world is full of inequities—some natural, some by choice, and some by design. I think for me, the biggest issue is that the youth of our country have access to equal opportunities, and if we get to a day when we can say every child is similarly endowed—where equality is the design—then at that point, it really just comes down to nature or choice, neither of which can be resolved via outside influence either from the state or society. Are we there yet?

Warmly,

Jen

Letter 20

Hi Jen,

We'll never have access to equal opportunities. That's just life. Consider "Chad." Chad is a classmate of a teenager I know. Said teenager, a typical black daughter of Ivy League–educated parents, is quite taken with Chad's charmed life. He is the son of Chinese immigrants. His father is very wealthy, and Chad's family has a spectacular home on the beach. Chad seems like a great guy, but he hasn't asked the teenager out yet. Just kidding. Just kidding. The point here is there's no way the teenager's opportunities in life will ever be equal to Chad's opportunities, let alone the same as poor children of unwed mothers.

If life is unfair, don't we have to accept equal opportunities will always be a pipe dream unless we live in a communist country, and, even then, the party bosses would have access to opportunities superior to worker drones.

Psychology professor Jordan B. Peterson talks about this. We should not compare ourselves to others. We should compare ourselves to who we were last week, last month, last year. That appeals to me as an achievable aspiration for everyone.

You conclude with the proverbial fork in the road, nature or choice.

Consider the last slave named Twyman, Scott Twyman (1848–1939).*

---

* Around 1845 in Madison County, Virginia, a slave owner named James Willis died intestate or without a will. Probate proceedings were filed by James Twyman to adjudicate the distribution of the decedent's property. The Chancery Court awarded two slaves named

Scott was born a slave and remained a slave until his liberation in around 1865 when the Union troops blazed through Madison County, Virginia. Scott was seventeen years old when freedom arrived. Now, in a Hollywood ending, this noble teenager's life would have been transformed by emancipation. He might have distinguished himself with education or property or wealth accumulation or visionary work as a founding father of free Twymans into the future.

And you know something?

There's nothing noble about the man . . . at all.

My paternal great-grandfather left no echo of enterprise across the ages.

There is only one trait and one story this man is remembered for among his descendants.

He was a mean man, a very mean man. One day, he was digging a well with his sons. He was so mean that his sons abandoned him at the bottom of the well to teach their father a lesson. That's it. Did Scott choose to be mean, or was that his nature? Since I know of several slave ancestors who were not reviled in their lifetimes, I'm inclined to believe meanness was in the man's nature. It was a genetic disposition. It is what it is. I would hazard no amount of therapy would have changed the man's innate character and personality. American slavery didn't transform Scott into a mean man worthy of being remembered for his meanness. He came into the world that way, I think. I like this story.*

Robert (1827–1880) and Smith (1822–1913) to the widow Susanna Willis. The decedent's surviving daughter, Mary E. Willis, was assigned a slave named Charlotte (1790–1880), the mother of Robert and Smith. The court assigned respective values to each negro: Robert $450, Smith $350, Charlotte $200. Robert's son Scott (1848–1939) was born a slave shortly after. All are ancestors of Winkfield Twyman, Jr.

* Unlike Scott Twyman and his father Robert, Smith Twyman left quite a trail in his life story:

1. Smith fought in the Union Army during the Civil War.
2. Smith was arrested for assault and battery in the Fourth Precinct in Washington, D.C., on October 12, 1863.
3. Smith sued a corporation to get paid for wages owed October 22, 1870. He won.
4. Smith was a depositor with the Freedmen's Bank from 1865 to 1871.
5. Smith secured a building permit to build a house in Washington, D.C., on May 9, 1872. (Notice how redlining was irrelevant then. I grew up among Twyman uncles who simply built their homes. Bank credit did not seem to be an issue, which may suggest that the

So, there you go. Not an uplifting, affirming ancestral story, huh? That's life. Just because one was a slave didn't make one noble. I oftentimes suspect activists attribute nobility to slaves. Nope, noble slaves are caricatures. Slaves were human beings with the full range of good and bad human traits, as historian Eugene Genovese reminds us.

I do appreciate your point on a family filter for reading *American Slavery as It Is*. Now, you should answer the question begged: would most read the book through the prism of tenacity and strength or through the prism of *white privilege*, *reparations*, and *white fragility*? What is the state of American junior high school kids today? Which prism is ascendant?

I love to hear about your distant black cousins. Making those connections is such a good thing to do. I wish more Americans would reach out to—and learn about—distant cousins from different races. Learning to embrace others is the wave of the future.

As always, I tend to be a contrarian, and so I notice bumps in the correspondence landscape where I pause, and reboot, what you have written. For example, you write, "many stories are replete with crime and poverty that are claimed as holdovers from slavery."

So, let's explore that connection a little. Name a slaver from the 1600s or 1700s who caused a mob of black teenagers to rob a drug store in San Francisco in 2021? What is the actual causation between, say, slave catcher Mr. Willis in the 1790s in Tidewater, Virginia, and the crime in the drug store in 2021? Even proximate causation would do for me. How does a slave transaction in New Orleans in the 1800s cause an overweight, undereducated poor black woman to assault a fast-food retail worker in 2021? Either actual or proximate causation would work. How did ownership of Charlotte Twyman in the 1840s in Madison County, Virginia, cause her descendants to have children with sketchy men in 2003? Once again, show me the actual causation. Show me in logical progression how the status of Charlotte's bondage creates a poor choice lead-

---

whole redlining consideration doesn't capture all of reality in the past.)

6. Smith had a will that went to probate. There was a major fight over Smith's estate in District Court.

Conclusion: while my great-grandfather Scott Twyman was a mean man and his father, Robert Twyman, left no lasting imprint, this Smith Twyman was leaving his mark even after his passing. This is life for any family—there are overachievers alongside siblings of no historical note or moment.

ing to poverty in a 3x great-granddaughter? Let's try another one. How does slave ownership of a 4x great-grandfather in Pittsylvania County, Virginia, "holdover" and compel a 4x great-grandson to steal a candy bar from a store and lie about it? Show me the logical, actual causation, not a sad song story of sorrow but a crisp, logical compulsion.

Show me how a broken spirit is passed down from parent to parent, particularly when intervening grandparents and great-grandparents were some of the proudest, most resilient, most indomitable people on the planet. I get a little testy when these sweeping conclusions are made without hard proof of causation, either actual or proximate.

So, that is my challenge to you. Connect the dots in a concrete, specific way.

Personally, so much of this is genetics and personality and character. Wealth rarely passes down through three generations (all praise to the Dead Hand of Daniel Brown). Why would crime and poverty pass down through five or more generations? Why would a broken spirit be an inheritance if intervening generations were building assets? I reject whispered poverty mindsets. American slavery has . . . absolutely . . . nothing to do with crime and poverty today.

Anyone who says otherwise can never prove direct and actual causation.

The comeback of American slavery in 2023, amazing.

Wink

Letter 21

Wink,

The *white privilege* storyline and the explosion of diversity and whiteness training is the prism in ascendancy. American slavery and its ills are making headlines daily. I think these are important discussions, but instead of these discussions resulting in a "coming together" ethos, it feels like they are another exercise in division.

There are several cultures colliding right now, creating the perfect storm. First, we have a digital culture that has isolated us from humanizing face-to-face contact (IRL—or in real life—as they say). As Brené Brown argues, "it's hard to hate people close up." We don't get close-up much any longer.

Second, we have the millennial culture that is now in its maturity. I'm not one to bash millennials. Every generation has its upsides and downsides. However, growing up in an era of "participation trophies" has led to attitudes of entitlement and increased sensitivity to perceived injustices. I know many millennials who are not burdened with the entitlement syndrome and others in older generations who suffer such symptoms. I don't want to overgeneralize, but entitlement has negative downsides that can lead to anger and rage in the face of a disappointing reality: life isn't fair.

When you add these two things together, it is unsurprising that a grievance or victimhood culture is the result. It is pervasive, and the millennials are but one group that is now awash in the trend.

Then we bring *racism* into the mix. Racism still exists (as does classism and ageism and sexism and so on), and it is something to get angry about. But if there are no overt signs of racism, well, dammit, let's find some—or so says the ascendant culture. So now we have racist capitalism, racist environmentalism, racist racists. You can't get through a day without a new racism revealed. It is a word that will define this decade. The "R" word is the new "scarlet letter" for white Americans.

And we are oh so very sensitive.

Sensitivity is a good thing. Sensitive people are typically more compassionate. And we definitely need more compassion. Wait, or is endless sensitivity a good thing? We are more sensitive, and yet we are angrier. Anger is good business, so bring on the stories of racism and slavery. Stir the pot. Fill the coffer. Repeat.

We coddle sensitivity and raise children who are unable to cope in a society that will never be equitable or fair, even under, as you say, a communist regime. And as it turns out, we now have a growing population pushing for communism. I wish we could have a time machine transport us back to Maoist China to revisit the "glories" of communism.

Anyways . . .

You ask that I trace the lingering effects of slavery on our current society. Let me see what I can do.

The story begins with slavery insofar as slavery instilled the idea that blacks were less than human. The Reconstruction Era held a lot of promise in its movement to address the inequalities of slavery, but it was short-lived. There may not be many black Americans today who can tell family stories of brutal slavery, but they likely can tell stories about the prejudice experienced under Jim Crow. This is where we can see more recent direct causes of inequality.

The *New York Times*' 1619 Project had an essay on the wealth gap. The essay begins with a black man who was thriving in Alabama before his murder in 1947. After his murder, whites plundered his wealth. I've heard similar stories over and over. They are heart-wrenching, gross injustices. Other instances of injustice highlighted in the essay are the dismantling of the Freedmen's Savings Bank, where the white trustees used the bank to offer speculative loans to white investors, and when the bank went bust, black savings went to dust. Then you have the stories of successful black towns and districts being attacked and looted, such as

Wilmington (1898) and Greenwood (1921).* And of course, there is the famous redlining that kept black neighborhoods poor and undesirable while not allowing black money to move into white neighborhoods.

Thankfully we are moving past all of this. But can we not trace these realities from the not-too-distant past to the influence of a poverty mind-set today? People who lived through these injustices are still alive today. There are many who are thriving regardless, but some who are not.

If your grandparents' wealth was plundered and your parents were not able to build upon any family wealth, let alone attend college, you were born into a family that still feels the sting of discrimination. Given all the new opportunities of the day, you can choose another route, but I can imagine how the stories mentioned above would generate indignation. And how that indignation could linger, even if the stories don't directly reflect your personal ancestral history. Does that mean that I might choose to carry this indignation into a life of crime? No, of course not. However, if you are uneducated and poor and your direct family descendants were left this way because of discriminatory policies, it is not a stretch to see how you may be affected.

The connection is not directly to slavery *per se*. However, slavery led to the institutionalization of racism, which led to discriminatory policies that continue to have an impact on some black families today (note: I'm not referring here to the type of imagined discriminatory policy we often hear about from popular "antiracist" authors and activists). Yet, many black families thrived nevertheless. So, even if everything else is equal, the environment provides barriers that aren't always easy to surmount. It can be done, but these barriers certainly appear higher for black Americans.

Asians have barriers. Jews have barriers. Hillbillies have barriers. There are always barriers. Asians and Jews, in large part, were able to overcome these barriers (this is a gross generalization, I realize). Hillbillies like J. D. Vance figured out the formula to overcome barriers, although the opioid crisis continues to be a formidable obstacle in poor white America. So, can the difference for those black Americans who haven't been able to hurdle these barriers be traced back to slavery? To a racism so fundamental that it continues to impact attitudes and shape choices?

---

* For an account of Greenwood and the Tulsa Massacre, see David French, "When Our Forefathers Fail," *Dispatch,* May 30, 2021, frenchpress.thedispatch.com/p/when-our-forefathers-fail.

With that said, it is interesting in the current discussion on race that we focus only on stories of loss and depravity. It's not that these stories aren't important and shouldn't be shared as we review and correct our history, but that the stories of overcoming are mysteriously absent. We seem to be purposefully and even consciously choosing to highlight, uphold, and promote a poverty mindset in black America and to fuel grievances. So much so it almost seems by design.

For example, one thing that the *New York Times* essay on the wealth gap failed to mention was that "black-owned banks turned down black applicants for home mortgage loans at a higher rate than did white-owned banks."[*] And, while statistics do show that inherited wealth and length of home ownership account for disparities in the white-black wealth gap, it accounts for only 32 percent of the gap.[†] Further, John McWhorter notes that the statistic that blacks earn only 60 percent of whites is "dragged down by welfare mothers and the preponderance of blacks in the South where wages are lower overall." He goes on to say, "many of the people most fervently embracing reparations are quick to condemn whites for thinking all black people are poor. Thus, we are brought to the savage irony—the reparations movement is founded in large part upon a racist stereotype."[‡] Can we talk about these statistics and realities, too, in an effort to try to solve these issues holistically, or are they off-limits? If we don't then we wallow in half-truths, anger, and division.

Disparities and inequities are not always the result of discrimination. But even when they are, we twist statistics and reality to match our mindset and the prevailing narrative, making it too easy to create the causation between slavery and poverty. Some threads are there that are necessary to explore to heal our country, but if we do so without a critical eye, the results are resentments and grudges that keep us in gridlock.

Your friend,

Jen

---

[*] Sowell, *Discrimination and Disparities,* 79.

[†] Hughes, "Black American Culture and the Racial Wealth Gap."

[‡] John McWhorter, *Authentically Black: Essays for the Black Silent Majority* (New York: Penguin Putnam, 2003), 68–69.

Letter 22

Hey Jen,

If one performed a side-by-side analysis in 1965, one would find the black Twymans living in red brick homes in relative comfort and the white Twymans shivering and left bereft of modern conveniences in a two-hundred-year-old wood-frame home, Oak Lawn. How does white poverty at Oak Lawn and black middle-class status on Twyman Road fit into your sentence about "the famous redlining"? I find this idea that all black neighborhoods were poor and undesirable alienating.

Now, I'm going to push back on your macro analysis of causation. You're just tapping into the common discourse about causation between long-ago American slavery and people with low impulse control today. I get that, but, as you probably suspect, I'm unmoved and unconvinced.

Let's start with my family, with the last slave named Twyman, Scott Twyman.

There are no stories passed down the line about American slavery. And that was my specific, concrete challenge to you—American slavery. I didn't ask about Jim Crow or stolen property or murder in Alabama in 1947. Nor did I ask about Reconstruction or racism or the Freedmen's Savings Bank or Wilmington or Greenwood. I know about these scars on our American past.

I asked you about American slavery (1655–1865).*

---

* A colonial Virginia court invested Anthony Johnson with the power of slave ownership in 1655, but slavery existed prior to this date in the colonies.

I asked you to connect with causation, actual or proximate, a slave's bondage in the 1840s with a descendant's choice to lie down and bear an illegitimate child with a sketchy (married) man in 2003. You skirted around my direct call for clear causation at the micro level.

I asked you to show how an ancestor's bondage before the Civil War compelled a teenage descendant today to steal a candy bar from a store and to lie about it. You offered me nothing in your response. Wilmington (1898) is not relevant or material to causation and the candy bar, be it actual or proximate.

I asked you to show actual causation between the slave catcher, Mr. Willis in 1790s Tidewater, Virginia, and the theft of a drug store in San Francisco. I got talking points from the Woke Academy.

We can't have an honest, quality conversation about the lingering effects of American slavery if we are not concrete and specific about the hand of the slaver driving the low impulse control of black teenagers who rob stores in 2023. You have not demonstrated causation, either actual or proximate.

And so, I am unconvinced. I conclude there is no causation. I will look for other causes and effects of crime and poverty today.

I guess this brings us to resentments.

I was hoping you would make light of post-traumatic slave syndrome. You haven't really done so. Where is the humor? The wit?

If I don't laugh about the comeback of American slavery today, then I just become resentful. I resent these discussions occupying space in the public discourse. I resent the manipulation and control of people vulnerable to seeing everything through the lens of race and tribe. Isn't it racial abuse to remind the descendants of American slavery over and over and over again that American slavery effects are ever present in our lives today?

That is a falsehood. I swear I have thought more about American slavery these past few years than I ever thought about American slavery between 1961 and when we began this correspondence in 2019. And I was born in Richmond, Virginia! Why is that? Whose agenda is being served when descendants of American slavery are spurred on to nurse old resentments and grudges?

I should bring in an illustration or two to highlight what I think is the problem. I know a young woman born to a single black mom who made foolish choices, such as having two children by two different sketchy men. So, that's strike one against this young woman. Through no fault of her own, this young woman came into the world handicapped by the foolish choices of others. In your mind's eye, imagine the young woman is light-skinned with freckles and "good hair."

This is the American Dilemma I know of. So, the Lord works in mysterious ways. While the young woman was handicapped in this way, she was blessed with high intelligence, very high intelligence. She grew up in poverty without a dad, but she had a card to play for a better tomorrow. She had brains.

There was constant drama in her life as her mom made poor choice after poor choice. And through it all—the lead-poisoning diagnosis, the lost apartment for nonpayment of rent, the abandonment by her father, a dim mother—she survived. Indeed, she was selected for the Governor's School for the Gifted. This would have opened doors, but she refused to accept the invitation. She did not want to work that hard.

Because this young woman was very intelligent and lived in horrible circumstances, and I was three thousand miles away, I thought about the A Better Chance (ABC) program as a precious opportunity. ABC is a program that selects gifted students who have the misfortune of living in low-income circumstances and makes referrals to the best boarding schools in the country. Schools like Phillips Exeter Academy, St. Paul's, Andover, Deerfield Academy. If the students are accepted for admission, the program will cover all the student's expenses for four years. It is a wonderful opportunity to rise into the professions for a life otherwise hemmed in.

I reached out to my contacts and urged this young, gifted woman to apply. "Apply and check out the program. Your life could change!" And you know what? She did not lift a finger. She did not deign to request an application. And so, she remained at her underachieving public school.

Did I give up? No. I didn't give up.

My wife and I, from three thousand miles away, enrolled the young woman in the local Kumon program in Chesterfield County, Virginia, so she could boost her skills, expand her vocabulary. She didn't know what terms like "cop-out" meant. Simple things that an assessment could fix.

We were paying full freight for her tuition, but she resisted. She rebelled.

I'm fighting this battle from the other side of the country. There was no support on the home front. She stopped attending the Kumon classes. There was no gratitude whatsoever.

By this point, my heart was broken. I washed my hands of the child. She had a mother. She had a father. They should be on the front lines. I forgot about the girl. You can lead a horse to water, but you can't make the horse drink the water. I did the best that I could, but I had to let it go.

And I did. I was resigned to the foolish self-defeating choices of this intelligent young woman. To be honest, I would not have cared as much except for the close relationship.

One day and months later, the teenager called me. She said she had been recruited by a boarding school. All expenses were paid. She had to fill out the paperwork. A young life was leaving a bad situation and on the way to a new world where she could fulfill her potential. The world was turned upside right.

A few weeks passed . . .

A close cousin called me. "I don't know if you heard, but [the teenager] isn't going to boarding school. She didn't complete her paperwork."

That young woman squandered an all-expenses paid admission for four years at a leading boarding school. She will be returning to her underachieving public high school this fall. And working in retail after school.*

Now, listen to me very closely, Jen. The *New York Times* will say American slavery is the most exceptional thing about America, that race and racism is the foundation of all that we know. That is the biggest lie in the countryside. The most exceptional thing about all of us is character—vision, ambition, confidence—having a high aim in life. When the teenager was blind to opportunity in front of her face, that was not *white supremacy*. No slaver caused the teenager to say "no" to the Governor's School for the Gifted, to say "no" to ABC, to say "no" to the Kumon program for self-improvement, to say "no" to recruitment from a boarding school with the promise of all expenses paid. That is a lack of character, of foresight. That is the American Dilemma today, not the slaver in 1619.

---

* To be fair, the story evolved. The teenager subsequently enrolled in college and even made national news for activism, but it appears she has since left college for an undetermined period of time. And so it goes.

I reject unbroken causation between American slavery in 1790 and impulse control today. Consider a boy I know. Imagine a dark-skinned middle schooler with dreadlocks who wears sagging pants. The father is sketchy, and several of the boy's half-brothers have served time in prison. In February 2017, a police officer told the boy—then just twelve years old—that he was caught on video in a fight at his public school. When questioned, the boy lied and said he was in the bathroom at the time of the fight. The video, however, clearly showed that he incited the fight. He was suspended for a day. A day!

The day of his suspension, the preteen boy appeared on the campus of the school in violation of school policy. A police officer warned him he could have been arrested for being on the premises of the school. This is an impulse-control problem. This is not a racism problem.

Later that month, the mom gave the boy a credit card (!) to buy shoes. Instead, the preteen purchased an $80 gold chain with the credit card.

The next month, the boy—now a young teenager—sneaked into a flea market with friends without paying a fee. Did the slave master control the mind of the youngster as he chose to break the law?

On or about April 1 that same year, the young teenager was caught on video stealing candy from a Family Dollar store. The store manager banned him from the store. He denied the theft even as the mom viewed the incriminating video.

Three months later, the young teenager was charged with larceny for the theft of a cell phone. The mom had to pay a $150 fee for the phone. The young teenager is now placed on probation. Jen, explain to me how this is racism. How is this mass incarceration?

Cousins now refer to the young teenager as *Baby Felon.*

Show me how bondage of a paternal great-great-grandfather compelled the young teenager to lie, cheat, and steal in the year 2017. Scott Twyman was a slave over 150 years ago in Madison County, Virginia. And if the lingering effects of slavery are suffocating, explain it to me and my immediate family.

I don't have time for falsehoods in the public square.

Regards,

Wink

Letter 23

Wink,

While I think you are being a little unfair (ha—life is unfair, I hear you say to yourself), I hear what you are saying. I think you are being unfair in the sense that I think that there is causation, albeit indirect. The causation is in a mindset that is passed down and molded from years of discrimination that impresses upon some people the idea that they are "owed." They were wronged by a system that they couldn't control, and now they are going to defy the system and defy the (white) man.

Your questions, asking to find the correlation between crime and slavery, remind me of my husband's insistence that crime is just innate, biological even. That there are no intervening factors. While crime may not be related to slavery *per se*, I'll give you that, I can't accept that people are just born criminals. Perhaps some are genetically more susceptible to such behavior (e.g., low impulse control), but our environments play an intervening role in how our genetic makeup develops and presents. I've been called impulsive on several occasions, and in certain circumstances, I most certainly am, but my impulsivity never resulted in criminal activity, as that just wasn't a part of my landscape.

So, could I provide direct causation? The impact of a 3x great-grandparent's slavery on a drugstore robbery in 2021? I can't, and you're right, I failed to do so. Moreover, many descendants of slaves refuse to adopt a poverty mindset. It is neither uniform nor ubiquitous, and destiny is predetermined only in the stories we tell ourselves. However, I don't think the story I told is so easily dismissed. Not necessarily because of causation, or lack thereof, but because this is the story that is fueling the resentment and grudges you mention. It is the story more directly, and not American slavery *per se*, that leads to division and even antisocial behavior. A story that can lock us into patterns that suggest a predetermined or even biological predisposition to accept the constant drumbeat of *oppression*, which expresses itself at best as resentment and grudges and at worst in criminal activity. Perhaps American slavery, in its extreme inhumanity, is just an easily cited justification for a pervasive narrative that permeates a present mindset.

It is the story that is fueling our revisit to the past and the Woke Academy. It is why American slavery is now omnipresent in 2023. And so, we need to discuss it.

You can dismiss it insofar as you believe that it is fallacious to make these ties. I wouldn't disagree with you, but I guess my question and challenge to you is: how do we change the narrative? How about the young teenagers you have discussed? They are obviously not living under the yoke of slavery, but might they be living in its shadow? Did their parents buy into the mindset and pass it on to them—that black Americans are "less than"? Might this result in one teenager failing to reach her full potential and another teenager opting for a life of crime? Maybe, as noted, genetics play some sort of role in developing character—maybe some are more inclined to be influenced externally and others internally, making a difference in how we operate in society. I can buy that. But I do think we are also molded by our respective environments. What might have made a difference in the lives and outcomes of the two teenagers?

In my own family, I have a half-sister who was given all the same privileges as myself in terms of resources. The biggest difference? Her mother remarried approximately five more times after her marriage with my dad failed. Her mother was a very successful professional and often made more money than her husbands, so her "polyamory" was not a result of financial necessity. As individuals with our own special genetic composition, we would be different no matter the circumstances; however, our starkest personality difference is her insistence that the world owes her. I reject this notion. This has had a direct impact on how we navigate the world, and I feel confident that our different experiences and environment are partly responsible for how we show up differently in society.

Can we choose our stories? Can we look above and beyond our experiences and environment to reflect always and only our best selves? Are we locked into a genetic blueprint that dictates how we interact in the world? Perhaps a criminal is simply born a criminal, and we chalk it up to DNA. Do you really believe that?

Let me run another thought by you. This doesn't get at anything directly causal, but I think it points to something that plays a role in perpetuating a poverty mindset. I wrote to you earlier about Robert E. Lee. You asked if he was the most evil man ever—if you should see him as Adolf Hitler. I think good and evil are too binary. This type of either/or thinking is what constitutes "tier 1 consciousness"—a consciousness that dismisses nuance and complexity in our humanity. The ways in which the South exalted Lee have been clearly problematic in this regard—the statues, the street names, and other monuments to his memory. Yet, as we've started to remove and dismantle images and statues of Lee across the United States over the past few years, I've really struggled with this issue. At first, I thought this move reflected a similar tier 1 consciousness—that we are only ever allowed to see the man through one lens.

My husband was in the irate camp. He claimed we were destroying history. He would point to crime numbers in certain cities and remark how the removal of the statues clearly had no impact on grievances and resentments, at least as they related to ongoing and even rising crime. As a law enforcement officer, he interpreted such moves as an attempt to mitigate the tensions that had led to looting, property destruction, and defacement and believed that ultimately they had no positive effect. I never had that type of visceral reaction, but I do think destroying monuments can illustrate a totalitarian bent, as we saw when the Taliban demolished ancient Buddhist carvings, and I cringe whenever we move in this direction.*

But as I sat with this some more, intentionally trying to empathize with those demanding Lee's removal from public spaces, I couldn't help but feel a different type of discomfort, even if I adopted a growth mindset that was not easily traumatized by perceived or even real slights at the glorification of someone like Lee. As complex a man as he may have been, Lee still led an army that fought, at least in part, to uphold slavery.

---

* For example, see Pierre Centlivres, "The Death of the Buddhas of Bamiyan," *MEI@75,* April 18, 2012, www.mei.edu/publications/death-buddhas-bamiyan.

If I truly put myself in the shoes of a descendant of slavery, would I really be able to "just get over it" and use slavery to fuel my achievement, as you think it should? Or would these monuments still play into an unconscious sense of not fully belonging or of having my own history degraded? I reached the conclusion that I might still try to excel in the face of such a challenge, but that I would be disgruntled.

Now imagine that you live constantly in the shadow of these monuments, that you are told that you will always be oppressed, and that you haven't had the resources or the guidance to develop a mindset that lets you move out of the shadow of someone who actively oppressed your ancestors. The ancestors might be long gone, but the memory of a man who fought to keep them enslaved continues to adorn state houses, schoolhouses, and so on.

In this regard, I understand why the dismantling of these monuments is necessary, even if the full benefits of their dismantling may take a generation or more to be truly felt. Yet, there is a near-term cost. Criminal behavior and general lawlessness may continue to rise as people come to realize that burning, looting, and rioting can produce wanted results with little threat of punishment. This concerns me. When lawlessness is rewarded in this way, we risk creating a vicious cycle that won't be easily arrested. Not to mention there are many grifters who are exploiting the trend for their own ends and adding fuel to the fire (sometimes literally). I don't have answers on how to interrupt such a cycle, but I do believe that future generations of children who are not constantly reminded of the past will be better able to grasp their full future.

No matter the impact of the symbols and monuments that inform our environment, the best way to change our mindset is through connection—such as through the connection we are making here, in our correspondence. This type of connection is the antithesis of segregation. When we connect, when we interact and share our stories and our lives and take the precious time to do so, we change our hearts. We can see ourselves in each other, despite the myriad differences and distinctions that make us unique individuals. This is monumental. Indeed, if our history had been built on connection rather than segregation, our monuments and symbols today would likely have a universal resonance.

I'm glad you pushed back on my letter. As a result, it encouraged me to think more deeply about these issues and to try to place myself in your shoes, much like I tried to place myself in the shoes of those who supported the dismantling of monuments. To see with your eyes. Even where we may disagree, I'm able to connect with you through your words and thoughts. Through your story.

Unfortunately, we aren't fostering connection through the resentments and grudges that emerge because of all our navel-gazing into the wider world of American Slavery, episode 2023. I may empathize with the removal of the likeness of Robert E. Lee, but we also shouldn't fail to celebrate those pre–Civil Rights successes and stories that don't align with the prevailing storyline about America's past. There must be a reckoning in some respects to remodel our "house," but tearing down the foundation doesn't make a better home.

Jen

Letter 24

Hey Jen,

I'm tired of sad narratives and excuse-making for low-impulse control people in the here and now. I appreciate your well-honed thoughts. Let's just agree to disagree. I remain unconvinced that causation, either actual or proximate, placed the gun in the black man's hand who killed a woman in La Jolla in the year 2018. And if folktales are sewed together to connect the slaver from the 1790s to the tragedy of a drive-by in 2021, then I regard those folktales as lies and falsehoods.

So, given the lack of proven causation, I will look for other causes of current poverty and crime. I will tune out the larger world engaged in mythmaking.

As for Robert E. Lee, my first cousin Rosa Nell Grace once said we should better integrate our past. The history we have is the history we have. We should focus on constructing monuments to John Mercer Langston, Oliver Hill, and Daniel Brown so that our history is complete. Why not a monument to entrepreneur Edward F. Mimms, Sr., the founding father of the Mimms Funeral Home dynasty, across from the Confederate soldier monument at the Courthouse? Destruction is not the way to the Blessed Society where divisions melt away.

Black people can handle the truth about the past, a complete past that sees Chesterfield County as an interwoven place in black and white. I lived two miles from Jefferson Davis Highway until I was eighteen, so I don't need to imagine the scenario you present; I saw no shadows.

I take this strong position because to do otherwise would suggest something uniquely weak and fragile about descendants of American slavery. I know that's not the case. If I came from a long line of troubled people in and out of jail, Black Fragility due to American slavery might appeal. But I'm sorry—imagined demons of cosmic harm are distasteful to me.

I think truth-telling is healing. And I don't mean light-hearted discourse. I mean Dr. Phil kind of stuff, the kind of stuff one shares with a therapist or mistress. Consider this passage from my manuscript, *On the Road to Oak Lawn: Truth, Reconciliation and the Twymans*:

> In psychiatry, there is this idea of drilling down to the bedrock truth as cathartic. A therapist keeps repeating a statement or question with a wounded soul until the wounded is freed of their demons. This is how one reaches a true answer. We see this method in the movie *Good Will Hunting* where Robin Williams as Therapist Sean Maguire repeatedly tells Matt Damon (playing janitor Will Hunting) that his child abuse wasn't his fault. Williams repeats the mantra "it wasn't your fault" over and over and over again until Damon breaks down and weeps. Damon had to pass through strong emotions to reach psychological relief.[*]

My friend Luis really liked this passage. (And notice I did not say my white friend or my black friend or my brown friend or my red friend. I just said, my friend.)

Have we drilled down to bedrock truth in our correspondence thus far? Have we experienced catharsis in our interaction? Do we know one another? And quite frankly, I think personality is more important than race. Have we kept repeating a statement with a wounded soul? I came close by repeating my demand for you to prove causation, not talking points. Am I the wounded soul? Are you the wounded soul? Are we both wounded souls? And, if so, what demons are we avoiding? I have shared some of my demons—kinship with Robert E. Lee, few close black friends, love-hate relationship with Jack and Jill. I have many more demons I will share over time, such as watermelon, the Harvard Club of San Diego, and dogma . . . We will get there in time. But my dear, wonderful Jen—what

---

[*] W. F. Twyman, Jr., *On the Road to Oak Lawn: Truth, Reconciliation and the Twymans* (December 1, 2018), 8, drive.google.com/file/d/1m1lRphmfWreEsglO6XseYjZtSA_hPlsl/view?usp=sharing.

are your demons aside from a *white savior* guilt complex? You will never be free of your demons until you acknowledge your demons and the resultant wounds and reveal yourself to others.

As we journey together on this path of anti-division, the fun times are the easy times. I love, love, love hearing about your distant black cousins. Warms my heart and makes me forget about Jack and Jill for a fortnight!

The real growing and healing lie in the dark times ahead. How were you abused racially? How did you respond? What were the lasting, lingering effects of said abuse? It wasn't your fault. It wasn't your fault that some of your ancestors owned American slaves. Been there, done that. We haven't reached our breakdown and weeping moment yet. But we will get there.

And when we do, psychological relief for us both lies on the other side. That is the place known as Octoroon Nation.

A toast to strong emotions ahead,

Good Will Hunting aka Wink

Letter 25

Dear Wink,

Americans need to come together for the journey of healing. The healing of a nation so bitterly divided comes from the sharing of painful stories, the generation of understanding and empathy, and the ability to see ourselves in each other.

With respect to racial divisions, I think there are a few things that make this journey more challenging. First is the current discussion on reparations. It necessarily pits people against one another and encourages the sense that someone is "owed" something. I actually believe in reparations, but not of the financial sort. The "owed" are black Americans and the "debtors" are white Americans, but this simple framing creates problems even if we can somehow manage to ignore the presence of all other races and groups in the country. There will be grudges and resentment if wealthy black professionals get a payout while poor whites are asked to contribute. If some black Americans can trace their descendants to slaveholders—either white or black—what should their payout be? Do we create a sliding scale of reparations? Finally, as you've said before, how do you put a price on a life? It is hard to start on a journey together on a landscape dominated by a growing Grand Canyon of division.

Second, the *white guilt/white privilege* mantra makes honest discussion difficult. White people have become ultrasensitive and are very aware of any language that could in any way be construed as racist. As a result, so many just stay quiet and avoid conversation altogether. Despite what our media feeds us, there are very few white people who are truly *racist*. Sure, we have our biases and prejudices, as does everyone. And we should check our biases, but the only way to do that is to engage in good-faith dialogue where people can observe and acknowledge biases—in a Dr. Phil kind of way! However, in the current climate where any perceived slight risks one standing naked in the public square, we pad ourselves in extra layers of protection and forgo the journey. I know you said to drop the dogmatic slogans, but it is precisely these slogans that are generating the silence, and so I mention them to underline the point. When we repeat slogans, we are only creating more silence.

I've read several essays where black authors say they appreciate the Ku Klux Klan (KKK) as they are at least honest and open with their racism. In essence, what I hear is that we white Americans are all just secret KKK members who have not yet recognized our biases. I sometimes feel that the only way some black Americans will be satisfied is if all whites just collectively shout, "I'm Racist!" And then we can move on. Is this appeasement enough, or will it lead to more vicious cycles? Does appeasement ever work?

The other day I was writing a text to my sister, and I told her she had my respect. On iPhones it will often give you a choice of an emoji to use when you type certain words. You know what my emoji choice was for the word "respect"? A black-power fist. Isn't this ironic? Even as we have boiled down all black-white relationships to *oppressed* and *oppressor*, our social landscape is filled with images and suggestions that black is "good" and white is not right. We even now have posters that decry "Amerikk-ka"! This social engineering would make even Mao jealous.

And yet, in the diversity-training class I attended, I was told that *racism* can only go one way. That is, only whites can be *racist* as they are the only group with power. The diversity trainer defined *racism* as bias + power (apparently, *Merriam-Webster* was not informed of this newly tweaked definition*). Accordingly, blacks can't be *racist* because they don't have power. This was a W.T.F. moment for me. I'm sorry, I know you don't like foul language, but since we are being honest, that was my honest response. This cloaked bigotry is the most insidious. This is where

---

* *Merriam-Webster* has since been informed. See Christine Hauser, "Merriam-Webster Revises 'Racism' Entry After Missouri Woman Asks for Changes," *New York Times*, November 3, 2021, www.nytimes.com/2020/06/10/us/merriam-webster-racism-definition.html

I fear the black mindset (or at least this is how diversity training lumps blacks together into a homogeneous group sharing a singular mindset) is being manipulated to embrace powerlessness. Have blacks historically been less powerful than whites? Of course. I don't think any sane person would argue otherwise. However, if we continue to impress this power-lessness on black citizens, it is truly an offense worthy of the KKK.

Maybe one solution is to enforce interracial marriages so that we all end up as some variation of a caramel hue, and then we won't have to talk about diversity any longer. Everyone would be black under the "one-drop rule." While we're at it, maybe we can all adopt the same haircut and wear the same green Mao suits as we march around waving our little red books on antiracism.

Maybe, Wink, this is the causation you were looking for in our earlier letters. Perhaps the causation is not that slavery caused a poverty mind-set in black Americans (although I still stick by my arguments!), but that slavery is revisited in the slogans of today: blacks have no power and need help. Never fear—iPhone to the rescue! Respect! In this mantra, we are actively encouraging a poverty mindset. To paraphrase Bob Marley's words in "Redemption Song,"* let's all emancipate ourselves from mental slavery and free our minds.

The road we are traveling on is segregated, and I'm not interested in this journey. If we are going to journey together on a path of healing, I think it is incumbent on all of us to channel our inner Dr. Phil. We need to be allowed the space to speak openly and honestly and with the hu-mility to search our biases through the eyes of our fellow travelers. I do believe this is the only way to slay our demons. Pain and hurt manifest in anger. And we are clearly a very angry nation.

It is a comfort for me to journey with you on the path to a national healing. I assume Octoroon Nation is a place where we all acknowledge our similarities and our mixed past and future. I hope we can pick up other travelers to come together on our trip to Octoroon Nation.

Your fellow traveler,

Jen

---

* You can find the music video of "Redemption Song" on the Bob Marley YouTube channel at www.youtube.com/watch?v=yv5xonFSC4c.

Letter 26

Good evening, Jen,

Those of us who are anti-division and anti-slave must contend with those who are pro-division and pro-slavery. And what I mean by pro-slavery today is not physical shackles and chains. What I mean is an intellectual movement that never recognizes a human being in descendants of a slave. That is a strong statement, and I mean it.

One can never make amends for the cruelties and barbarities of American slavery. We have both read a thousand eyewitness accounts of American slavery, and the horrors are sickening. "But my soul sickens at the remembrance of these things."* There were around four million slaves as of the start of the Civil War. Now, multiply one thousand eyewitness accounts by four thousand. And this hell of floggings and mutilations and castrations and rapes and runaways burned alive and decapitated heads left on stakes as a warning to others is something we really want to make descendants whole for today?

It is a disgusting, offensive, shameful thought from a humane standpoint. And this is why those who push for reparations are no better than slave owners. Reparations are incompatible with recognizing a human being in a slave. Reparations treat slaves as property.

Such Marxism and socialism! It's just about transferring wealth and using the ugliness of American slavery as an ATM machine.

What is the price to make whole a beautiful mulatto teenage girl

---

* Weld, *American Slavery as It Is,* 49.

from Charleston, South Carolina, whose healthy front tooth was removed? What is the price to make whole slave babies fed to alligators as bait in the Deep South swamp land? What is the price to make whole six African girls driven to self-hanging? What is the price paid to the runaway George hacked to death limb by limb? What is the price to be paid the slave mistress and her quadroon daughter sold away at the slave market in Richmond, Virginia? I'm not talking about the price of unpaid labor because these were human beings. What is the price of the pain and suffering of that mother sold away from her daughter on the auction block in New Orleans? What is the price to be paid a slave cook whose eyeball was knocked out because she displeased her mistress? What is the price to be paid a teenager bred with some random black buck in the slave pen? What is the price of pain for hundreds of years of living hell on earth?

No price is sufficient. No amount will ever do. Forty acres and a mule? That would be blood money for my 3x great-grandmother Phyllis, used as a bed warmer by faceless white men.

And so, I recoil at this reparation talk. I really do.

How does all of this help me "Come to the Table"?* Well, I can't come to the table until I am authentic with myself. I don't like talking about American slavery. I long for a different American past, one where we could unite behind flawless Founding Fathers. As a country, we need reverence for our Founding Fathers. They might not have been flawless, but we are the inheritors of singular documents like the Declaration of Independence and the Constitution of the United States. Imperfect men of vision created documents aimed at a more perfect Union.

Today was the first day I "came out" in my office.

What do I mean?

A colleague was in my office, and we were talking about Virginia and its rich, deep history and slave markers in Northern Virginia. I talked in

---

* Coming to the Table is a group dedicated to bringing together descendants of slave owners and slaves. Jen is unfamiliar with the group, but Wink has attended two meetings, one in Santa Monica, California, and one in Richmond, Virginia (virtual). While Wink supports the group's aims of truth and reconciliation and admires the individuals involved, he found the group protocols to be a bit strange and cult-like and has no plans to participate in the group again. As a condition of attendance, Wink swore never to reveal what was said in the meetings. Thus, he will not reveal anything further here or elsewhere.

generalities about how slavery was just part of the backdrop in Virginia and how I had a high school classmate who proudly wore a "Son of the Confederacy" lapel pin when we met last Christmas at a Starbucks in Chester, Virginia. And then it seemed like the most natural thing to say, "You know, people are really close with deep roots in Virginia. Robert E. Lee was my fourth cousin, three times removed." My colleague seemed surprised, but he didn't, like, fall out of his chair. A few hours later, he came to my office and asked about the pictures on my office wall. I proudly said, "This guy is Col. Richard Lee I. He was my 9x great-grandfather. And this guy is George Twyman IV. He was my 5x great-grandfather's son." Alongside these portraits are a large color picture of Thurgood Marshall circa 1952 and Richard Holloway, Sr., the earliest existing color portrait of a black person from Charleston, South Carolina.

And just like that, I came out of the closet and embraced my full genetic self. The world didn't stop. The colleague didn't run away screaming. I embraced my full ancestry for the first time in a face-to-face conversation with someone outside of my family.

This is Coming to the Table for me. Authenticity. It was difficult because of learned villains. Every group has villains. Robert E. Lee would be foremost in the cast of anti-black American villains. And there is the fear of what others might think. The difficulty wasn't shame. Shame would be the wrong word. The better term would be unspoken norms and mores, guardrails of race consciousness and fidelity to race. What is the meaning of a genetic relationship to a villain of your group? That is the deep question I'm drawn to, and I don't have a satisfactory answer thus far. My friend, Trina, says it just shows we are closer than we might want to admit. Trina is right, and she is also my friend. Friends don't judge. They understand.

You're already there. You've had no internal struggles with embracing a multiracial past.

So, there you go. Does American slavery cause *white guilt/white privilege* mantras today? That is an interesting question. Why were these mantras not on the table in 1961 or 1968? Shouldn't there have been more *white guilt* and *white privilege* the closer we were to actual slavery? Something happened between 1961 and today that was an intervening factor. Was the intervening factor "antiracism"?

I ask because causation generally requires an unbroken chain of causal events. *White guilt* and *white privilege* were simply not on the radar screen in the 1950s. We are talking about American slavery from 1655 to 1865. (And still, you make no jokes or quips about the comeback of American Slavery today.)

With Pietas,

Wink

Letter 27

Wink,

I think the introduction of *white privilege/guilt* is a result of what John McWhorter would call "third-wave" antiracism. The first wave was the anti-slavery movement—a movement for basic human rights. The second wave was antiracism—a movement for equality and desegregation. And now we are in a third wave—a movement to stamp out unconscious biases and any remaining conscious stereotypes and caricatures.

The first two waves had religious underpinnings. According to McWhorter, so does the third wave, but without the religious terminology: "The idea that whites are permanently stained by their white privilege, gaining moral absolution only by eternally attesting to it, is the third wave's version of original sin." Further, he goes on to say: "the new religion, as a matter of faith, entails that one suspends disbelief at certain points out of respect to the larger narrative."*

So, to answer your question, there is causation insofar as the continuation of a movement from basic freedoms to equality undoes stereotypes and caricatures. Undoing stereotypes and caricatures and recognizing what roles we may play in perpetuating them is not an effort in futility *per se*, but the problem with this third wave is that it is not moving in the right direction.

---

* John McWhorter, "The Virtue Signalers Won't Change the World," *Atlantic,* December 23, 2018, www.theatlantic.com/ideas/archive/2018/12/why-third-wave-anti-racism-dead-end/578764/.

One could argue, as my first-year philosophy teacher did when I was an undergrad, that in order for a movement to successfully progress, you need those on the extreme edges to pave the way first, and then those who follow need to reel in the extreme edges while pulling the original status quo with them. I've thought a lot about this idea over the years. In fact, it may be one of only a few lasting takeaways from my undergrad education. It resonates.

Nonetheless, we have come to embrace virtue signaling, victimization, and grievance as the primary vehicles for this new third wave. As I've said before, I believe this is largely due to the convergence of the third wave with a digital era, making it all too easy to broadcast even a hint of a slight—whether perceived or real—to garner the support of a tribe. You don't even have to leave your lounge chair.

I want to digress here to tell a story—not of racism, but of how I saw this victimhood culture in action the other day. A very good friend of mine who has never exuded a victim mentality was offended by what another friend of hers said in a personal interaction. Instead of having a discussion with her friend, my friend posted about the incident on Facebook in her search for consolation. They were FRIENDS. Wouldn't a better way to solve the problem between friends be to explain the offense and the resulting pain? To give the friend the opportunity to see her pain and taste her own words? That is what Coming to the Table means to me. To have both the courage and vulnerability to look someone in the eye and share a moment, even a painful one.

I don't think my friend even recognized that she was playing into the victimhood mentality, and, if I had pointed it out, I believe she would've been appalled with her social media reaction. But my point is that this mentality is so pervasive and pernicious it often manages to sneak into our culture without our own recognition.

Third-wave antiracism plus social media has engendered a victimhood culture that has reached the heights of performance art. Even when we don't actively participate, we are participants. In this instance, I didn't chime in myself because I was too busy microwaving popcorn so I could watch the show. And it didn't disappoint as waves of supporters piled into her Facebook story, sloppily apologizing for the fact that she had to suffer such an egregious offense. Oh vey! One thing I can attest, I am never bored in our new-found world of outrage. You don't have to buy pay-per-view to get a front-row seat to a cage match.

The problem is that this hypersensitivity and performance art has gotten us off track. We are no longer climbing the ladder to the fabled utopia of genuine equality. Not that we could ever get to this utopia, because well . . . it's utopia and doesn't exist. Nonetheless, true progress has stalled. And we may even be backsliding.

For example, we've become so obsessed with these new pursuits that many schools have decided that instead of teaching the classes that force us to think critically and thoughtfully, they should focus their energies on teaching social justice to eradicate any vestiges of bigotry. In many classrooms, teachers have decided that directing students on social activism is a better endeavor than teaching them basic fundamentals. Washington and California are leading the charge in the proposal to teach students that even math is *racist*.*

And God help the child who doesn't suspend disbelief. Critical inquiry into the narrative would result in some children receiving a detention slip for not sticking to the script.

One of my teacher friends was beside herself recounting stories of swastikas and such found drawn in school bathrooms and carved onto desks. She was adamant that this was the result of President Trump. I won't discount that his influence may have emboldened closet bigots. But it's also the rebellion against the new social justice curricula. I honestly think that there is a portion of these offending kids who don't even

---

* Several examples include: Lee Ohanian, "Seattle Schools Propose to Teach That Math Education is Racist—Will California Be Far Behind?" Hoover Institute, October 29, 2019, www.hoover.org/research/seattle-schools-propose-teach-math-education-racist-will-california-be-far-behindseattle; George Packer, "When the Culture War Comes for the Kids," *Atlantic* (October 2019), www.theatlantic.com/magazine/archive/2019/10/when-the-culture-war-comes-for-the-kids/596668/; Susan Edelman et al., "Richard Carranza Held 'White Supremacy Culture' Training for School Admins," *New York Post,* May 20, 2019, nypost.com/2019/05/20/richard-carranza-held-doe-white-supremacy-culture-training/?utm_source=url_sitebuttons&utm_medium=site%20buttons&utm_campaign=site%20buttons; D. J. Buck, "Schools Need to Teach Patriotism," *Areo Magazine,* October 2, 2019, areomagazine.com/2019/10/02/schools-need-to-teach-patriotism/; John McWhorter, "The Show-Trial Rhetoric That Took Down a Charter School Founder," *Atlantic,* November 10, 2019; www.theatlantic.com/ideas/archive/2019/11/ascend-charter-school-petition/601696/; and Rochester, J. Martin, "Social Justice Miseducation in our Schools," Fordham Institute, November 1, 2017, fordhaminstitute.org/national/commentary/social-justice-miseducation-our-schools.

know what a swastika is but see it as an act of subversion to authority. What if, instead of overreacting in dramatic displays that we recount on Facebook and Twitter (or any other social media platform), we actually use the opportunity to teach kids history. This is what one teacher did to great success, so much so there is even a book and documentary on her class: *The Freedom Writers Diary.* And this was well before Harvard offered a free "social justice certificate."† Ever wanted to say you went to Harvard, folks? Now's your chance!

Further, I know in many high schools today, the N-word is used more frequently now than it ever was in my day, often in jest between black and white friends, precisely because they are told how horrible it is. It has become a joke. It is a joke because the woke narrative's performance is a tragicomedy. (By the way, "woke" is just another slogan word. But unlike almost all the others in use today, this one is now deployed by those opposed to cancel culture and speech policing. I myself am guilty of using this term at times, because I know of no better word to describe those who see *everything* through an oppressor-oppressed lens, essentialize race and gender, and demand illiberal and even authoritarian solutions to the often wholly imagined problems they identify.) After the murder of George Floyd, one of my son's white friends told me he wished he was black. They were getting all the ladies and all the attention. We don't do history any longer. We do drama in the name of social justice.

To create a durable change and to really engage in true reparations, we need to drop the tragicomedy and drama and take actionable steps that matter. Financial reparations are pandering to the black vote and promoting division. Should black Americans have received financial reparations after slavery? I think so, even though, as you note, it would have devalued human life with a price tag. Arguably, however, if enacted in the Reconstruction Era, it could have been seen as back pay for uncompensated labor. Sadly, this didn't happen. To go back and revisit reparations today not only is messy, but it also devalues everything black Americans have fought to achieve.

---

* Erin Gruwell, *The Freedom Writers Diary: How a Teacher and 150 Teens Used Writing to Change Themselves and the World Around Them* (New York: Broadway Books, 1999).

† For more on the Harvard certificate, see www.extension.harvard.edu/academics/professional-graduate-certificates/social-justice-certificate.

True reparations are only achieved in an authentic Coming to the Table, minus the slogans that create caricatures and avatars devoid of real meaning. In order to do this, we need to stop segregating into *affinity groups*—a frequent practice in colleges, social circles, and a favorite activity in diversity training that now also abounds in public schools. We need to tell stories and share experiences without the fear of blame or guilt. We need to see and hear someone's pain (and joy) and to see ourselves in them. This will eventually lead to a more common identity in multiracial arenas, especially in schools, and it will carry through life. It won't always be pretty or even civil, and some people will refuse the invitation, as it is sure to be uncomfortable.

Oh, and it will take a while, so buckle up for the ride.

Resisting American Slavery in the present day,

Jen

Letter 28

Hola Jen,

How do we create belief in the idea of a shared American identity? For starters, let's start thinking of the history of slavery as a common history between black and white Americans. Don't you think Old Americans share a common history in American slavery? My daughter may wish to deny them, but her ancestors in Virginia date back to Peter Montague in the year 1621. You and I share a common history in our antebellum past, don't you think? Or, maybe not, as you do not have slaves in your direct line. Does that matter, and if so, in what way does the absence of slaves in your direct line render your history of slavery different from my history of slavery? Remember, as Eugene Genovese said in *Roll, Jordan, Roll: The World the Slaves Made*, we cannot understand the slaves without the slave owners, and we cannot understand slave owners without the slaves. Why do you think there is no overlap in the common history of Old Americans—Americans, for example, who can trace their ancestry in Virginia back to the year 1621?

Cool breeze in San Diego,

Wink

Letter 29

Wink,

How do we create a belief in the idea of a shared American identity? That's the question I'm trying to answer as well. Indeed, I believe it is the reason why we write. You have presented me with a solid solution in my quest—to do more research on my own family history and find ancestors across the color line.

In your quest, you have found ancestors as far back as the indentured servant George Twyman (1661–1703) from Kent, England, and Peter Montague, the first schoolteacher in the Virginia colony in 1621. This is a powerful testament to a common American identity and the realization of a common American history.

We have both shared old documents attesting to a common history in American slavery. The difference is that I don't know of any slaves in my direct line. You have both slaves and slave owners. I can only claim the latter. Should this matter?

I've spent a lot of time grappling with this question. I believe that to claim a common history, a common responsibility, if you will, would be viewed by many as a way to sidestep history. I appreciate that you recognize that there are slave owners in your family tree. We should embrace the fullness of our history and ancestry. As I said before, we all have sinners and saints. However, I think many black Americans are in search of recognition for their contribution to American history. At least this is my most benevolent reading of the 1619 Project. Or this is just a veil

Nikole Hannah-Jones very effectively used to mask her agenda to center America in racial oppression and slavery and ultimately make a case for reparations. At a time in history when a postmodern lens and social media screeds fog our perception, we are ripe to consider such an act of duplicity. As we zoom in on slavery, there is no room for Peter Montague in the picture. All relationships are a power play in this colorless world of black and white.

Practically speaking, what would it look like for us to claim a common history? Would it be the recognition by white Americans of their full family trees and the contribution of slaves and slavery to the building of America? Would it be a recognition among black Americans that they share a genetic history with many white Americans and that they should embrace their genetic relationship to early white Americans?

You speak a truth—that many black Americans have slave owners in their family, either through white ancestors or free black men and women who owned slaves. And yet, it was our white ancestors who created a system with separate classes of people that really only started to dissipate in the past fifty years or so. What kind of national therapy do you propose to get over this hurdle?

Given that the average black American has 24 percent European ancestry, is it okay to simply claim that we all come from the same stock and call it a day? Can an average black American take that information and embrace their likely ties to slave owners, not to mention the country's forefathers? I know that you like to choose uplift over despondency, so this solution works for you, but is it really this simple? I look forward to getting your insight and guidance.

Let me throw some figures at you. According to a Pew Study, 44 percent of black Americans felt *racism* was a problem in 2009. That figure had increased to 81 percent by 2017.[*] (I'm going to guess the percentage has grown even larger since then.) I'm not really sure what definition of *racism* we are using these days as it seems so fluid, but Pew doesn't offer any enlightenment on the evolution of this new slogan word that has become increasingly weaponized. As we move even further away from slavery and Jim Crow, the number of black Americans claiming to feel *racism* has grown dramatically in a very short time. What happened be-

---

* Kristen Bialik, "5 Facts about Black Americans," Pew Research Center, February 22, 2018, www.pewresearch.org/fact-tank/2018/02/22/5-facts-about-blacks-in-the-u-s/.

tween 2009 to 2017 or even today that has created such a change in perception? Could it partly be the imposition of woke ideology, the spawn of Critical Theory? From our letters, I know you don't believe that *racism* has increased, but you're in the minority. At least according to Pew. I'm sure you're okay with that!

And so, your elegant solution to our racial dilemma seems out of reach, at least in this current cultural moment. The bigger question is, is this current cultural moment just a spasm? Is it something that will eventually burn out?

Let me throw another figure at you from yet another Pew Study. Seventy-six percent of black American adults say that race is extremely important or very important to their sense of self, compared to 15 percent of white American adults.* I think you are onto something in addressing the complexity and nuance of American slavery and our mixed heritage. I have joined you on this mission to seek out distant cousins with different genetic heritages.

However, I believe that the hardships that black Americans have either directly faced or heard in stories of oppression have resulted in tribal enclaves. You attest to this even within the bonds of your own immediate family. Despite your openness to tracing your lineage back to the likes of Col. Richard Lee I, Peter Montague, and even Robert E. Lee, your beautiful daughter apparently refuses to acknowledge these connections. If one's ancestors can be so easily denied or disavowed, how can we expect to will a sense of common history into reality? On that note, I guess in some ways our current slogans have forced a certain national consciousness that has become a reality, so maybe we can. Sadly, these sloganeers seem to be holding the cards today. And so, perhaps we write not for today but for tomorrow.

I am no sociologist or psychologist, but it is my understanding that humans are a tribal species and that our group bonds and boundaries become stronger during a crisis, whether perceived or real. Yet, throughout history, there are notable characters who, like you, have looked beyond the tribe and accepted their full genetic history. In the modern context,

---

* Kiana Cox and Christine Tamir, "Race Is Central to Identity for Black Americans and Affects How They Connect with Each Other," Pew Research Center, April 14, 2022, www.pewresearch.org/race-ethnicity/2022/04/14/race-is-central-to-identity-for-black-americans-and-affects-how-they-connect-with-each-other/.

consider Jean Toomer or even Thomas Chatterton Williams. It is this acknowledgment and acceptance that could lead to racial healing, but these suggestions and the role models who have made this trek are too often ignored or even maligned in the public square for breaking with groupthink and group identity. As Erec Smith would say, they are erased and replaced.*

According to Pew's statistics, black Americans have a strong connection to black identity (again, Pew doesn't offer any insight on how exactly this is defined). You don't buy into group identities, but this suggests that there was and is a real or perceived crisis. Arguably, today, it is a crisis of the spirit, not of past slavery. A crisis that, once again, has the fingerprints of postmodern meddling.

Elite institutions and educational systems have bought into the neo-Marxism of Critical Theory, and grifters have profited from its spread. This is one of the reasons I would suggest that we see the sharp rise in *perceived* racism from 2009 to 2017 and beyond. Add to this trend the centrality of race for black Americans, which may be, at least in part, a holdover from years of segregation, and I just don't see how we can apply your prescription effectively. Getting everyone to read *American Slavery as It Is* might be a start, as we've noted in our earlier letters.

Into this mix is the irony that the purpose of such neo-Marxist ideology is not a search for truth and reconciliation—something that could be a valuable part of the healing of America and lead to a shared American identity if done correctly. Rather, it seeks the wholesale destruction of American values, perhaps even of America itself. This does a great disservice to the likes of Jean Toomer and John Mercer Langston, who refused to erase the blackness from their ancestry and, in so doing, were paragons of an authentic American identity. Old Americans, indeed.

While I think the recognition of historical truths that have been whitewashed is important, the reconciliation part is trickier. I would argue that ineffective efforts at reconciliation, in the form of purposed reparations, for example, will have unintended consequences that result in more damage and segregation. The question is, can there ever be reconciliation? As you say, the past is the past, but we continue to keep it in the present, and when we do so, no true reconciliation will ever emerge.

---

* See Erec Smith, "Authenticity: Erased & Replaced," YouTube video, posted by the Institute for Liberal Values, September 27, 2021, youtu.be/1AU9n7VH8Q8.

We are caught in a negative feedback loop. American slavery 2.0.

We need to let history be history. Let it all hang out—the good, bad, and ugly . . . truths. Let's realize that if we cannot bring ourselves to forge a new American identity based on our common humanity, we are opening the doors to new evils from which we may not have the opportunity to recover, and our binary tier 1 consciousness will be our downfall.

A higher consciousness, a tier 2 consciousness, would be the acknowledgment of a common slave history, as you suggest. We recognize the horrors and heroes, the contributions, and the setbacks. We insist on reaching out to the individual through the muddle of collectivization, breaking away from group identification and rigid affiliations that mask authenticity.

We take our seats at the table we set together. How do we invite others to join us?

Jen

Letter 30

Jen,

Let me begin with a simple acknowledgment that all you say about the Pew Research Studies and the primacy of blackness to one's sense of self for the majority of black Americans is true. It is undeniable. As I've written elsewhere, the prevailing "attitude among Blacks that relationships with whites must be kept at arm's length maintains a silent us-against-them mindset. Blacks who appear too friendly and comfortable around whites are viewed with suspicion; their blackness in question."* My life vision has been to live beyond boundaries of race. You and I share this vision; however, you seem more willing to accept the prevailing perception ("it would be viewed by many as . . .") that an appeal to a common American past, a common slave past, represents an attempt to sidestep history. I see shared blood and ancestry as a gateway to a better tomorrow where a silent "us-against-them" mindset can die off.

For me, it is unacceptable for any American, regardless of race, to perceive the recognition of a common American past, a common slavery past, as sidestepping history. Did I read you right? If so, I am surprised you didn't immediately cast out that limited sight, that limited vision, as odious and distasteful. I give the limited perception of a common American past no quarter. You share my vision and say so by the end of your letter. However, I am more hostile to perceptions of sidestepping history

---

* Twyman, *On the Road to Oak Lawn,* 63n10, drive.google.com/file/d/1m1lRphmfWreEsgl-O6XseYjZtSA_hPlsl/view?usp=sharing.

than you are. I am very sensitive to sidestepping history as a reason to reject a common American past. A common past is the exact opposite of sidestepping history. I will be direct with you as my whole life, since the age of eight, has been one of embracing the larger world. I have always embraced all of history. I have never sidestepped discomforting history.

I read your letter several times. I looked for specific narrow answers to my specific concrete questions. I didn't ask about tier 2 consciousness in my questions to you. Nor did I ask about horrors and heroes, contributions, and setbacks.

I asked, "How do we create belief in the idea of a shared American identity?" Well, how do sports teams create a shared identity? How do fighting regiments under attack create a shared identity? How did Alexander Hamilton create a shared American identity as he led the black 1st Rhode Island Regiment to victory at Yorktown? These are concrete pathways for the creation of a shared American identity in the past. Your answer was not as on point as it could have been.

You are not sidestepping history, Jen, but you write that a common American past could be seen as sidestepping history. I think I read you right. If so, I question the values and attitudes of those who would see our good work as sidestepping history. I have seen too much sidestepping in black culture and consciousness over the years to not respond to your use of the word "sidestep." Sidestepping connotes for me memories of limited and self-defeating thought. Those who sidestep lead us into cultural and racial cul-de-sacs. That is the opposite destination of where we should be heading as a society. I don't really care about the current cultural moment. My reaction to sidestepping history remains the same regardless of the times I live in.

In your letter, there was no mention of your Richmond or my Twyman ancestors. I was surprised that you didn't do a side-by-side analysis of the two families in black and white. There are plentiful similarities and distinctions between the Richmond and the Twyman families that you might have reviewed and examined. We won't reach the promised land where divisions melt away until you and I think of our past as a common past:

As the meeting ends, hundreds of Twymans shake hands and embrace as is the custom in church. Nathan, Deb, Patty, Anthony, Jim, Elizabeth, Connie and I lead countless Twymans down an old country road towards Oak Lawn. George Twyman III built Oak Lawn in 1750 upon a land grant of 1,100 acres from King George II. The road is filled with family, cousins from all parts of the country. There are all shades of humanity imaginable, from the darkest-skinned African-Americans to brown-skinned, light-skinned and white-skinned cousins. Color doesn't matter today in this hour on this country road. Color has ceased to divide.[*]

This commonality in our American past is my vision. I reject side-stepping history as we all have ownership of our collective past as Old Americans. While you are not sidestepping history *per se*, you are ac-knowledging that others would perceive a common American past as sidestepping history, and I have a strong quarrel with that perception. Like the abolitionists and civil rights litigators of yore, one must never surrender one's moral vision to the vagaries of the moment. Bari Weiss has called upon Americans to be more courageous and less cowardly in the face of conformity and dogma.[†] If one accepts the limited sidestep-ping vision of others, is one on the philosophical side of abolitionists or slave owners in antebellum Virginia? Wherein is the vision for the ages?

I asked how, and in what concrete way, did not having slaves in your direct line render your history of slavery different from my history of slavery? It doesn't matter at one level because neither you nor I were slaves. We both only know what we know from reading history books, al-though I have a nugget or two of oral history from my grandmother, and you have a nugget or two of oral history in family lore. This letter would have been a great opportunity for you to compare and contrast your oral history with my oral history and whether the difference in nuggets of oral history made a difference in our respective life trajectories. I read none of this possible depth in your letter.

Finally, and out of genuine curiosity, I asked why you thought there was no overlap in the common history of Old Americans—Americans, for example, who can trace their ancestry in Virginia back to the year 1621. This idea of Old Americans can be central to a vision of race in the

---

[*] Ibid, 60.

[†] Bari Weiss, "We Got Here Because of Cowardice. We Get Out with Courage," *Commentary* (November 2021), www.commentary.org/articles/bari-weiss/resist-woke-revolution/.

United States. I was hoping for more engagement on the psychological dimension of self-conception as an Old American. For example, why do you and I have more in common than I have in common with my immigrant friend from Hong Kong?

I could end my letter now as a simple critique of failure to answer my specific and direct questions with specific and direct answers. But that would not be fair to you or to me. We grow the most when we completely hear from others, so here are my additional concerns with your letter. Let me be clear I am not interested in personal attacks. I am interested in earnest revelation. This notion of others sidestepping history troubles me to the point of distraction, so I wanted to fully express myself before we can move on further in our correspondence. Let's disagree without being disagreeable.

Reasonable people can disagree without being disagreeable. So, I don't care so much about a particular position as long as the position flows from one's premises. You write a common history is a common responsibility. No, that statement doesn't hold up. I share a common history with other Twymans and Malcolm King of Scotland. Do I and other distant cousins carry common responsibility for any atrocities ordered by King Malcolm? Of course not. A common medieval history doesn't impute common responsibility on common descendants in the present. You write that "many black Americans are in search of recognition for their contribution to American history." How does it sidestep history to recognize one is a direct descendant of Thomas Jefferson or Ralph Quarles or Col. Richard Lee I? Those people are a part of oneself, and only Jim Crow genealogy would fence off black Americans from the fullness of American history. How is it congruent to support a unified American identity and yet bless a Jim Crow conception of one's past?

Now, you may argue that I have cherry-picked your words in a single paragraph of a single letter. Perhaps I have misread the spirit of your letter and you agree with my vision. It is those other limited people who don't see the better path ahead. You are pointing to some nameless, faceless group of people for whom a common past, a common American past, must mean a sidestepping of history. It is the phrase "sidestepping history" that I reject as a history major and as an American Native to Virginia. Internalizing a common past is the exact opposite of sidestepping history.

So, let's develop this point for a while. Why am I bereft with emptiness upon reading the words "sidestepping history"?

In a previous letter, you wrote that we must acknowledge the painful past with an introduction of a variety of lessons that explore all dimensions of American history from different perspectives. You wrote that, and it is sound. How do you square that vision with discrediting acceptance of one's full history as sidestepping history? I know of an influential black lawyer in D.C. whose family is descended from a French immigrant family. The family proudly embraces their French immigrant past and their black American past. This integration of their family past into a unified American whole is a beautiful thing. You suggest that many would cast out this family's self-conception as sidestepping history? Am I reading you correctly? Any characterization of what this beautiful black family has done as sidestepping history does not sit well with me.

Doesn't the call to acknowledge all dimensions of our painful past compel you to argue against those who would reject a common American past? How can you acknowledge all dimensions of a painful past on the one hand and, on the other hand, give people a pass when it comes to rejecting a common American past? Doesn't the logical extension of your urgent demand for acknowledgment lead you to decry and oppose those who would perceive a common American past as sidestepping history? Don't you oppose an inflexible mindset, which is a fair categorization of those who are closed to a common past as sidestepping history?

You have written about the importance of "encouraging critical thinking." Great, and I agree. So, do we encourage critical thinking about one's genetic truth if we look the other way when fellow Americans reject a common past as sidestepping history?

You have also written against "neo-segregation" in the classroom. I agree. We're on the same page for a better world. So, I would suggest that those who reject a common past are implicitly blessing neo-segregation in family trees. Shouldn't your principled opposition to neo-segregation in the classroom apply even more so to anything that denies genetic truth and our common American past? Isn't it even more central to one's sense of self to not be segregated at the level of one's DNA?* Don't

---

* According to Ancestry.com, some of the exact genes that were in the daughter-in-law of Col. Richard Lee I (1613–1664) are in me and keep me alive. That realization is chilling and reminds me that we are so close to one another as Old Americans. There is no room for

we all have a human right to be free of racial segregation in one's genetic construction?

Further, if the aim is to create "a new American identity," as you describe it, there is nothing new in a divided American past, a divided history. Shouldn't you stand against the currents of the day and write, hey, there is a better vision for us, and we're not there when we can only think of whites as having American History and blacks as having Black American History? You might have written that we do not sidestep history when we conceive of slavery as part of our common past. In other words, I was hoping you might more zealously critique the view of the "masses" and not just serve up the view of the masses. We are embracing history, warts and all, when we conceive of our common past. And then you might have debunked those who reject a common past as sidestepping history. Just a thought.

I have written, "there's a unity in the American Experience which we possess." That's our vision. When one appeases the 76 percent of black Americans for whom blackness is extremely important or very important, one is ensuring that racial silos in experience will continue and continue. That's not an American experience. That's a silo experience of race.

I have also written, "Do constant reminders of American slavery sever black culture and consciousness from the rest of American culture and consciousness?" We both disagree with siloed thinking. Jim Crow genealogy is the way of the past, Jen, not the future. We need to be on the side of the future. I suspect, in a hundred years or so, all people will accept all our common past as our common history, and this will just be accepted as truth, a given.

Conclusion

There is power in the single story we tell ourselves as Americans. It is the single story, not the divided story, that will lead us to a better purpose and meaning in life. We talk about race so much in this correspondence. It is easy to forget that we, you and I, are people first and foremost. For both of us, a sense of closeness creates rootedness. Rootedness creates belonging. Old Americans, regardless of race, need their rightful belong-

---

social construction of race at the level of one's chromosomes.

ing in our complete American past.

Jen, what threw me for a loop in your letter above all else were the words "sidestepping history." I hoped for more vigorous criticism from you of the 76 percent view of the world. In this instance, there is no truth in between. In the year 1822 in Virginia, there was a vision of slavers and there was a vision of abolitionists. There was no truth in between. One vision had to win out. Similarly, the vision of sidestepping history is inconsistent with a greater genetic and authentic truth. This latter vision will win out in the end, just as the vision of abolition won out over the vision of slavery. It was my hope you would critique without reservation or qualification the sidestepping vision, but that was not the case.

In 1932 in Virginia, there was the vision of Jim Crow segregation in public schools. And there was the vision of Howard Law School Dean Charles Hamilton Houston that schools must not be segregated by race. There was no truth in between. The visions were inconsistent. And the vision of public school desegregation in the South won out. I reaped the benefits of that better vision.

Today, in San Diego and Austin, two visions again are clashing. One vision says we must acknowledge we live in a fact-based world of Jim Crow genealogy and to do otherwise is to sidestep history. The other vision says we are more complete as a people if we internalize our common past as a unified whole. Which vision will win out?

In her *Disagreeable Jews* podcast series, Dara Horn confronts a cranky old Holocaust survivor who claims Jews shouldn't have to be agreeable to survive.* This take on Jewish identity at first takes Horn aback. She reflexively disagrees and sets out in a sense to write a book and make her case for being agreeable. As Horn digs deeper and deeper into her work, she reviews the famous movie *Gentlemen's Agreement*, the premise of which is that a Gentile passes as a Jew for six months to discover what it is like to be Jewish. Of course, in late 1940s America, all non-Jews are anti-Semitic more or less. So, Gregory Peck goes undercover as a Jew and presses the issue at every turn. "I'm Jewish and I would like a room at your hotel," etc. No Jew would have done such a thing in late 1940s America, but Peck wants the Jewish experience, and he presses the point. In the end, he discovers he is not Jewish since Jews know the

---

* See the *Adventures with Dead Jews* podcast, episode 7, "Agreeable Jews," podcasts.apple.com/us/podcast/agreeable-jews/id1582119175?i=1000538688340.

score and do everything possible to blend in, like changing their names. Even the author of the underlying *Gentlemen's Agreement* novel used the Christian name of her divorced husband for professional purposes. The author did not deny her Jewish parents if asked, but no one had cause to ask, you see.

Horn sees a lot of this agreeableness, and yet there seems to be no protection in being agreeable against anti-Semitism. In the end, Horn comes full circle and comes to agree that Jews should not erase their traditions dating back thousands of years simply to please others. There is integrity in living life from the inside out.

I see the ethical and life thoughts of black Americans as hemmed in by the values and attitudes of the 76 percent. This is a sad state of affairs for any group, since we are in greatest harmony when we are true to ourselves and not the group. And like Horn felt at first, the whole life strategy for many black Americans is to be agreeable with the 76 percent. But being agreeable is no guarantee of the abundance of life's pleasures. Being agreeable doesn't protect one from moral panics or thought-policing. Perhaps, and as Horn grew to accept, the highest calling of any minority in any society is to be disagreeable, to not erase truths about black achievement and a mixed ownership in our common past. Maybe, just maybe, the conscience of the citizen means breaking away from the 76 percent and, in that sense, living a life as a Disagreeable (Jew) Black individual. Even better as a disagreeable human (shout-out to Erec Smith).

Becoming an Old American means holding two ideas in one's mind at the same time: one can be a descendant of a slave, Charlotte Twyman, and a direct descendant of Peter Montague (arrived at Jamestown in 1621) at the same time. Think of it this way. I am equally a descendant of the Twyman and Womack families. These families are different, but I am a part of both. Being an Old American means one accepts and embraces that one is part of all the various strands in our American past. This way of being seems more coherent, congruent, and authentic to me than pretending one is not part European.

How one thinks of oneself carries one through the highs and lows of life. If one thinks of oneself *only* as the descendant of faceless and agentless American slaves, what does that self-identity mean for one's sense of self? Inspiration comes from triumph over adversity. Stories of tenacity, resilience, and mental strength among slaves and former slaves are legion. This mindset is why Daniel Brown (my grandmother's grandfather) speaks to us through the ages. Now change the mental programming and take this all a step further. Suppose one is taught that one is the product of a rich tapestry—African slaves who survived the First and Middle Passages, an English indentured servant who ran away from his master Thomas Lee into the Virginia woods, a free black immigrant from England who founded the elite Brown Fellowship Society, and the first school teacher in the Virginia colony? See how a complete and full accounting of everything in one's family history might bolster and lift one's sense of self? Nothing beats the full story of all ancestors. See generally *Migrants: Our Family's Immigrations to America, From All Over the World* by J. E. Smith, III.

Wink

Letter 31

Wink,

This is a powerful response, and you give me a lot to consider. I will only say, in my short response here, that the incongruence between our ideals and reality is why we write.

To the coming of a better time,

Jen

Letter 32

Jen,

While you consider, I'm curious, what's your "origin story"? Any key moments from your childhood or life that inform your views and made you who you are today?

Wink

Letter 33

Dear Wink,

Yes, I like it! This question I can answer.

My formative years are marked by the Cold War. At the height of this era, in the early 1980s, we played hopscotch to a popular jingle: "Kill a commie for your mommie." Brightly colored chalk was used to outline the hopscotch squares. Little ditties are a necessary accompaniment to the hopscotch craft. The Cold War defined much of my early childhood, including schoolyard games. It was the first "us vs. them" narrative I can remember. Coming from a military family, the Cold War kept us in a constant embrace, influencing much of our perception and interpretation of the world.

It was probably in second or third grade, after discussing the nuclear threat in elementary school, that I asked my dad, "Do you really think we will have a nuclear war?" I thought for sure my dad would say no. After all, parents are supposed to ease and alleviate their children's fears, right? To tell them there is no monster under their bed. To turn on the lights and show them that all their fears are merely murky shadows that can be chased away with the simple flick of a light switch. Right? Right?

He replied, "Maybe."

That "maybe" gripped me in fear. That "maybe" made the shadows come alive and gave substance to their fuzzy outlines. That "maybe" had a name: the Russians. It had a name, but it didn't have a face. While these Russian shadows had substance, they didn't have characteristics. Well, except for one. They were the Other. They were evil.

And then I heard a story that changed everything. I don't know if it was propaganda or not, and sometimes I wonder where this story originated as I, myself, cannot recall. I heard that an American student, probably only a little older than me, had written a letter to the Soviets. In this letter, the student asked the leadership not to start a nuclear war. They (not sure who specifically) read and responded: "The Russians love their children too." (Perhaps Sting heard this story too, prompting him to write his song "Russians"?*)

This one simple sentence floored me. I remember the words and the reality they conveyed. They did not slowly seep into my consciousness, silently unfolding a gentle truth; rather, they careened toward me head-on, screeching like a truck with burnt-out brakes. The Russians have families. They love like we do. Their children have hopes and dreams and aspirations.

Mind-blown.

Shortly after this revelation, my little insular world was upturned yet again. I remember my dad sitting after work in his olive-green Air Force flight suit on a high-top stool at our kitchen counter in Beavercreek, Ohio. He looked down at me as I sobbed, trying to find ways to console me. "You know," he said, "Burma has tigers."

After coming home to tell us that he was taking the Air Force Attaché position in Rangoon, I thought my comfortable little world was crumbling. But hold up, tigers? Perhaps Burma wouldn't be that bad after all.

As it turns out, it was the watershed event in my life.

In a country ruled by a military junta, what we were allowed to do and see was highly curated. At the time, I thought the constant presence of military guards meant we were special. VIPs. In a country that strictly limited tourism in the 1980s, we were special, but in hindsight, I know the guards were there, in part, to dictate our experience.

And even so, what we saw and experienced would never be erased from my memory. But it wasn't just the men who walked on coals or hung suspended with hooks in their flesh at the Hindu festivals—although those memories will forever be seared in my brain, literally and figuratively—it was the people. The day-to-day lives.

---

* You can find the song's music video on Sting's YouTube channel at youtu.be/wHylQRVN-2Qs.

We had a Buddhist, Muslim, Christian, and Hindu who intermingled in our house daily. The education I received in their presence was richer than any in the hallowed halls of academia. Beyond the house, we frequently engaged in international events with attachés from other countries. One of my favorite attachés was Russian. Stereotypes aside, he was truly a bear of a man, and I will forever remember the bear hugs he gave. As his squeeze lingered, I always walked away from his embrace in contemplation—the Russians love their children too. In the light of this truth and the clasp of this Russian bear, Russians emerged from the shadows in my mind to have characteristics as distinct as my own. The "us vs. them" veil was lifted. The light switch was turned on.

As a result, the veil was lifted not only in my simple understanding of the dynamics behind the U.S.–Soviet Cold War but also in my appreciation of differences. During my Burma days, I not only was exposed to a new culture in the Burmese experience, distinct from anything I'd encountered before, but I also, in my international school, came to know the friendship of those from a multitude of cultures with disparate histories, politics, and norms. I learned about the importance and sanctity of a cow to my Indian friends. I learned how to tie a traditional sash called an *obi* from my Japanese friends. I learned about the delicacy of a hundred-year-old egg from my Chinese friends (never mind that my mother had to cover me choking down this egg with a firm pat to the back at a dinner with dignitaries). Pretty much the only people that I never interacted with were the North Koreans, which in and of itself spoke volumes about their society and politics.

I remember one of my birthdays in Burma (was it my eleventh or twelfth?) I traipsed into our kitchen to check on the preparations for the festivities. As I stood there enveloped in the smell of freshly baked bread, thinking to myself, if I died now, I had lived a full life . . . I had an epiphany. It lasted less than a second but still stopped me in my tracks. It was one of those divine moments where the mystery of the world is exposed. Perhaps these flashes are so brief because our human brains can barely conceive of the magnitude of the universe. In that moment, I saw everything connected and the peace that was cradled in the connection. And then it was gone, and I was left grasping for meaning. I hesitate to get too metaphysical in a world that demands we acknowledge our senses, tying us to the mundane, but the imprint of this connection, plus the connections I had made in the temporal terrain, set in motion a quest to connect across cultures.

At the onset of this quest, I felt blessed to be born into a culture that was considered a "melting pot." Although that term is now considered a "microaggression,"* what the term meant to me at this time was a place not where we were all the same *per se*, as it is now interpreted, but rather a place where we found commonality in our differences. A multicultural Mecca. I've spent the rest of my life studying and immersing myself in other cultures. And I came to find that in the process, I became more acutely aware of my own culture and how it has shaped my perceptions.

Influenced by these early life experiences, I went on to study Asian culture. I learned Mandarin and have spent most of my career studying and working in China. With this focus on the largely homogeneous Chinese landscape, coming back to America to see the unfolding tensions, especially in our race relations, took me off-guard. While being fairly well-versed in American history and politics, I always had a bit of an outsider's perspective. I held our multiculturalism and our liberties and freedoms on a pedestal. I had seen too many instances in places like China where one word against the government could result in exile, a prison sentence, or even death.

One Beijing summer drove this message home. I climbed a six-story flight of stairs in a sterile concrete apartment building. Cigarette smoke suspended in the humid air, wafting lazily around our heads as we made our way up. Three of us trudged up together. Two suits followed behind as their smoke crept ahead of us. Relieved to finally make our destination, the three of us burst into the air-conditioned room to get a beer and shut the door. After cracking the beer, I wanted a smoke. A bad habit a lot of us picked up in China in the 1990s.

Being young and overly confident, I decided to ask one of the two Ministry of State Security officials parked outside the door if I could bum a cigarette. He leaned calmly against the railing, within a foot of the door. He showed no surprise when the door opened suddenly, and I asked in

---

* See, for example, the list of microaggressions posted by the University of Minnesota's School of Public Health, which refers to the statement "America is a melting pot" as a microaggression: sph.umn.edu/site/docs/hewg/microaggressions.pdf. The list was adapted from Derald Wing Sue et al., "Racial Microaggressions in Everyday Life: Implications for Clinical Practice," *American Psychologist* 62, no. 4 (2007): 271–286.

Mandarin to share a smoke. He stared coldly and slowly took another puff of his cigarette. I was neither getting a cigarette nor a response.

I've been told that the Chinese keep dossiers on all foreigners. If they didn't have one on me already, I'm sure the week I spent that summer in Beijing with a Tian'anmen dissident—allowed home for the first time to visit his ailing mother after years in exile—was a reason to start. And my dossier expanded greatly over the course of the next decade.

As a foreigner, I was bold. Perhaps too bold. But the authorities pretty much left us alone. In some ways, living in China as a foreigner felt freer than living in America. There was no drinking age, and at the time, we could even smoke in movie theaters—can you imagine? And I still get a laugh out of the times that I would go to class or out to grab a coffee in my pajama bottoms. Why not? I would generate stares no matter my attire. The day-to-day regulations, at least for a foreigner, were minimal. The authoritarian regime did not influence us. I didn't know what it meant to be afraid of your own government until that summer in 1995 in Beijing.

Several years later, while working for a geopolitical firm and after meeting with a high-profile former U.S. intelligence director in Beijing, I got a glimpse at my dossier.

The phone rang around 10:00 p.m. in our hotel room. I had just returned from a long day at a conference. My colleague said the call was for me. What? No one knew where I was staying. And it was late.

I was told, in Chinese, to come to the hotel room directly below mine on the floor below. Of course, I said no. I was told it was not a request.

My colleague joined me on the ninth floor, where three plain clothes officials waited. My colleague protested, but it didn't do either of us any good. I reluctantly went with the officials, with my colleague promising to call the room every thirty minutes.

It was two weeks before Christmas, and I worried I wouldn't make it home to see my son. After two hours of questioning, where years of my activity in China were laid out, they let me go. But it wasn't the end of my relationship with the Ministry of State Security. For two years, they'd continue to meet me in random places, taking me by surprise with an "invitation to tea," which is code for interrogation.

After every one of these encounters, I would touch down back home, grateful. Despite our troubles, I always thought of us Americans unified around the values of liberty and freedom. It gave me the feeling of safety and security that no longer defined my China experiences.

However, about the time of the 2016 U.S. presidential election, fear and division started to grip the American psyche in a way I hadn't seen before. In many ways, I feel that the 2016 election results were a reaction to a fear that had been percolating in an unstable world. Today, that fear has long since bubbled to the surface. Fueling this fear is the media's hyper-focus on our differences and on race in particular. Tribes coalesce around fear, and identity politics become the norm. New jargon is introduced—*white privilege, white fragility*, etc. The "us vs. them" ethos typically reserved as a foreign policy tool is internalized, and a growing Cold War emerges domestically in a new clash of cultures.

Despite the social media landscape that has me joyfully reconnecting with my friends from my Burma days whom I thought long lost, I see disturbing trends. As communication and connection transform into angry vitriol in short clips and 280 characters, our world is now both more connected and more tribal. A white professor tweets that all cops should be killed.[*] A California teacher proudly announces on TikTok that she has taken down the American flag in her classroom and that she has told her students that there's another flag in the classroom they can pledge their allegiance to: a Gay Pride flag.[†] How we land in the ensuing debates over these divisive posts has torn friends and families apart and entrenched tribes. Even in my own family, talking politics has become taboo when we come to rely on sound bites to formulate arguments instead of good-faith dialogue.

What started as a desire to connect across international boundaries—to explore and exalt the differences across the cultures of countries—has turned inward as a new Cold War materializes. A Cold War that is too often interpreted through child-like binary simplicities, masking the Other in hazy shadows that belie the complexity and nuance of interconnected and overlapping realities. And yet, despite these complexities, I know we

---

[*] Nick Irvin, "A UC Davis Professor Thinks Cops "Need to Be Killed," *California Aggie,* February 25, 2019, theaggie.org/2019/02/25/a-uc-davis-professor-thinks-cops-need-to-be-killed/.

[†] See the report by Lauren Lyster, "Orange County, California, Teacher Investigated for Joking Students Should Pledge to Pride Flag," *KTLA 5 News*, August 31, 2021, available at www.youtube.com/watch?v=qUnOAn064fY.

can start with a foundation that underlines our common humanity.

I know you love your children too.

Jen

P.S. This was a fun one to write. Now that you know mine, what's your "origin story"?

Letter 34

Dear Jen,

The New South defined my childhood. While the segregation of public life had once kept black Virginians from white Virginians, the final step toward desegregation was taken when I was in elementary school. During my earliest education, I attended an all-black segregated school in the Hickory Hill neighborhood of Chesterfield County. After I completed second grade in that school, black schools and white schools in the county became, simply, schools.

Unlike writer Ta-Nehisi Coates, I have been called the N-word due to racial prejudice in public school. The first time was at E. S. H. Greene Elementary School, a formerly all-white school in which I found myself as the only black student in my third-grade class. Abusive white classmates there repeatedly called me the N-word. One day, I simply sat down on the playground and thought about why these classmates were abusing me so. I knew from growing up on Twyman Road that there was no correlation between intelligence and skin color. The most important adults in my life—Mom, Dad, Grandma, Uncle Robert Daniel Twyman, Aunt Juanita Twyman, Uncle William Womack—were all black, and they came in a range of colors. It dawned on me that my classmates were dumb. They were not smart. And since I prized intelligence as a young kid, I concluded I would ignore and dismiss these tormentors. This realization armored me well for life ahead in the 1970s.

But the funny thing is I was never gripped in fear like you were, Jen, about nuclear war. I was far more concerned about learning and knowledge and achievement. Prejudiced classmates never held sway over my soul and spirit. And that meant I chose to focus on my goals in life, not the prejudice of others.

Did I hear a story that changed everything for me? I don't have a story comparable to the Soviet story that you share. For me, the story that changed everything would be stories of my mom being an orphan as a teenager and having to leave school for shelter at her brother's home in Hickory Hill. My mom would always remind me that I had more opportunities than she had had, so it was my duty to achieve in life. My mom saw my life as an extension of trampled possibility in her own life. And this maternal aspiration remained my North Star, just like an immigrant family often pushes their children because often that's why they come to the United States. They come to America for their children to have more opportunities than they did. My mom had a relentless optimism reminiscent of black American immigrants. My mom viewed pre-1970 as the Old Country and post-1970 as the New Country.* This one simple sentence—that I had a duty to achieve because I had more opportunities than my mom—grounded me. I remember the sense of purpose and meaning life had. I always lived my life like I was running out of time in those days—to paraphrase a lyric from the musical *Hamilton*. I did not have girlfriends in grade school or college, as they would have been a distraction. I had focus.

Mom gave me a search for meaning in achievement.

One day in the fourth grade, I was sitting outside waiting to see my family doctor, Dr. Lush. By this point, my parents had moved from Twyman Road to Jean Drive deep in Chesterfield County, Virginia, where I attended Bellwood Elementary Annex, a formerly all-black school that became mostly white following desegregation. My thoughts turned to United States Presidents. I'm not sure why, although I had been captivat-

---

* For an example of conflicting visions within a single black American family about whether the United States is a land of oppression or opportunity, see Clarence Page, "Is Affirmative Action on the Way Out? Opportunities Still Endure," *Chicago Tribune*, October 4, 2022, www.chicagotribune.com/columns/clarence-page/ct-column-affirmative-action-supreme-court-bollinger-immigrants-page-20221005-3kfreqipsrg7xfwryjwnzyajry-story.html. A native-born husband thinks of "America as a land with a history of oppression," while his immigrant wife "tends to see it as a land of opportunity."

ed by presidents for some time. I enjoyed learning about them and memorizing them. There were only thirty-seven, Richard Milhous Nixon being the then current president. I settled upon the idea that I would like to be president one day. I had no one to tell me to stop dreaming, to have common sense. The idea just appealed to me. Even in first and second grade, I had a sense of leadership and making my own way. I would chastise my best friend, Kevin Robertson, because he had a girlfriend. I felt girlfriends were bad news because they took time away from studying. Even now, there are echoes of the child in the man. For example, once in the first grade, my teacher, Mrs. Lucille Walker, rapped my knuckles with a ruler for saying "son of a gun," a phrase I had heard on the television show *Gunsmoke*. I was six years old, and that remains the closest thing to a curse I have ever uttered in my life. I decided then and there I would never use profanity. My wife often says I must not have been a normal child. It's true. At the time, I didn't take my cues from the outside world of other children. My ideas came from within, and if they felt right, I went with them. I made my mom very happy as a kid.

I knew one didn't wake up one day and become president. I needed a plan, a series of goals to achieve along the way. I decided to work backward in time. It would be important to serve as governor or U.S. senator before becoming president. This was what history showed me. And most governors and senators had served time in a state legislature, so it would be necessary to serve as a state senator or state delegate. How would I make a living while doing this? What kind of job would I need? I remembered that the most popular occupation of members of the Virginia legislature was attorney, so I would have to attend law school and college before serving in the legislature. Of course, I would need to develop practice in running for office while in grade school, so I set out in my mind an eight-year plan: (1) Student Council Secretary in fifth grade; (2) Home Room Delegate in sixth grade; (3) Student Council Senator in seventh grade; (4) Student Council Attorney General in eighth grade; (5) Student Council Governor in ninth grade; (6) Student Council Delegate in tenth grade; (7) Student Council Vice-President in eleventh grade; and (8) Student Council President in twelfth grade.

I reviewed the milestones two or three times and committed them to memory. By the time Dr. Lush was ready to see me, I was the same person on the outside, but on the inside, I was a nine-year-old with a purpose, a mission in life. I had divined and created a calling.

Did it ever occur to me that race would stop me in pursuit of my dreams? No. Why did race never enter my mind? I didn't see the world that way. Sure, I was aware of racial differences, but my job was to achieve my goals. I had a dim view of prejudiced students and was not inclined to let others steal my joy. As the legendary Reginald Lewis once said to his family, *"Why Should White Guys Have All the Fun?"* I never said those words, but those feelings infused my soul and spirit from my earliest encounter with prejudice. My resolution is all the more noteworthy when you consider public schools had been desegregated for only one completed school year when I divined my mission in life. My new elementary school was around 8 percent black, my future junior high school was just under 4 percent black, and my future high school was 8 percent black. Circumstances demanded that I learn how to communicate with all students, many of whom probably heard a healthy dose of prejudice around the dinner table every night.

As a backdrop to my origin story, I loved to read and learn about the past. I started to read second-grade books in the first grade as a personal challenge and kept up this advanced reading pace throughout elementary and middle school. My second-grade teacher, Mrs. Dorothy Taylor, taught the class how to speed-read news stories, and this skill enabled me to read more and more books above my grade level with ambition and confidence. I was curious about the larger world and driven to learn for the sake of learning.

All the students at my new school lived in the same general area, which helped with racial understanding, particularly since the lower-middle-class and middle-class black neighborhoods were roughly on par with the nearby white neighborhoods with red brick homes and a cut above the white trailer parks. Still, I suffered sporadic harassment on the playground as intolerance died hard.

I lack the words to describe the promise of the New South. When I talk about segregation and desegregation and the distinctions between *de jure* and *de facto* segregation, my Brooklyn-born wife doesn't quite get it. She learned about segregation, but she didn't live it like I did. She used to say that she forgot I attended a segregated all-black school in my early years. These were never issues for my wife in private schools in Brooklyn. Consider that, for centuries, whites and blacks did not attend public or private schools together in the South. Let that thought sink in for a moment. This meant a total isolation of social worlds. Blacks and whites only came together and met in positions of white supremacy and black inferiority. Generations of black people could never call a white person a classmate. My father never called a white Virginian a classmate.

By the time I was in the eighth grade and my service as student council attorney general had begun, I had won every office in my eight-year plan except for student council senate in the seventh grade. I recall being very focused on keeping my campaign promises and trying to better align our school constitution with the Constitution of the Commonwealth of Virginia. This was the reason why I inadvertently brought the student council secretary, an Asian American classmate, to tears. Under our school constitution, she ranked third in the line of succession for student council governor after the lieutenant governor. I felt this was wrongheaded since the state attorney general was ranked third in the order of succession for the Virginia governorship under the Virginia Constitution. I, therefore, argued I should rank third, ahead of her. It wasn't personal. My drive was to conform our constitution to the Virginia Constitution, but she took it personally.

At the end of the school year, it was time for me to run for the next office on my list: governor. I distinctly remember talking about my plans with a white classmate on the school bus. We were approaching my home. I said I was going to run for governor. He replied, "Who ever heard of a black governor?" I could not have cared less. I had my goals, and my classmate could pound sand. This kid was an outlier. I received several expressions of warm support from other classmates. Julie, a tall, white eighth grader with red hair, dimples, and freckles, wrote in my yearbook: *"To a real smart and skinny dude. Hope you run for office next year. Good luck. Julie."* I had a crush on Julie, and I greatly hoped her autographed well wishes were genuine.

I wrote up a speech emphasizing our commonalities as students. I remember settling upon an emotional hook. If students were looking for someone who could solve all problems, I told them not to vote for me. I consciously urged my classmates not to vote for me if they had pie-in-the-sky desires. However, if they wanted a governor who would work as hard as he could, who was passionate about student government, then they should vote for me. It was a novel approach and placed the onus on my classmates to vote for—or against—me in a conscious manner. I won the race. I was the political leader of my school. I was caught totally by surprise when I won the Award for Best All-Around Eighth Grade Student during the end-of-the-year assembly.

This part of my origin story has a happy ending. In the spring of 1978, I announced my bid for student council president of my high school. I was arrogant and drunk with my past successes. I didn't campaign at all. I had no campaign manager. I didn't put up any campaign signs. I assumed I would win with the power of my speech. Ha! My opponents were an unremarkable white student and a very attractive black teenager, Marva Felder, the daughter of an architect. I gave the speech of my life, and Marva turned on the charm. To my horror, no one won a majority of the vote. There had to be a runoff between Marva and me. My life flashed before my eyes. I immediately went into panic mode. I appointed a campaign manager and plastered the hallways with campaign signs. I was no longer arrogant. I was scared straight! And the heavens smiled on me. I was declared the winner of the runoff election by a slim margin.

I had fulfilled the mission of the nine-year-old outside my doctor's office years ago. I had been elected president of Thomas Dale High School, having defeated the most attractive black female in school. I had inspired other black students to vie for student office. During my administration, my vice-president, the senior class vice-president, and the sophomore class president were also black. And what became of Marva? She would one day become the first black Homecoming Queen at Virginia Tech University.*

I was the New South, and the New South was me.

Was my world insular growing up compared to your world overseas? I don't think so. I lived in all-black neighborhoods, started school in a segregated system, and eventually attended schools where the student body was anywhere from 92 percent to 98 percent white. So, I stood astride in black and white worlds, and I would grow to have a sense of ownership in the larger world. I never shied away from raising my hand or asking questions or seeking political office because I was the only black kid in the class. I focused on achievement.

---

* For more about Marva, see her interview with Tamara Kennelly, "Oral History with Marva LaJeune Felder Davis," Virginia Tech Special Collections, March 27, 1999 (Ms1995-026), https://digitalsc.lib.vt.edu/Ms1995-026/Ms1995_026_Davis_Marva.

Did the tension between a black world and a white world create anxiety and trauma for me? Absolutely not! I was on my mom's mission in life. I didn't have time to major in the minor.

But surely there must have been some watershed event in your life surrounding race, you might ask?

Yes, of course. As a writer, I can create a narrative, an impression. I can cherry-pick from hundreds of moments in my life and create a positive image or a negative image due to race. I am an open-minded person, contrary to what others might think, including my wife and daughter. (For example, my wife sometimes refers to me as "Archie Bunker.") While they see closed-mindedness because I no longer, for example, reflexively embrace any and all black social events like Kwanzaa celebrations, Black Family Day, the MLK Day Parade, and Juneteenth get-togethers, I instead see growth into my authentic self—someone who is more concerned about the individual. I find that as an American adult in the twenty-first century, a shared personality serves as a stronger basis for a relationship than a shared race. Today, my closest friends come from all races, and only one, a fellow Harvard Law School graduate, is black.

So, what are some watershed events in my life comparable to your moving to Burma and learning about the Russian bear and all types of different cultures?

For starters, as I mentioned in an earlier letter, I lived within two miles of the Jefferson Davis Highway until the age of eighteen, when I left home for the University of Virginia in Charlottesville, Virginia. I have never been to Burma or even Asia. My son has traveled to Japan, and that reflects the greater opportunity for the younger generation. I never mingled with Buddhists, Muslims, and Hindus in my home. I only mingled with black Protestants in my home. I cannot remember a white person ever stepping inside my home until after I started college. The most exotic people I met were at school, and I'm not talking about Japanese, Chinese, or North Korean exchange students. I'm talking about Catholics, who were considered different from us Protestants. Catholics were perceived as progressives. We had one Spanish American and one Cuban American in my high school. But they shared the same culture as everyone else. There were no Mexican Americans or Puerto Rican Americans. There were no Jewish students. The first Jewish person I ever met was Mr. Levy, who lived in Windsor Farms, a leafy neighborhood in Richmond,

Virginia. Levy interviewed me at his comfortable home in his capacity as a member of the Harvard Admissions Alumni Committee.

I never experienced this type of intermingling as any kind of cultural watershed event. Why? We all shared the same culture. We were all Southern small-town culture, living through one of the most unsung social transformations in American history. Black and white schools were becoming just schools after centuries of social isolation. (Without digressing too much, this might be why I recoil at the idea of separatist black social associations. They seem to be a step backward in time to me.) To be honest, I don't remember hearing the word "culture" until college. The real differences in my hometown were racial. So, my watershed moment was different in quality and character from your watershed events. While yours were based on culture, mine were based on race.

As I mentioned earlier, I remember when a white classmate on the school bus said to me that he had never heard of a black governor. I paid him no mind and won the race for governor. This was a watershed event for me personally as it confirmed that my goals and aspirations mattered, not the prejudices of others.

And remember Julie, the signer of my yearbook? I eventually mustered up the courage to ask her out on a date. Julie said she had to ask her dad. Her dad said no; Julie could not go out with me because I was black. This rejection was not so much a watershed racial event for me but an inflection point. Julie's dad's "no" told me that, no matter how much promise I had in life, it would not matter to Julie's dad. Only race mattered to Julie's dad. I still remember that racial rejection to this day.

I remember the day after Henry L. Marsh III was elected the first black mayor of Richmond. This was great news for black advancement in politics. Even though I lived in Chesterfield County, I felt energized by the news. This was a high moment for me.

I remember standing by the kitchen sink as my mom washed dishes. She asked me how come I wasn't dating girls. I must have been in high school. I said none of the black girls were intellectual. My mom suggested that maybe I should put aside those prejudices. I sternly told my mom I would not date a girl just because she was black. A girl had to be intelligent, an intellectual. This was a racial moment for me as it told me that my mom wanted me to date—and marry—a black girl. That was her hope for me.

While moving into 313 Watson, my dorm room at the University of Virginia, I met my roommate, John, from Tupelo, Mississippi. John seemed like an okay guy. His mom took one look at me, pulled John aside, and said John did not have to live with a black student if John didn't want to. I guess mom was concerned about appearances back in Tupelo. To his everlasting credit, John told his mom to "butt out." John and I lived together for a year, and we had no issues with one another. If John is out there somewhere in the world today, much love out to you, guy. Wahoowa. The reaction of John's mother to me was a racial point of awareness for me.

While at the University of Virginia, I discovered a class of light, bright, and almost-white black students from Washington, D.C. I won't mention any names, but their families were at the top of the social pecking order in Black America. They all had the same physical appearance and lived in the Gold Coast, the upper 16th street neighborhood in Northwest D.C. I remember driving up to D.C. during the summer and just driving through these neighborhoods inhabited by the Black Elite—doctors, lawyers, dentists, professors, entrepreneurs. To see black affluence in the Gold Coast was a racial apex event for me.

My father objected to me attending Harvard Law School. He wanted me to attend Howard Law School. Imagine two introverts, dad and son, fighting the fight of their lives in the summer of 1983. He said I was "acting white." I won the battle but we both lost the war. Our ties of father and son were irretrievably severed. This was the most important racial inflection event in my life, even more than entering a formerly all-white school in the third grade.

What happened, you might ask? I asked my dad to sign the student loan papers for law school.

"No, I refuse to sign those papers. I'm not going to go into debt for you for law school," he said. Four years earlier, on April 14, 1979, I had opened a thin envelope from Harvard College in response to my undergraduate application and felt the burn of major rejection for the first time. It wouldn't be the last time I knew failure. "Dad, it's the best law school. I've worked long and hard for this opportunity. Most fathers would be proud to have a son attend Harvard Law School." I had powered my way through the University of Virginia with a personal goal of admission to Harvard Law School. Picture me as James Hart in the movie *The Paper*

Chase, brooding and intense. "I'm not most dads. Have you looked at Howard? Howard is a black school." I made it my mission to be the first in the study hall in the morning and the last to leave the study hall at night for three and a half long, long years. I sought out the smartest three students I could find to be my roommates for maximum peer pressure at home to study.

"Howard is not in the same league as Harvard. Harvard Law School opens doors."

I thought back to my personal admissions essay about triumph over adversity, my small-town roots, and my desire to contribute to the study of race, racism, and American law. I revised draft after draft after draft of my personal statement. I rewrote my essay twelve times for maximum polish and impact. On February 9, 1983, I received a fat envelope from the Harvard Law School Admissions Office, and I ran for pure joy throughout the hallways of my dorm, yelling and screaming from sheer triumph. I burned with concentrated effort and won my prize.

It did not matter to my dad, a middle-aged black man who came of age in the segregated South. When my dad thought of lawyers, he thought of Thurgood Marshall, distant cousin lawyer and Richmond Circuit Special Justice M. Ralph Page, City of Richmond Mayor Henry L. Marsh, III, Virginia State Senator L. Douglas Wilder—all black and all graduates of Howard Law School.

"You're acting white. You've been around whites for all these years, and you think you're white." I seethed inside. I was being me and pursuing my life goals. This was the opportunity of a lifetime, and I could not imagine turning my back on it. I lived next to a cow pasture, and within a month, I could be studying among the brightest minds in our country. This was the American Dream personified! Why couldn't my dad give the race thing a rest for once?

"All I need is your signature. This is my dream, not yours!"

"You encouraged him," I heard, as the man whose name I bear turned to my mom. "At every turn, you supported him. Harvard Law School is his God, his Bible."

"You Blame the Man too much," said my mom turning toward my dad. "I wish I had had the opportunity Winkfield Jr. has now. Are you jealous of your own son?"

This was my summer of 1983. What should have been a sublime time of affirmation became an epic fight for my future.

When I met the family of my first girlfriend for the first time at a top restaurant in downtown Richmond, Virginia, they were excited to meet me. Their vocabulary and mental processing speed were at level 10. As I began to engage them, I sensed they were downshifting their words to level 7. This was the first time in my life a black family (not my girlfriend) had talked down to me so that I could understand. This lunch was a racial moment to be remembered for me.

Commentator Shelby Steele recently remarked that he still feels a sting of discomfort when he approaches a top-quality hotel. Steele was born in 1946, so he can recall being rejected from public accommodations because of his race. Before the Civil Rights Act of 1964, traveling across the country was dangerous for African Americans. In 1948, a black driver named Robert Mallard was lynched in his brand-new car in front of his wife and child by a white mob in Georgia. Mallard was "not the right kind of negro" and "n----- rich."

Imagine the year is 1949. You are black. You want to soak up the sun and surf in San Diego. Where would you spend the night in San Diego? According to *The Green Book*, you would have three selections—Douglas Hotel at 206 Market Street, Simmons Hotel at 542 6th Avenue, and the YWCA at 1029 C Street.* That is it! Suppose your growing family is hungry, and you want to eat. Where can you just relax and enjoy your meal? *The Green Book* says you could dine with your family at two places—Sun Restaurant at 421 Market Street and Browns Hostess Restaurant at 2816 Imperial Avenue. That's it! I don't mean to pick on San Diego. Only 6 percent of the more than one hundred motels that lined U.S. Route 11 in Albuquerque, New Mexico, admitted black customers. Only three motels in the entire state of New Hampshire served African Americans in 1956.

The Civil Rights Act of 1964 silenced this madness. There are many, many important legacies of the Civil Rights Act of 1964, but the most important element was to outlaw race and color discrimination in public accommodations—in hotels and restaurants. Both "Cabins for Colored" and "We Cater to White Trade Only" signs came down.

---

* From his Harlem community home, postal employee Victor H. Green created *The Green Book* as a directory of which hotels, camps, road houses, and restaurants would serve African-American travelers. *The Green Book* was an instant success with the black consumer. Within one year, Green was distributing his book on a national level.

My life began in 1961 in Richmond, Virginia. I have no memories of "Colored Only" or "Whites Only" signs. By the time of my first memory in 1965, the Civil Rights Act of 1964 had already been passed. My folks lived in an insular black enclave, and they probably did not have the money or desire to tool around the country. I love five-star hotels, and my most cherished memories are of overnight stays at the Fairmont Hotel in San Francisco, the Jefferson Hotel in Richmond, the Harvard Club of New York, the Plaza Hotel on Central Park South in Manhattan, the Sheraton Commander Hotel in Cambridge, and the Study at Yale. I am of a different age and generation from Shelby Steele and my father.

I continue to have inflection moments. At a desert resort in Palm Springs, California, my mother-in-law and I argued for two hours about a proper understanding of blackness. I perceived my mother-in-law saw the negative in blackness: slavery, underfunded urban schools. I lived in Black History from an early age and learned to see blackness as relentless enterprise and triumph over adversity. I interpreted my mother-in-law's vigorous disagreement as the opposite of affirmation. I felt bullied for two hours and left the argument awash in anxiety. This was a racial event for me as it told me there was no middle ground possible in the Cold War of ideas on race. Where is the hope for common humanity if one is at war with one's mother-in-law?

Like you, Jen, I love my children, and so do family members who reject all that we hold most dear, an idea of common humanity more than racial identity.

Wink

Letter 35

Wink,

I loved learning a bit more about your background and reading about your early experiences. We should have exchanged these stories sooner. Now I feel like our journey has officially started.

Jen

EPISTOLARY II

Letter 36

Jen,

So, I went outside toward the garage. There was an early morning chill in the air. I turned the corner and opened the door to the garage. Inside was a landscape of the debris of life—old bicycles, old bed frames, unused and chipped flowerpots, plastic cups and bowls, folding chairs. I took a deep breath. I knew what I wanted, but there was an avalanche of stuff to clear away. Fortunately, I was determined and driven. I began to methodically remove items between me and my goal. Piece by piece and step by step, I created a path of order out of chaos. I wasn't going to remove the bed frames, so I had to bend down and reach over to the file cabinet. I pulled the second drawer in the file cabinet. It wasn't there. I removed the first drawer, and I recognized the old papers immediately. I pulled out the pregnant folder labeled "FAMILY/BROWN FAMILY Rainey Twyman."

I opened the folder, and, of course, the very first item was the national hymn/lyrics for Jack and Jill. Next was a handwritten document titled "The Lawrence Family Reunion Saturday, July 18, 1981" stapled to a paper named "Lawrence Genealogy 1776–1949." And then I see it, a weathered, old obituary for my daughter's ancestor, George Shrewsbury. The date is March 8, 1875. The paper is the *Daily News* (Charleston, S.C., March 8, 1875). These and many other papers about Shrewsbury were entrusted to me by my wife's grandparents, Mr. and Mrs. Walter Lawrence. They were in their eighties at the time and knew I would cherish forgotten ancestors like George Shrewsbury.

Who was George Shrewsbury? And why does he matter?

My family finds racial innocence in relative ignorance of their free black past. My daughter lauds the oppression of her slave forebears to acclaim and remains silent about her free black ancestors in the public square. That is wrong. In fact, I would wager the majority of my daughter's maternal ancestors were not slaves at all. She has many free black ancestors worthy of remembrance—Edward Rainey, Joseph Hayne Rainey, James McGuire Rainey Jones, James Mitchell, Richard Holloway, Sr., Richard Holloway, Jr., Susan Cooper, Paris Cooper, Peter Mann. Perhaps the most unsung of my daughter's free black ancestors is George Shrewsbury.

Shrewsbury was born free and poor in 1820. He learned to read and write as a young man, and he was a mulatto. He embarked upon a trade of butchering and achieved a notable level of success remembered by historians to this day. Historian Eric Foner has described Shrewsbury as "[a] wealthy free black butcher and realtor in antebellum Charleston."[*] Shrewsbury's membership in the Brown Fellowship Society, an elite association of free blacks, was a foregone conclusion.

Upon conclusion of the Civil War, the Episcopal Church in Charleston, South Carolina, faced financial distress. The future of the Church was uncertain until Shrewsbury dug into his own pocket and gave Rev. Anthony Toomer Porter sufficient money to stay afloat.[†] The priest approached Shrewsbury about terms of repayment, but Shrewsbury refused. Survival of the Church was repayment enough.

After the Civil War, local residents from both parties recognized Shrewsbury's leadership. He ran unsuccessfully for Congress in 1872 as a Democrat. In 1873, he was elected as a Republican to the Charleston City Council. The city awarded Shrewsbury two city contracts for the provision of meat, which only added to his wealth. He died on March 7, 1875, in Charleston with a sizable estate that continued to grow after his death for years to come.

---

* Eric Foner, *Freedom's Lawmakers: A Directory of Black Office Holders During Reconstruction* (New York: Oxford University Press, 1993), 194.

† Shrewsbury handed over to Rev. Porter a roll of one hundred dollars, which is roughly equivalent to $1,598 in 2022 dollars.

Given all this, why did I say he's "unsung"? Shrewsbury is not remembered in the family because he owned slaves. He owned twelve slaves in 1860, according to the U.S. Census. He was the fourth largest free black owner of slaves in Charleston. On September 27, 1844, Shrewsbury purchased two slaves named Cyrus and Isaac from G. W. Cooper. The slaves were tailors by trade. In the same year, Shrewsbury sold five slaves for $1,100. On September 5, 1845, Shrewsbury filed a petition against another free man of color, James Norris, who claimed ownership of three slaves. Shrewsbury sought to quiet title for himself in the three slaves whom Shrewsbury had acquired in a gambling transaction.* Shrewsbury's slaves were hired out to the Charleston Work House. In the 1850 U.S. Census, 83.1 percent of black masters were mulattoes, while 90 percent of their slaves were dark-skinned. Kinship between free black slave owners and black slaves was not common, although it was clearly present in many instances.

Upon his death, the local paper remembered Shrewsbury for the ages:

DEATH OF ALDERMAN SHREWSBURY. — The subject of this notice, who died suddenly of heart disease on Sunday night, belonged to a colored class in Charleston who have long been equally distinguished by their high order of respectability and their perfect devotion to their native State and city. They are well known for the temperance of their opinion and conduct and unobtrusiveness of their manners, and for their quiet, persistent industry. Their relations to their white fellow-citizens were of the kindest long before the war, and were not only not disturbed, but, indeed, confirmed and strengthened by the issue of their struggle. Mr. Shrewsbury began life as a poor man, but by steady and well directed labor he had succeeded up to the time of his death in amassing a handsome fortune. His days were passed in the retirement of his home, and amid the activities of private pursuits, and

---

* "A quiet title action, also known as an action of quiet title, is a circuit court action—or lawsuit—that is filed with the intended purpose to establish or settle the title to a property. Quiet title actions are particularly prevalent in cases where there is a disagreement on the title and the lawsuit is meant to remove, or 'quiet,' a claim or objection to a title. The result is a clear title." Will Kenton, "Quiet Title Action: Definition, How It Works, Uses, and Cost," *Investopedia*, September 15, 2022, www.investopedia.com/terms/q/quiet-title-action.asp#:~:text=A%20quiet%20title%20action%20is%20a%20legal%20action,outside%20entities%20to%20acquire%20the%20property%20in%20question.

he never entered public life until at the last municipal election, without any solicitation on his part, he was chosen an alderman. He was serving in that capacity, and also as commissioner of the Almshouse, at the time of his death. His face and form, betokening, as they did, the quiet, and substantial citizen, will be missed in our markets and upon our streets; and we are satisfied there are none who will not feel that, particularly at the present juncture, the city has suffered severe loss in the death of one who was effecting so much good by his teaching, and especially by his example.*

If we abhor slavery, must we erase four generations of free black slave owners from our family memory?† That is the question. On the one hand, an equal opportunity shunning of black and white slaveholders is defendable. There is certainly no reason to discriminate based on race. However, whites held all the power in antebellum South Carolina. Blacks did not. Does the power imbalance suggest some recognition of the struggles and triumphs of four generations of a free black family? There is much to admire in the perseverance of my daughter's free black ancestors over the course of nearly one hundred years.

One of the papers in our family folder proudly proclaims:

HARNESS REPAIR SHOP 39 Beaufain Street Charleston, S.C. Five Generations of Artisans Located at the Same Place for over a Century "Let your moderation be known to all men" in charges. Faithful Work Guaranteed, Your Patronage Solicited, "Know Old' Charleston? 'I Hope you do! Born there? Don't say so, I was, too. Born in a house with a shingle roof: Standing still, if you must have proof, And has stood for a Century."‡

---

* *Daily News* (Charleston, South Carolina), March 8, 1875.

† Four generations of a free black family:

George A. Shrewsbury (1820–1875) = Georgiana Muriel Holloway (1837–1902)
Richard Holloway, Jr. (1807–1888) = Muriel (?–?)
Edward Shrewsbury (1795–?) = Anna (?–?)
Richard Holloway, Sr. (1776–1845) = Elizabeth Mitchell (1785–1866)
James Mitchell (1758–1821) = Diana Caywood (?–?)

‡ Document is a two-sided, single-page copy of a business card (date unknown). The front of the business card reads, "Taken from the Records of Brown Fellowship Society. The 17th Anniversary Meeting was held at the house of Richard Holloway, Beaufain Street, November 5, 1807." On the back of this business card, the pride in family dynasty comes through live

Jen, these black men were building a family dynasty unique to black American history. I cannot think of a single black family that has transmitted enterprises and property over one hundred and twenty years in the South, save for the descendants of Daniel Brown in Chesterfield County, Virginia. Please correct me if there are other black generational success stories over the course of five or more generations in the former Confederacy.

Is it possible to separate the great from the deplorable? Wouldn't my daughter be more truthful in her writings and public addresses to recognize slaves in her past *and* free blacks who achieved in imperfect times? To cancel multiple generations of success as an American feels wrong. The difficult chore is providing psychological context for why the success of George Shrewsbury matters in a healthy, constructive way. If we can unravel this conundrum, we as a family will be closer to our imperfect truth, and truth is always liberating. Perhaps the conundrum can be unraveled by holding two ideas in one's head at the same time. Value achievement always, even if in imperfect times. Respect one's ancestors for doing the best they could with what they had. I draw upon the wisdom of Joe Louis and Thurgood Marshall in this regard. Both Louis and Marshall made a similar remark when reflecting upon their own lives.

Sincerely,

Wink

---

and clear. It reads, "Taken from the records of Brown Fellowship Society, July 5, 1805. First Generation—The Monthly Meeting of Society was held at the workshop (Carpenter) of James Mitchell on Beaufain Street. Second Generation—Richard Holloway learned his trade with James Mitchell, married his daughter and succeeded to the business stand in 1807–1845. Third Generation—Charles H. Holloway, son of Richard, learned his trade with his father and continued at the same place from 1845 - 1885. Fourth Generation—James H. Holloway, son of Charles, learned the trade of Harness Maker and continued at same place from 1885 to the present. Fifth Generation—Harry H. Holloway, son of James, is associate with his father in the Harness Business. If you value Reliability, give us your Patronage." This document is in the personal possession of Winkfield F. Twyman, Jr.

Letter 37

Wink,

What I wouldn't give to go back in history and meet George. I would love to walk down the street with him and see how he was received. Did he lament slavery, but under the circumstances, played by the norms of the day? Did he treat his slaves any differently than white slave owners?

Other questions that came to mind include: How did he escape slavery? Did his lighter skin color give him a "pass"? I wonder, how many freed blacks owned slaves? Slavery's origins weren't necessarily racial, as I understand it. Once the Portuguese were able to navigate their ships to West Africa, they took advantage of the warring tribes that were willing to trade their own captured slaves. If Africa had been inhabited by light-skinned people operating under the same societal parameters, would we be today talking about a past of white slaves in the New World? Would the dynamics have been any different if their skin color was the same as their captors?

Marx would've argued that the European poor became slaves under the industrial revolution, and of course, true white slavery did exist, especially in the Middle East. Slavery was common the world over, so it doesn't necessarily surprise me that a black man owned slaves. If you said he lived in Africa, that would make perfect sense to me. However, given the specific nature of discrimination in the United States at that time, it is still quite surprising to me that a black man living in South Carolina in the 1800s owned slaves.

What else is surprising is that these stories are never shared in the public square. Of course, many more whites were responsible for slavery in America—Shrewsbury was surely in the minority, so it makes sense to focus on white slave owners when reviewing our country's history. However, the story is incomplete without an accounting of the lives of Shrewsbury or Anthony Johnson. There is a complexity to slavery that is missing in the American review of our past, not only in the incomplete history of global slavery but also in the agency of free and freed blacks in America.

How do you feel about George? Do you feel any more saddened that your family ancestry includes both black and white slaveholders? Would you feel proud to have someone like George, who thrived despite the odds, as an ancestor? Do you suffer from black guilt and black privilege? What is the psychological context for why George Shrewsbury matters?

If nothing else, I would argue that George Shrewsbury matters because all history matters. While we need to work in community to overturn discrimination, individual stories that take agency into account matter so that we can construct a holistic archive of all history—not just black history. Blanket histories that lump people into tribes flatten our past. We should also keep in mind there are forty million distinct versions of black history being written today.

This isn't to say there shouldn't be a general accounting of our history. You already know my feelings on this. Many argue that our review of history is flawed in classrooms that gloss over slavery. I would argue it's an egregious flaw, even. It is equally egregious to gloss over stories of the indelible spirit to overcome. We do a disservice not just to black Americans but also to all Americans when we bury the stories of Shrewsbury and others.

To overcoming,

Jen

Letter 38

Good evening

The hour is late, and this will be my last e-mail of the evening. I wanted to offer a quick rejoinder to some of your questions before retiring for the night.

Did he lament slavery? I suspect Shrewsbury played the hand he was dealt in life. He lived in a slave society, and he was going to compete on those terms. I don't have documentary evidence on Shrewsbury, but I have read the account of a wealthy free black barber who owned slaves in Mississippi. That barber played by the norms of his day and his community.

How did Shrewsbury escape slavery? Well, he was born free. I suspect his mother was a free woman, but I'm speculating. Odds are either both of his parents were free, or his mother was free. Had his mother been a slave, Shrewsbury would have been born a slave.

Did his lighter skin color give him a pass? Yes, there is no question more opportunities were available to Shrewsbury due to his light skin color. That's the way the black and white community rolled in Charleston, South Carolina, between 1820 and 1875.

How many free blacks owned slaves? Hmmm . . . I read somewhere that 28 percent of free blacks owned slaves in the South, but I would have to confirm that figure.[*]

---

[*] One-third of free blacks owned slaves in Charleston, South Carolina, as documented in the 1790 U.S. Census. See Loren Schweninger, *Black Property Owners in the South 1790–*

Would white slaves be possible as a mind experiment? I would say yes. I don't think slave traders cared about skin color. They cared about profit.

How do I feel about George? I feel George Shrewsbury did the best he could in his place and time. I respect black achievement a lot, and I have the power of discernment. I can separate the great from the deplorable. One can be great and a slave owner. One status doesn't cancel out the other. I wouldn't characterize this understanding as a reckoning *per se*, as it misses the mark. Reckoning connotes a foreboding, and that's not what I'm feeling as I reach this realization. For me, this understanding represents psychological coherence and authenticity.

Do I feel any more saddened that my family ancestry includes both black and white slaveholders? I feel more American. Everyone was caught up in an immoral system. Oddly enough, that forces us to see the humanity in everyone, regardless of race.

Would I feel proud to have someone like George, who thrived despite the odds, as an ancestor? Yes, I value triumph over adversity most highly.

Do you suffer from black guilt and black privilege? Answer: What are those terms? I am unfamiliar with those terms. Have you been making up jargon again, Jen? Tsk, tsk.

What is the psychological context for why George Shrewsbury matters? Answer: All ancestral achievement matters. We are impoverished to the extent we are not honest about flawed achieving ancestors in our past.

We can't erase black antebellum lives and hope to live in truth in the here and now.

Time for sleep,

Wink

1915 (Chicago: University of Illinois Press, 1997), 23.

Letter 39

Hi Jen,

An academic at the University of San Diego (USD) once said to me that he was not aware of free blacks before the Civil War. I didn't say anything, but it was a sad reflection of how we, as Americans, have forgotten the inspirational stories of black people who were not slaves. We seem all too eager to romanticize Harriet Tubman, Nat Turner, and Frederick Douglass at the expense of lettered men, professional men of enterprise. What does it say when even well-educated men like the USD academic are unaware of black enterprise and achievement before the Civil War?

I once wrote about a trailblazer, George Boyer Vashon (1824–1878), who deserves to be remembered more in the public square today.

Born July 25, 1824, George B. Vashon grew up in a Pittsburgh home steeped in abolitionism. His father, John Vashon, was the wealthiest black man in antebellum Pittsburgh and a national leader against slavery. John had extensive relationships with prominent abolitionists resolved to ending slavery. One such abolitionist, Walter Straton Forward, was a Pittsburgh lawyer, congressman, and U.S. Secretary of the Treasury Department. Forward would later sponsor George Vashon's legal career.

When not strategizing with abolitionists like Forward, John Vashon might be found running the Underground Railroad from his barbershop or organizing the community to support a private school for Pittsburgh's black youth. George Vashon attended that school, where he soon exhausted the knowledge of the sole instructor. When the public schools there temporarily integrated, the young Vashon left the black private school for the better resources of the public school. He excelled and gained admission to Oberlin College in 1840, becoming the first black graduate of Oberlin four years later.

Inspired by his father's activism, Vashon decided in 1845 to become a civil rights lawyer. He sought out Forward for an opportunity to study law. Black Americans faced grim conditions at the time. More than 90 percent of blacks toiled in bondage. Free blacks faced the loss of suffrage and citizenship rights. To sponsor a black for the practice of law marked a white lawyer as a radical, regardless of wealth or influence.

Forward felt an affinity for black struggle. He knew struggle himself, having arrived in Pittsburgh as a young man with little more than the clothes on his back. In all likelihood, Vashon's father had kept Forward informed of the young man's progress in school, his leadership in forming the first Juvenile Antislavery Society in Pittsburgh, and his graduation near the top of his Oberlin class.

Forward opened his law office to Vashon so that he could study law. The recent graduate proved a quick study and brilliant student. After two years of reading law and observing Forward, Vashon applied on February 17, 1847, for the examination required for admission to the Allegheny County Bar.

Vashon did not receive a warm welcome.

A majority of the examining committee refused to examine Vashon "because his complexion was a shade darker than their own," according to an account in the *Pittsburgh Telegraph*. Stunned by this turn of events, Vashon applied to the court "for a rule upon the Committee, directing them to examine him." The judge, Walter H. Lowrie, denied Vashon's request. Lowrie would never consent to colored people being citizens because Pennsylvania Chief Justice John Gibson had so decided in a prior case.

Vashon left Pittsburgh for greater opportunity in the majority-black Republic of Haiti. While en route to Haiti, he stopped in New York and requested an examination for admission to the New York Bar. Vashon passed the examination with ease and became New York's first black lawyer on January 11, 1848.

Haiti proved unable to support a legal practice at the time of Vashon's arrival in 1848. He worked teaching languages in local schools. In 1851, he returned to the United States and set up a law practice in Syracuse, New York. Within three years, he left his practice due to a lack of patronage from white clients. He became the third black college professor at New York's Central College before returning to Pittsburgh and a teaching job in the late 1850s.

Vashon gave the Allegheny County Bar a second chance after the Civil War on July 13, 1867. The presiding judge asked every member of the bar for his opinion on the admission of a black man. The question was debated at a raucous bar meeting attended by the entire bar membership.

Thomas Bayne championed Vashon's cause with the argument that no reason whatsoever existed for denying Vashon admission. Bayne had served as a colonel in the Union Army during the Civil War. Fearless in battle, Bayne led his command, the 136th Pennsylvania Volunteer Infantry, in the December 1862 Fredericksburg and May 1863 Chancellorsville campaigns. Having risked his life for the Union, Bayne might have believed that the 1866 Civil Rights Act, a federal law granting citizenship to U.S.-born persons, trumped state constitutional law.

John H. Bailey took the opposing side, arguing that if a white Pennsylvania citizen could eject a black from a public accommodation for whites, then the white bar could reject a black member. Bailey would later become an associate law judge of the Allegheny County Court of Common Pleas.

The three-judge panel denied Vashon's application without racial comment on March 28, 1868. The court refused Vashon's application because two certificates had not been produced, although Vashon's attorney, P. C. Shannon, demonstrated "two recent similar instances in which the court had allowed admission."*

At the time the court of common pleas denied Vashon's motion, the first black Americans who would eventually be admitted to the Allegheny County Bar, William Maurice Randolph and John W. Holmes, were still youngsters.

---

* J. Clay Smith, Jr., *Emancipation: The Making of the Black Lawyer 1844–1944* (Philadelphia: University of Pennsylvania Press, 1993), 152. ("Even though he had been a member of the New York bar since 1848, Vashon's application for admission to the Allegheny bar was again rejected by the three-judge Court of Common Pleas, but this time on the technical ground that he had not submitted two character references with his application.")

Like many northern blacks, Vashon felt a sense of duty toward freed blacks in the South. He relocated to Washington, D.C., in 1867 and became an unsung leader in black history. He lived the life of a trailblazer as he achieved these milestones:

- First black professor at Howard University on October 8, 1867

- Admitted to the U.S. Supreme Court Bar on April 6, 1868

- First black admitted to the District of Columbia Bar on October 26, 1869

- Admitted to the Mississippi State Bar on June 8, 1875

- Professor of ancient and modern languages at Alcorn University from 1873 to 1878

By December 19, 1891, the idea of black lawyers did not provoke open rancor in Allegheny County. The bar admitted Randolph and Holmes upon the recommendation of former Judge C. S. Fetterman. No one objected.

George B. Vashon had been dead for thirteen years.

Vashon's descendants take pride in their ancestors, both black and white. Yet they remember the Allegheny County Bar's refusal to examine Vashon with sadness. "I think George B. was heartbroken. That's why he wandered from New York to Haiti and back to New York," said his great-great-granddaughter, Janet G. Davis. She hoped his memory could be honored with an apology or a posthumous admission. The Pennsylvania Supreme Court admitted Vashon to the state bar on October 20, 2010.

Today, there are over three hundred black lawyers in Pittsburgh. That the first black American lawyer from Pittsburgh would gain admission to the New York, District of Columbia, Mississippi, and U.S. Supreme Court Bars but never the Allegheny County Bar is more than ironic. George B. Vashon died on October 5, 1878, far away from home in rural Mississippi.[*]

The life story and accomplishments of Vashon always inspire me.

---

* Wink Twyman, Jr., "A Career in Exile," *Pennsylvania Lawyer* (September/October 2007): 54, www.pabar.org/members/PALawyer/SeptOct07/ACareerinExile.pdf.

Against the wind of raw and naked prejudice, he persevered and triumphed. That he was never admitted to his hometown bar in his lifetime was on the Allegheny County Bar. Are you also inspired by the true grit of Vashon? Why do you think the name of Vashon doesn't resonate in the public square today? Does the example of Vashon further our understanding of black self-reliance? Who might be opposed to a greater celebration of Vashon's memory?

Watching TRADING PLACES,

Wink

Letter 40

Dear Wink,

Vashon did persevere and triumph. He should be upheld in black history as someone who refused to bow down to the dictates of the pervasive discrimination that characterized his era. I do agree that more stories of the likes of Vashon should fill our textbooks. However, that he never received admittance to his hometown bar harkens back to the injustices that black Americans long had to endure. That he persevered is testament to the resilience and self-reliance of black America, but that he was constantly overlooked despite his credentials is also testament to a pervasive anti-black racism.

I'm guessing you're suggesting that Vashon doesn't resonate in the public square because, Allegheny County Bar aside, he was a story of success. The public square likes to highlight stories of weakness wrought at the hands of *white oppression*, and Vashon doesn't fit the bill. Someone who exudes strength doesn't fit the revolutionary agenda of a total systemic overhaul. Without sympathetic martyrs, the Black Lives Matter movement would lose its momentum. And yet, while Vashon comes across as anything but weak, he was a victim of oppression nonetheless.

And so, like you, I find his personal story inspiring, but his struggles anger me. If I, as a white American, am angered with the injustices he faced, wouldn't a black American who shares his heritage of struggle become more enraged? How do you propose that we view Vashon in an effort to instill strength and character in black American youth, without it being tinged with the division that colored his history? Can and should these two be separated?

In search of unity,

Jen

Letter 41

Dear Jen,

I love black achievement. Stories of perseverance always inspire me and give me an extra charge for engaging the world. I've been like this since grade school. Vashon is one of many storied pioneers in our past.

You raise the suggestion whether black Americans who shared Vashon's heritage of struggle should be enraged, whereas you, as a white American, are angry. What's the difference between anger and rage? Prejudice is just a historical fact. It is a part of our past. One might even argue that black Americans might be more blasé about Vashon's treatment since prejudice is well-known. "Blasé?" you might be asking. Here's what I mean. When my distant cousin Deb (Andrew) Maddox discovered the oppressive labor contracts enforced by the Freedmen's Bureau against my paternal great-great-grandparents in 1866, Deb was genuinely shocked and angered to use your word. I was not because I have studied black history for much of my life. Oppressive contractual terms in an 1866 labor contract did not faze me. So, I suggest black Americans may be less prone to anger than you concerning Vashon's treatment because prejudicial treatment based on race is old news. Just something to consider.

You ask how Vashon should be viewed. He should be viewed as a model, a template for black achievement in this country. The keys to achievement are simple—gain as much education as possible despite prevailing norms and mores, aim high for professional success, and never give up. That's the Vashon way.

Finally, the story of Vashon can be told without division. The elements of achievement are universal. The keys to triumph over adversity are timeless. Focus on the things that unite us, not the things that divide us. And that approach will eliminate the division.

More people should know of George Boyer Vashon.

Regards,

Wink

Letter 42

Dear Jen,

On April 21, 2018, a teenage relative declared, *"Race Is All About Culture. Blackness Is All About Oppression. Nothing Else Matters."* How could a member of my family believe nothing else matters but oppression? It would be one thing if this person had grown up poor in a public housing project with no dad and a mom strung out on drugs and older brothers in prison. Maybe I could understand their perception of the world. But this is far, far from the case. The relative is privileged to live in a coastal town, to be the descendant of four generations of free black slave owners and the first black congressman, to be the child of two Ivy League–educated parents and a Harvard-degreed auntie, to have been educated in private schools all their life save one crazy year in sixth grade, and to be studying now at an Ivy League institution.

In what alternative universe can the family member fervently believe blackness equals oppression and nothing else?

I believe part of the problem is how we educate children about the antebellum past. The relative once said that her "school only teaches me about slaves." How wrong.

Imagine how different the mindset of the young would be if we gave free blacks before the Civil War their due, if we practiced a little diversity, inclusion, and equity in how we teach about black achievement. All blacks were not slaves.

As you intuit, Jen, we need more stories about achieving free blacks in the public square. We need more stories about men like John Mercer Langston (1829–1897).

To begin his life story, John Mercer Langston wrote, *"Self-reliance [is] the secret of success."* He did not begin his life story bemoaning white privilege. He did not commence his life story Blaming the Man. He chose his words with care. Langston was sixty-four years old at the time of publishing his autobiography, *From the Virginia Plantation to the National Capitol.* He had lived through the death of his beloved parents; pioneered student success at Oberlin College; been rejected from law school because of his race; trailblazed triumphantly as the first black lawyer in antebellum Ohio; served as the General Inspector of the Bureau of Refugees, Freedmen and Abandoned Lands, the founder and organizer of the law department at Howard University, the Acting President of Howard University, the Minister to Haiti, and the first President of Virginia Normal and Collegiate Institute (now Virginia State University); and been voted in as the first black congressman from Virginia.

In 534 pages of his life story, one will find no mention of *institutional racism* or *structural racism* or *white privilege.*

Did Langston not understand oppression?

To ask the question is to answer the question. Born on December 14, 1829, in Louisa County, Virginia, Langston entered the world with slaves all around him. Langston's mother was a free mixed-race woman, and his father was a white slaveholding planter. His parents lived in a common-law marriage arrangement. If *blackness is oppression*, Langston knew blackness as oppression up close and personal more so than any living person can possibly know oppression. Langston's own brother, Charles Langston, was incarcerated for his opposition to the Fugitive Slave Act, and Charles thundered against the Fugitive Slave Law with an eloquence worthy of the ages.* Social Justice Warriors today do not

---

* The Wellington Rescue occurred on September 13, 1858, when a group of men rushed to Wellington, Ohio, to rescue a runaway slave, John Price. The U.S. Marshals were enforcing the Fugitive Slave Law, but thirty-seven men took it upon themselves to enforce moral law. The men rushed a hotel where the marshals had hidden Price. Price was liberated and taken to Canada, forever free of slavery. The federal government indicted Charles Langston for his part in the rescue. Upon sentencing in federal court, Charles delivered one of the greatest speeches of the 1800s: "When I come to be claimed by some perjured wretch as his slave, I shall never be taken into slavery. . . . We have a common humanity." As the transcript of the proceedings note, his words were followed by "Great and prolonged applause,

know oppression. They dishonor the memory of courageous heroes who fought honest-to-goodness slave catchers in the back alleys of northern cities. There is something offensive in equating the oppression of a captured free black returned to slavery with the arrest of two black men at Starbucks. There is no moral equivalence here.

If Langston understood real oppression during real slavery, why does he begin his life story with self-reliance as paramount, as the secret of success? Langston tells us why. Self-reliance fitted Langston mentally and morally for those trying and taxing duties that awaited him in life. "Whoso would be a man must be a nonconformist." Self-reliance is the importance of avoiding conformity and following one's own ideas and instincts. Truth is inside a person, and this is authority, not institutions. Do what you think is right no matter what others think. Truth is within oneself. Reliance on one's own efforts and abilities will see one through. This is how Langston understood the world.

Psychology professor Martin E. P. Seligman has speculated that the words running through one's head may correlate to psychological health and well-being.[†] Seligman recounted how a research team scanned Facebook posts to assess well-being as a factor of word clouds. Word clouds predicted the gender of the poster a staggering 92 percent of the time. Women prominently used words like shopping, <3, excited, and yay! Men thought distinctively different thoughts like f---ed, f—k, f---ing, wishes, and he. What I found more interesting were word clouds associated with low neuroticism (emotional stability) and high neuroticism (emotional instability). High emotional stability correlates with psychological health and well-being and the use of words like success, opportunity, church, beautiful, blessings, blessed, and greatness. High neurotics seemingly cannot help themselves as they use words like hate, nightmare, depressed, depression, and stupid.

How does a real hero like John Mercer Langston fare in a word cloud

in spite of the efforts of the Court and the Marshal to silence it." Charles Langston, speech at the Cuyahoga County Courthouse, Cleveland, May 12, 1859, available at www2.oberlin.edu/external/EOG/Oberlin-Wellington_Rescue/c._langston_speech.htm.

* Ralph Waldo Emerson, *Self Reliance* (1841), 3.

† Martin E. P. Seligman, *The Hope Circuit: A Psychologist's Journey from Helplessness to Optimism* (New York: Public Affairs, 2018), 344–346.

analysis? A check for words in his autobiography revealed low neuroticism (emotional stability) and psychological health. Words like success, opportunity, church, beautiful, blessings, blessed, and greatness are associated with well-being. In relating his life story, Langston used these words the following number of times:

Success—103
Opportunity—70
Church—65
Beautiful—47
Blessings—7
Blessed—6
Greatness—5

If these words are running through one's head every day, wouldn't success be more probable than not?

What about the words often used by those with high neuroticism, words like sick, hate, depressed, depression, stupid, and nightmare? Langston did not think of the world in these terms:

Sick—7
Hate—4
Depressed—0
Depression—0
Stupid—0
Nightmare—0

In a time of unimaginable racial hate to the modern mind, a black forerunner of his race gave "hate" bare mention in his 534-page life story! How would a modern public intellectual like Ta-Nehisi Coates use words to describe the world? Using his iconic *Between the World and Me* as a prism into the mind of Coates is illuminating. A man born in 1975 in Baltimore, Maryland, uses the word "hate" when describing his life at almost (but not quite) twice the rate of a man born on a Virginia plantation in 1829. Who is more neurotic about race in America? I would place my bet on the writer who never graduated from Howard University in lieu of the first black Acting President of Howard. This is the uncomfortable truth about race in modern-day America. Conditions are so blessed today that writers tip over into unhealthy, unbalanced tomes to make a splash. Coates has tipped his hand on this score: "Hate gives identity."* Once again, John Mercer Langston would never have used these words to think about his life story. He was a great American success story because he thought about success more than anything else. His word cloud does not lie.

As for Coates? I counted one use of the word "success" in his life story.[†]

I've read *From the Virginia Plantation to the National Capitol* several times. It is always a pleasure to peer into the mind of an achiever free of stereotypes and unthinking service to political agendas. As a nine-year-old orphan bereft of his guardian family, Langston faced the crisis of his young life. A gloom settled upon his spirit. His new guardian, Richard Long, asked what Langston could do? Langston honestly answered, "I can't do anything." Long asked the nine-year-old, "How do you expect to live?" When I read those words, I think of my grandmother Rosa Nell Brown Twyman Jackson or Mrs. Lucille Walker, my first-grade teacher, or Mrs. Helen Friend, my fourth-grade teacher. One was never too young to learn the importance of strict and severe discipline. Long immediately put Langston to work driving the horse and cart and hauling brick. Years later at the age of sixty-four, Langston expressed gratitude for the "instruction and training given him, in the ways of industry and self-reliance."[‡]

During his early years at Oberlin College, Langston was invited to join a literary society. He accepted and was immediately assigned to debate a question: *Do the teachings of phrenology interfere with man's free moral agency?* When the date of the debate arrived and Langston was announced as the next speaker, Langston ascended the platform only to have the unimaginable happen. His mind went blank! He could not find the words to express himself. After what seemed like an eternity, he sat down and began to cry. Classmates offered their sympathies, but

* Ta-Nehisi Coates, *Between the World and Me* (New York: Spiegel & Grau, 2015), 60.

† Ibid., 96.

‡ John Mercer Langston, *From the Virginia Plantation to the National Capitol* (Hartford: American Publishing Company, 1894), 58.

sympathies only compounded the problem. Mortified beyond all comprehension, he ran home and wept, the tears soaking his pillow, bed, and clothing. All the faith placed in him by his brothers and grammar school teachers seemed for naught. As the morning bell rang at 5:00 a.m., Langston turned course. He vowed he would never, ever fail again in any effort at speech-making. He would never allow to pass any opportunity to make a speech unimproved. And when Langston returned to the society the following week, he delivered a speech with "ease and spirit" received with transforming applause.* Never again would words fail Langston.

Truly, character is the best measure of a man.

Upon graduating from college in August 1849, Langston decided upon his life's profession. He would practice law. Consider the inner certitude of the man. There were only two other blacks practicing law in the United States at the time—Macon Bolling Allen (1816–1894) and Robert Morris (1823–1882). There is no evidence Langston was aware of Allen and Morris as Langston clearly wrote there were no black lawyers anywhere and there had never been black lawyers.† Langston faced "no prospect of success"; he had "no example of a daring and courageous forerunner" to offer guidance and encouragement.‡ The judges and juries were all white men, and most Americans at the time opposed the idea of a black lawyer.§ Even those favorable to Langston's ambition offered no encouragement. An old wise black man advised Langston not to think of studying law, because even white men had a hard row to hoe in making a living as a lawyer. A white abolitionist lawyer and friend of black people counseled Langston to leave the United States and live in the British West Indies. There, he might be able to eke out a fair living.

---

* Ibid., 95–96.

† Ibid., 104.

‡ Ibid., 104.

§ There is a reference to Allen's admission to the bar in a Maine newspaper. The reporter observed that, if whites didn't oppose digging for potatoes beside negroes, then they shouldn't oppose working beside a negro lawyer. "Is the practice of law so much more respectable than hoeing potatoes that a lawyer can be disgraced by contact with a black man, and not a farmer?" *The Daily Eastern Argus,* July 15, 1844, as quoted and cited in John Clay Smith, *Emancipation: The Making of the Black Lawyer, 1844–1944* (Philadelphia: University of Pennsylvania Press, 1993), 93.

A prudent black man might have considered the landscape, thought better of ambition, and pursued a career as a teacher or minister. There were clear, concrete demands for black teachers and ministers to serve free blacks in antebellum Ohio. But Langston persevered.

Langston applied for admission to law school at Ballston Spa, New York. The head of the law school, J. W. Fowler, was frank with Langston. He said the Board of Trustees and Board of Faculty were unanimous in their decision—that Langston could not be admitted because of his color—but he nonetheless invited Langston to the school for a look-see. After meeting Langston, Fowler said he would resubmit Langston's application to the Board of Trustees and Board of Faculty. Within twenty-four hours, the Board of Trustees and Board of Faculty again denied Langston admission based on race. Fowler explained to Langston that the school had an interest in working with U.S. Senator John Calhoun to bring more South Carolina students to the school. These students would be uncomfortable with a black student in their midst.

But it was not the denial in which Langston's character was revealed. It was in the enticement.

Fowler suggested that Langston might "edge his way" into the school if Langston could pass as a Frenchman or a Spaniard. This lure excited the greatest moral indignation from Langston. "I am a colored American; and I shall not prove false to myself, nor neglect the obligation I owe to the Negro race!" Fowler offered his sympathies, which only added to Langston's fortitude: "I do not need sympathy. I need the privileges and advantages of your law school."[*]

We need more black heroes like Langston. John Mercer Langston was standing up for his race when few others saw the long game of race elevation and uplift. Refusing to be denied his goal, Langston found an Ohio lawyer, Judge Philemon Bliss, who agreed to train Langston as a law clerk. Bliss drew no distinction based on skin color and openly gave his all to Langston's training in the law. On September 13, 1854, Langston achieved the unimaginable. He was admitted to the Ohio Bar. His achievement is all the more remarkable when one notes blacks could not then vote, serve on juries, or testify as witnesses.[†] Where did

---

* Langston, 108.

† Ibid., 163.

the steadfastness, the iron will, within Langston come from? Langston would answer with two words above all others—*self-reliance!*

It is hard to imagine how strongly the odds were against Langston. He was marked and set apart from all other lawyers due to skin color. How would he make a living? Would he starve for lack of business? Was the white abolitionist right about better opportunity in the British West Indies? These fears did not speak to Langston. This was a man trained in self-discipline and racial pride. "A thousand times he had been warned that the fate of the negro was sealed, and in the decree which fixed the destiny of the blackhued son of the race his own position was determined and settled."[*] Langston defied the expectations of thousands. Within a month of admission to the bar, he won a unanimous jury verdict in favor of his client.[†] And within one year, he had a prosperous practice. His clients were all white! The year was 1855, and across the Ohio River, blacks remained slaves.

A determined purpose can always, always move mountains.

What would Langston say to Coates today? First, Langston would chastise Coates for not completing his college degree at Howard. Too many freed slaves gave too much for their descendants to squander higher education. The former Acting President of Howard University would be stern with Coates.

Second, Langston would repeat the timeless principles he spoke of at innumerable platforms, halls, barns, schools, and fields throughout the South before former slaves: "education, labor, thrift, forecast, economy, temperance, morality."[‡] Above all things, "Get education! Get money! Get character!"[§]

Third, I wonder how many times Coates has heard the N-word in anger and out of race prejudice. Coates was born in Baltimore in 1975, so I have my doubts. One will find eight references to the N-word in Langston's life story. Langston doesn't sugarcoat his life experience. One's heart is drawn to the young man, the ambitious lawyer, and the hard-driving congressional candidate who had to endure these racial

---

[*] Ibid., 130.

[†] Ibid., 132.

[‡] Ibid., 240.

[§] Ibid., 244.

slurs. Knowing the full breadth of his story only enhanced my appreciation for all that Langston accomplished. I was born in 1961 in Richmond, Virginia, and I cannot comprehend the raw vile Langston faced. I submit that a writer born in 1975 in Baltimore, Maryland, has even less cause to draw the race card.

I hope my relative grows to see there is more to blackness than oppression.

Sincerely,

Wink

P.S. Not entirely by coincidence, April 21, 2018, is also the date that I decided to continue work on my novel about the first black lawyer. My family member's words of racial despair drove me to the keyboard to tell a story in which blackness represents enterprise, triumph over adversity, and all the other positive traits we've discussed through our exchange.

Letter 43

Dear Wink,

I think this may be one of your most powerful letters. The two things that resonate the most are, first, your relative's focus on oppression. Your relative is more privileged than most of the white children I know in terms of access to resources, and now they are enrolled in an Ivy League institution. (Congratulations to this person, by the way!) Let me ask, do they feel oppressed? They talk about oppression, but do they have stories of personal oppression? Have they ever felt uncomfortable as a black person in their classes, or have they ever had insults thrown at them due to the color of their skin? Or is this just a general oppression they've adopted from the oppression mantra?

Do you think they will participate in outrage demonstrations at their Ivy League institution, such as the 2015 protests against Nicholas and Erika Christakis?* Are you worried that Ivy League faculty and staff are lacking in self-admitted viewpoint diversity?† If you do have these worries, how do you discuss them with your relative? Do you think your viewpoints register?

I think it is important to continue to push forward an agenda that

---

* See, for example, "Silence U Part 2: What Has Yale Become?" YouTube video, uploaded by We the Internet TV, March 22, 2017, www.youtube.com/watch?v=xK4MBzp5YwM.

† See, for example, Greg Piper, "Yale Faculty Agree It Has No Real Political Diversity," *College Fix,* December 10, 2019, www.thecollegefix.com/yale-faculty-agree-it-has-no-real-political-diversity/.

recognizes the history of black Americans and seeks to reconcile a dark past with a bright future. As we've discussed before, I'm just not sure that the way we are going about it supports a Coming to the Table moment. Eric Kaufmann, in his book *Whiteshift*, suggests that we support ethno-traditionalist nationalism. That is to say, a viewpoint that recognizes minorities and minority struggles, with the idea that we are all Americans and responsible for creating our future . . . together. To value our history and founding and to take responsibility for maintaining a larger national identity while embracing our differences and struggles. I find this "solution" to our current polemics enticing. I think you'd agree with this. In fact, I think this may be what you mean when you suggest a common "Old American" identity. Although I earlier wrote that your suggestion risked "sidestepping history," maybe it's true that those of us who cannot see our common ancestors are really the ones sidestepping history, as you passionately argued. I wonder what both your relative and Langston would think about such a solution.

I believe that thinkers such as W. E. B. Dubois and Martin Luther King, Jr., would subscribe to such a view. Both fought for the values of this country to be applied to all. The oppression mantra today seems to suggest that we "throw the baby out with the bath water." Instead of taking everything down to the foundation to rebuild, this thinking seems to revolve around total destruction. Within this storyline, we've built walls between us that seem insurmountable.

This leads me to the second point that resonated with me: Langston's idea of "self-reliance" as a critical part of his mindset and, arguably from your letter, the key ingredient to his success. This idea of self-reliance seems to have become a conservative buzzword and a sentiment that many progressives would label as *white supremacy*. Given that black Americans have faced oppression for their race, there are issues that need more than just personal grit and determination to resolve.

Yet, as someone who does not believe a big government is agile enough to work in the best interests of our diverse population, I don't know that systemic and blanket solutions are the best way forward. And so, at the end of the day, we are left with more regional and localized solutions.

One thing that I would support as a national initiative would be the full recognition of our past, including an education platform that not only included the darker narratives in our history but also simultaneously upheld the stories of uplift and overcoming. That is, we get in front of our past, so to speak, to recognize and teach of our overall failings while also underlining stories of Langston, Vashon, and Shrewsbury to highlight self-reliance and grit and to promote a broader picture of how our history unfolded.

Would Coates approve of such an initiative? If it doesn't include a dominant language of hate, I'm guessing not. The fact that he only mentions "success" once in his book is a stark contrast to Langston's personal story. How can we responsibly account for our past while also instilling a personal identity, outside of the tribe, of strength and character? Is it possible to do both?

Yesterday I attended a holiday show that had a jazz band composed of two white men (piano and sax), a black man (upright bass), and an Asian woman (drums). As I sat in the audience, I couldn't help but smile. This is my America, I mused, playing together in perfect harmony. Am I too naïve to think that we can replicate this nationally?

I'm looking forward to hearing your next story on black achievement. Maybe it is these stories that we need to lift us out of our history of oppression.

Feeling hopeful,

Jen

Letter 44

Dear Jen,

Unlike George Shrewsbury (1820–1875), George Boyer Vashon (1824–1878), and John Mercer Langston (1829–1897), Congressman Joseph Hayne Rainey (R-SC) (1832–1887) is well remembered in the public square. Congressman Rainey vaulted from slave to the Speaker's Chair of the U.S. House of Representatives in one lifetime. Congressman Rainey is my wife's paternal great-great-grandfather.

Joseph Hayne Rainey was born on June 21, 1832, in Georgetown, South Carolina, the child of Edward L. and Theresa Rainey. Joseph was born a slave. He died on August 3, 1887, in his hometown at the age of fifty-five after living an extraordinary life.

He persevered against all odds.

In 1846, Joseph's father, Edward L. Rainey, purchased the freedom of his family with savings from barbering work. Joseph was fourteen years old and suddenly free due to his father's enterprise. Joseph learned barbering and practiced the trade alongside his father at the Mills House in Charleston, South Carolina.

During the 1850s, Joseph moved to Philadelphia, Pennsylvania, where he married Susan Cooper. He violated South Carolina state law by returning with his wife to South Carolina in 1859. It was against state law for a free black to leave and return to the state. Only the intercession of white friends in high places averted criminal prosecution of Joseph.

Conscripted by the Confederacy to work on fortifications surrounding Fort Sumter, Joseph escaped on a ship through the Union blockade, went to New York City, and then on to the island of Bermuda, where he settled. He first found work as a waiter in a hotel before setting up residence and a barbershop in the Governor's Mansion called Tucker House. To this day, the alley behind his room is known as "Barber's Alley" in honor of Joseph's reputation and high regard. Susan joined her husband in Bermuda, and she established herself in the clothing-pattern business.

After the Civil War ended, Edward L. wrote his son and argued that many opportunities were opening up back home in Georgetown, South Carolina. While reluctant to leave his beloved Bermuda, Joseph was a man of ambition and civic awareness. In 1865, Joseph returned to South Carolina and rapidly began his ascent in the era of Reconstruction. He attended the state black convention that same year. In 1868, he represented Georgetown County in the State Constitutional Convention, and his constituents and neighbors elected him to the State Senate, where he chaired the State Senate Finance Committee. He served in the State Senate from 1868 to 1870.

In December 1870, he was elected to the U.S. House of Representatives, where he served from December 12, 1870, until March 3, 1879. Rainey was the first black congressman and the longest-serving black congressman during Reconstruction. In 1871, Rainey delivered a powerful speech on the floor of the House. He spoke movingly about the Ku Klux Klan Act of 1871 and the need for a constitution to protect the humblest of citizens.

In May of 1874, Rainey served as Speaker of the U.S. House of Representatives on a *pro tempore* basis. Rainey was the first black congressman to do so. Sometimes, I imagine Speaker Rainey wielding the gavel over former Confederates asking for recognition from the Chair.*

In 1875, Congressman Rainey was appointed brigadier general in the South Carolina militia. Rainey was one of the first five black brigadier generals in U.S. history.

Congressman Rainey had four children with Susan. Of the four,

---

* In an odd quirk of history, Rainey's nephew, James McGuire Rainey Jones, served as a bodyguard to General Robert E. Lee during the Civil War. See "Georgetown Negro Was General Lee's Bodyguard in War," *Georgetown Times,* September 20, 1929. ("Who was the body guard for Gen. Robert E. Lee? James McGuire Rainey Jones of Charleston, S.C., a loyal colored man from a loyal colored family.")

three survived into adulthood. The surviving children were Joseph Hayne Rainey II, Herbert St. Claire Rainey I, and Olive Rainey. Rainey maintained a second home in Windsor, Connecticut, partly because educational provisions for blacks were so lacking in South Carolina. We visited the Windsor home a few summers ago, and it was a thrilling experience for my daughter to walk along the same long and big floorboards as her ancestors.

When federal troops were withdrawn from South Carolina in 1877, Congressman Rainey realized that his opponents would defeat him by any means necessary. He lost the election of 1878 as a result of fraud, intimidation, terrorism, and violence at the polls. On March 3, 1879, the congressman served out his last day in the U.S. House of Representatives.

Congressman Rainey had been promised a position as Clerk of the U.S. House by leading Republicans, but this promise was not kept. After a series of setbacks and struggles, the congressman returned home to Georgetown.

Congressman Rainey died on August 3, 1887, in his hometown. His body lay in state in the family parlor before interment. The ancestor of my children had risen from slave to the Speaker's Chair in one lifetime.

"Very like leaves upon this earth are the generations of men—old leaves, cast on the ground by wind, young leaves the greening forest bears when spring comes in, so mortals pass; one generation flowers even as another dies away." *

With pietas,

Wink

---

* Homer, from *The Iliad,* as quoted in Nelson W. Aldrich Jr., *Old Money: The Mythology of America's Upper Class* (New York: AA Knopf, 1988), 10.

Letter 45

Wink,

The family stories you share are stories of strength and agency in black America at a time when slavery, literally, colored the landscape. They are stories we rarely hear in today's race-obsessed America, in which everyone is either a victim or oppressor. I don't have a problem revisiting the past, you know this already, but I believe that glossing over it does nothing to really impart true healing, and our country is desperately in need of healing. However, in revisiting our past, the stories that make headlines in our national narrative do not account fully for the agency so evident in your own family stories. Similarly, they put all white actors into the same category, failing to account for the poverty and struggle in many white families throughout our history.

We dismiss individual agency for a larger group narrative. Critical Race Theory and cultural theorists give short shrift to individuality, and where it goes against their established dogma, they dismiss it as anomalous or demonize it as an alt-right talking point. As the idea of individual agency threatens the current groupthink, it has now become categorized as the enemy in order to weaken its impact. In so doing, we abandon the stories of Congressman Rainey to the Borg (thought you'd appreciate the *Star Trek* analogy), or in common-speak, to the hive-mind.

The truth is, as much as I admire and uphold individuality, I also believe in community. It's not an either/or dichotomy; it's both/and. I think we try to simplify our chaotic lives and lean toward either/or binaries to avoid too much complexity—tier 1 consciousness. There is strength and healing in community. As we become more digitally isolated, we seek homogeneous communities to provide us with a group identity to ease our seclusion. Race has become one of the strongest identities anchoring our new binary communities.

Communities that tether us to only one identity lack dimension and strangle individuality. The two—individuality and community—can coincide, but it requires us to stretch the parameters of community. In order to create more heterogeneous communities, we need shared narratives that cross racial boundaries. Can we cross this divide with shared narratives of weakness and strength without the harness of race? How can we reconcile our history in our search for some commonality in a shared American identity? Your idea to embrace slavery as a common history of Old Americans is a solution, but as you already know, I don't know if it is one that would resonate in our current landscape.

At the moment, our new homogeneous communities give a sense of in-group camaraderie, providing quite the challenge to any brave individual willing to buck the trend. Through exploiting our differences, a zero-sum game evolves alongside an "us vs. them" ethos. This ethos becomes a salve for our loneliness. To go against the grain threatens exclusion. To create something novel requires a courage of individual agency that can coalesce into a new community.

The other day a very progressive friend said something that I thought was interesting. He said, amidst the chaos, we've started to have a conversation that is long overdue. Perhaps our current racial chaos is just a temporary spasm, taken to the extremes to force a conversation. I believe he may be onto something. My hope is that the conversations force us to create a new communal identity in the American mindset. My fear is that a new civil war will erupt before we come to this conclusion.

Congressman Rainey believed in a new America, even when all the odds were against him. His individual agency and belief in the idea of a shared American identity drove his ambition. What can we do to create such momentum today?

From Mumbai,

Jen

Letter 46

Hello Jen,

Earlier in our correspondence, I wrote about my ancestral connection to slavery through my grandma's grandfather Daniel Brown (1833–1885). It wouldn't do to repeat his life story of accomplishment and achievement as a former slave. As with Congressman Rainey, Daniel's past enslavement had no bearing on his drive for success. One might even surmise that his past enslavement motored his lifelong drive to prove himself.

Daniel was a founding father for me and my sister and first cousins, second cousins, and third cousins. What Daniel did was to start from nothing and, over a lifetime, acquire over 400 acres of land in Chesterfield and Charlotte Counties, Virginia.* He not only lifted his children and grandchildren above the tumult for survival, but he also—through

---

* My wife rejects the story of Daniel Brown as our Horatio Alger, and this disagreement is fine. She writes, "You say Daniel Brown started with nothing, but he inherited quite a bit of money. This isn't starting from nothing! Yes, he had to do something to make sure that money wasn't taken from him, and he probably wisely gave up claim to the property he was supposed to inherit to avoid a fight or having everything taken from him. Very wise. But he didn't quite start with nothing as most did. Edward Rainey, for example, earned everything by barbering and had to purchase the freedom of himself and his family. So I think you need to acknowledge that Daniel Brown didn't quite start with nothing. But through his smarts, he was able to keep and grow what he inherited." When I write that Brown started from nothing, I mean he came into this world as someone's property. He was not born with an inheritance in 1833. He was born a nonperson under Virginia state law. My wife and I can disagree about the story, and meaning, of Daniel Brown without being disagreeable.

his foresight and vision—ensured his grandchildren would not be starting from scratch as Daniel did. My grandma and her cousins would take property holdings for granted, and, like many Old Money families, this gave their descendants a head start in life. The acreage was modest and rooted in past generations. Ownership was the tradition in Hickory Hill for the descendants of Daniel. The tradition, with some exceptions, was not renting or sharecropping.

When I read a book like *Old Money: The Mythology of America's Upper Class* by Nelson W. Aldrich, Jr., I recognize stories of past ancestors and the possible elevating influence of foresighted grandparents of grandparents. What I find disaffecting are those who seem so marinated in "systemic" and "structural" analysis that they seem incapable of hearing my truth, that Daniel was a founding father in the best sense of the word, and that his life story undercuts the force of institutional racism. There has always been a place for black foresight and vision. Why wouldn't the Left be absolutely thrilled that a former slave—a man who could not read nor write—bent the world according to his will for the benefit of generations into the distant future. The man died in 1885, and we still live in his wake 135 years later.

When I share the Norse tales of Daniel's triumphs, the woke say Daniel was an outlier, an anomaly. They say his triumph against adversity is of no value to oppressed black people today!

Diminishing and discounting my ancestor doesn't sit well with me. He's not just my ancestor. For a couple of hundred close and distant cousins, Daniel informs how we perceive and understand the world. How prejudiced must someone be to tell me my ancestor must be discounted and dismissed in the name of social justice.

Slave owners never saw the humanity in the descendants of slaves. When the woke turn a blind eye to an achieving black ancestor, it causes me to wonder whether the woke are incapable of seeing the humanity in black Americans.

Before one can be an ally of black Americans, one must see the humanity in the descendants of American slaves.

Stuck in a snowstorm in Mammoth, California,

Wink

Letter 47

Wink,

I remember when I was very young, my mother had a rattan swinging chair. The kind that suspends from the ceiling. It was in my parent's bedroom, next to the bathroom, where she would spend time getting ready. I spent hours there as a child, swinging back and forth and twirling around and around in much the same way as she twirled her blond hair around old metal curlers.

My mother, born into an era that applauded housewives as pinnacles of American morality, played her role dutifully, but you could tell there was an underlying tension in her narrative. I believe she resolved it in the narratives she created for me. On a rather normal day that held no particular significance, I sat bouncing in the chair as my childlike mind explored my future. Maybe I'd be a nurse, I mused aloud. After all, that was a profession many of my preschool playmates envisioned. Not one to buck the trend, it seemed good enough for me.

My mother stopped her grooming to look at me—to pause and really see me, bouncing there in my Underoos. I don't think my mother had any problem with my preschool nursing ambition *per se*, but she quietly—and with much determination—told me, "You can be anything you want to be. You can be president." I think that is the first time that I realized my own agency. Really? President? I really had no idea.

Of course, being president was going to take some work on my end. My mother's high expectations of my endless possibilities generated a determination on my part, not necessarily to be president but to find my potential.

Soon after the idyllic days of the rattan chair is when my dad decided to take the Air Force Attaché post in Rangoon, Burma. This was perhaps the second biggest development in my personal narrative. My little world expanded as I attended school with Koreans, Filipinos, British, and a cornucopia of other nationalities. My first two "boyfriends" were Thai and Filipino. I had the hots for the son of a Burmese Air Force liaison. I got in the most trouble with the Koreans.

At an age when stereotypes often develop and solidify, I was exposed to our common humanity across cultures. And ultimately, this exposure determined my trajectory, not to become a nurse or president but to connect with others as an international citizen. Like you, the slogans of *oppression, systemic racism,* and *white supremacy* were just not a part of my experience. Granted, my experience was not your average American experience. However, having witnessed the brutality of the totalitarian Burmese junta coupled with the common humanity I found in the dreams and aspirations of my multicultural posse, I returned to America forever changed.

Perhaps this is why I find so much unease with our current dogma, or at least the dogma that our media likes to highlight.

For example, I've been reading about a new movement in education that claims math is racist: 1+1 may equal 2, but if a child reaches a different conclusion and you correct them, you are contributing to racism.[*] I read these stories in disbelief. I can't help but wonder if the media is only picking up on fringe movements like this or if this is really something that has wider appeal.

When I read such stories, there is sometimes a small element of a movement that does make sense, no matter how bizarre it otherwise sounds. We create stories for ourselves from our experiences. For example, if some teachers teach down to students of color over time, assuming that math is not their strength, or if children are born into families that do not support educational pursuits, then this can have an impact on the narrative that starts to play in the minds of those kids. They start

---

* See A Pathway to Equitable Math Instruction, *Stride 1: Dismantling Racism in Mathematics Instruction* (May 2021), equitablemath.org/wp-content/uploads/sites/2/2020/11/1_ STRIDE1.pdf.

to believe that they can't compete educationally, leading to a cycle that recalls the saying, "Whether you think you can, or you think you can't, you're right."

What I've found in all my travels is that the ideals of liberty and freedom are universal human values that transcend culture. I witnessed it in the yearnings for liberation that eventually surfaced shortly after we left Burma, resulting in a massive crackdown in 1988. We saw it again in China in the 1989 Tian'anmen Square protests and in the "color revolutions" in Eastern Europe.

And what I found so remarkable was that our country, in particular, and other Western countries, in general, was where these ideals originated. Due to these values, the only foreigners with whom we didn't interact during our time in Burma were the North Koreans. Coming from a despotic nation fearful of value contamination, they were not allowed to commingle in any expat community where Westerners were present. Heck, we even hung out with the Russians, and this was at the height of U.S.-Soviet tensions during the Reagan administration. In fact, it was those true Russian bear hugs from the Russian military attaché that perhaps did the most to solidify our common humanity in my young mind.

Despite the fact that these values did not extend to everyone at our founding, we have constantly evolved to expand their reach to women, people with varying melanin, those of different sexual orientations, and so on. It is because of these values and the agency of abolitionists like Frederick Douglass that we fought a civil war. And these values spurred Martin Luther King, Jr., in the Civil Rights Movement (as an aside, MLK is not a role model in many of the new antiracism curricula as he is considered too passive).* While not always timely and often marred with bloody struggle, we continue to expand these values.

The challenge to these values is the institutionalization of oppression. This emerging pedagogy locks us into patterns that are hard to unravel. Indeed, unraveling the institutions that upheld racism has been

---

* Jamila Pitts, "Bringing Black Lives Matter into the Classroom Part II," *Learning for Justice* no. 56 (Summer 2017), www.learningforjustice.org/magazine/summer-2017/bringing-black-lives-matter-into-the-classroom-part-ii. Pitts writes, "Romanticizing the civil rights movement is a particular concern when it comes to what students have already learned. Prevailing narratives praise 'respectable,' seemingly passive, docile, nonviolent black leaders."

a historic challenge. Instilling the mindset of oppression and "learned helplessness" is akin to the dumbing down of students of color and is itself an egregious form of racism. Teaching oppression and helplessness breeds a lack of agency.

Liberation, freedom, and equality—which I used to assume were the goals of our new activists—are suffocated without agency. But we can change the story.

The stories of your ancestors are a start. The stories of daughters who were told they could be president are a start. Young boys, like yourself in 1970s Virginia, who simply decide they *can* be president, are a start. The story of a black man who *did* become president is a start.*

As we engage in a more honest review of our history, we must wrangle with oppression but not forget the stories of uplift and strength, the stories of Daniel Brown.

In transit from Hyderabad to Dubai,

Jen

---

* In a quirk of fate and fortune, Wink did not become President of the United States. However, Wink decided to become a lawyer because most members of the Virginia General Assembly earned a living as lawyers. And he aimed for Harvard Law School because Harvard was the most popular college and university for presidents. While there, Wink served as a Black Law Students Association (BLSA) Big Brother to Michelle Robinson. One day, Michelle would serve as First Lady of the United States. A few degrees of separation.

Letter 48

Jen,

On May 1, 1866, a race riot broke out in Memphis, Tennessee. "The riot began when a white police officer attempted to arrest a black ex-soldier and an estimated fifty blacks showed up to stop the police from jailing him."* Who began the shooting? No one knows for sure. "Mobs of white residents and policemen rampaged through black neighborhoods and the houses of freemen, attacking and killing black soldiers and civilians and committing many acts of robbery and arson."† How bad was the mayhem and devastation? "46 black and 2 white people were killed, 75 black people injured, over 100 black persons robbed, 5 black women raped, and 91 homes, 4 churches, and 8 schools (every black church and school) burned in the black community." The effects of this terror were long-lasting. "Many black people fled the city permanently; by 1870, their population had fallen by one quarter compared to 1865."‡

"Your Old Father Abe Lincoln is Dead and Damned," an Irish police officer had cried out to black soldiers as the riot commenced.§

---

* MacKenzie Lanum, "Memphis Riot, 1866," *Black Past,* Nov 20, 2011, www.blackpast.org/african-american-history/memphis-riot-1866/.

† "Memphis Riots of 1866," *Wikipedia,* en.wikipedia.org/wiki/Memphis_riots_of_1866 (last accessed September 6, 2022).

‡ Ibid.

§ Kevin R. Hardwick, "'Your Old Father Abe Lincoln is Dead and Damned': Black Soldiers

What kind of man, regardless of race, would step into Memphis as every black school and church smoldered in ashes? Who stepped into despair and did the hard work of reconstruction? One such man was Horatio N. Rankin, the first documented black lawyer in Tennessee.

> Horatio N. Rankin, a free black missionary from the North . . . traveled north to raise funds for the rebuilding of the independent black Methodist church and school of South Memphis. Meanwhile, the congregation appealed to the local black community. They bought a lot and began building a new church. And, in the fall of 1866, the members of Avery Chapel organized a fair to raise money for "paying off the debt of the church for the lot and building now complete." In order to rebuild their church, they made it clear they were relying on the "charity" of "every generous colored citizen." They were successful.*

There is not much backstory available on Rankin. Rankin enrolled in the preparatory department of Oberlin College from 1861 to 1864.[†] We know this fact. Rankin attended the influential National Convention of Colored Men held in the City of Syracuse, New York, on October 4, October 5, October 6, and October 7 of 1864. Most of the influential free blacks in the United States attended the convention; their objective was to communicate to the American people a bill of wrongs and rights on behalf of black Americans. Frederick Douglass was present and garnered much applause for his eloquence and oration.

I am particularly moved when I read the words of successful Ohio lawyer John Mercer Langston at the event—his vocal and active profile befitted a future college president and congressman. A stirring oration on the next to last day of the convention was offered by attorney John S. Rock. Rock's words spoke to the ages. As a delegate from Memphis,

---

and the Memphis Race Riot of 1866," *Journal of Social History* 27, no. 1 (Autumn 1993): 109–128.

* Brian Daniel Page, "Local Matters: Race, Place, and Community Politics after the Civil War" (PhD dissertation, Ohio State University, 2009), etd.ohiolink.edu/apexprod/rws_etd/send_file/send?accession=osu1249417207&disposition=inline.

† Like a good many colleges in the nineteenth century, Oberlin maintained a pre-college preparatory department from 1833 to 1916. The prep school established a mechanism for funneling black Americans into Oberlin's regular Bachelor of Arts degree program. Many black students attended the prep school before entering Oberlin College proper.

Tennessee, Rankin did not speak. I was disappointed when I read that Rankin was silent. His silence disappoints me, but, as we shall see, silence has no bearing on the moral courage and fortitude of a man.

The Memphis Massacre brought out the measure of the man.*

---

* When one reads the 1866 report of race relations in Chesterfield County, Virginia, one must face and understand the stark contrast between Chesterfield and race conditions in Memphis, Tennessee in 1866. There was a localism to the reality of race on the ground in the defeated Confederacy. Consider the raw racial animus in Memphis: "Shortly after, the City Recorder (John C. Creighton) arrived upon the ground (corner of Causey and Vance Streets) and in a speech which received three hearty cheers from the crowd there assembled, councilled [sic] and urged the whites to arm and kill every Negro and drive the last one from the city. Then during this night the Negroes were hunted down by police, firemen and other white citizens, shot, assaulted, robbed, and in many instances their houses searched under the pretense of hunting for concealed arms, plundered, and then set on fire, during which no resistance so far as we can learn was offered by the Negroes. . . . The city seemed to be under the control of a lawless mob during this and the two succeeding days (3rd & 4th). All crimes imaginable were committed from simple larceny to rape and murder. Seven women and children were shot in bed. . . . The City Recorder Creighton in his speech on the evening of May 1, said 'That everyone of the citizens should get arms, organize, and go through the Negro districts,' and that he 'was in favor of killing every God damned n-----' . . . 'Boys, I want you to go ahead and kill every damned one of the n----- race and burn up the cradle." Charles F. Johnson & T.W. Gilbreth, *The Freedmen's Bureau Report on the Memphis Race Riots of 1866*, submitted May 22, 1866, from House Divided: The Civil War Research Engine at Dickinson College, hd.housedivided.dickinson/edu/node/45502. Conditions in Chesterfield were not ideal for black people, but there was no overlap with the murderous state of affairs in Memphis: "I have the honor to submit the following report of the conditions of the affairs of the Freedmen in this county during the month ending February 28, 1866. The rations during the month issued to Destitute Freedmen. . . . The Freedmen have no source of supplies, generally seen to be seeking employment and making contracts for the year. Yet there are a number reported to me who do not seem to have any employment whatsoever but living about in idleness. — The feeling existing between the Whites and Freedmen in this County are as friendly and mild as could be expected under any circumstances. The number of complaints weekly tried by the Freeman's Court for the size of the county and the number of its population are comparatively few and most of those cases are for small debts and insignificant complaints as they turn out on investigation. There is only one rare case of importance which has occurred in this County and came to my notice during the month. Case of Fraud Larceny a freed-woman robbing the house of a gentleman of his property valued one hundred and fifty Dollars. The woman is now confined in the jail at this place. Proper charges and specifications have been made out and forwarded to Captain J. Barnes for trial by Military Commission in Petersburg, VA." Report of Office Assistant Superintendent and Provost Marshal, Chesterfield County, Virginia, February 28, 1866 to Colonel O. Brown, Assistant Commissioner, Bureau R.F.& A.L., Richmond, Virginia.

Once the rebuilding of the black church and school had taken place, Rankin applied for admission to the Municipal Court in Memphis in December 1867 so that he might provide better leadership for his people. Rankin, at the time of his application to the bar, was "the colored Principal of the Rankin High School."

Within twenty months of the arson of every black school in Memphis, Principal Rankin was presenting himself to the Court as the face of black education in Memphis. One often hears about profiles in courage. We have no grasp of the real-time courage of a man like Rankin in the shadow of debris all around him.

As was customary for all pioneer black lawyers, Rankin had the sponsorship of courageous white lawyers who attested to Rankin's age and character, men like "Messrs. J. B. Woodward, W. Vernon and D.L. Griffin, Esqs." A committee was duly constituted by the Court to examine Rankin on his qualifications for the practice of law.

Two weeks later, in January of 1868, Rankin was admitted to the practice of law. "Rankin practiced law in Memphis, created the West Tennessee Colored University and advised Congress on the freedmen's laws." From his office at Linden and Causey Streets, he helped establish an independent Methodist Church. *

Rankin was a registered Republican in Shelby County and later became a justice of the peace.

I cannot tell you much more about Horatio Rankin. I do not know of his family. I cannot share with you his birth date or the date of his passing. I don't even know whether he married or what happened to his children. I don't know what Rankin looked like, as no images exist of this profile in courage. What I can tell you is that, in the darkest hour of burning, looting, and murder in Memphis in early May 1866, at least one man pulled back the veil of fear and led with his heart so that blacks in Memphis would be educated and would know the Lord in places of worship. I know that, in the face of good and truth, the wicked men of

---

Every city and county was unique in its own way after the Civil War. One couldn't paint with a broad brush even one year after the Civil War. Why would all black experience be the same 160 years later today? It is laughable to me, and you should laugh too.

* Stacey Shrader, "Law Professor Looks at Tennessee's Black Pioneers in the Law," Tennessee Bar Association, February 12, 2021, www.tba.org/?pg=LawBlog&blAction=showEntry&blogEntry=60070.

evil ultimately fled while true grit walked again in Memphis.

Let us hold fast to what Rankin must have felt in his heart when evil stalked the streets of Memphis and the later days of triumph when churches were raised from the ashes, school bells rang again, and a missionary from up North led the way of hope as he practiced law at Linden and Causey Street . . . in the land of the Delta blues.

Wink

Letter 49

Dear Wink,

A true American hero. As I read your account of Horatio Rankin, one thing stuck out in particular. There were also white men who supported Rankin and helped him to excel. While I do tend to emphasize and maybe even overemphasize the white sins of slavery, as much as we forget stories of Rankin in our Hunt for Oppression, we also forget stories of non-black heroes.

I don't know anything about the attorneys who helped Rankin succeed, but I do know about the abolitionists like Theodore Weld and the many others who helped to ensure the success of the Underground Railroad, such as Levi Coffin, who at age seven fed fugitive slaves. How many of these unsung heroes made it into the 1619 Project or are part of California's Ethnic Studies Model Curriculum?* As I mentioned in an earlier letter, we don't even acknowledge the likes of Martin Luther King, Jr., in many ethnic studies curricula these days, so it is no wonder that we forget about the heroism of white abolitionists.

You have asked me in previous correspondences if we could come together over our common history of slavery. Why don't we come together over our common history of American heroism? Most of the credit for ending slavery belongs to the many rugged black souls who believed in the promise of freedom and liberty for all. I honor those American an-

---

* You can find information on the California Ethnic Studies Model Curriculum at www.cde. ca.gov/ci/cr/cf/esmc.asp.

cestors. We discredit all these souls when we are hell-bent on destruction masquerading as truth.

Despite the indomitable black spirit so evident throughout American history, black freedom simply wouldn't have happened if there also wasn't a formidable force in non-black America that was also willing to fight and die for these values. I have my problems with the glorification and romanticization of figures like Robert E. Lee, but in order to create this new American identity we've mentioned, perhaps we erect statues to both black and white heroes. Those who fought for these freedoms. Those who saw humanity in the Other.

Ah, but I'm sure, were we to do that, some would revert to another favorite slogan: *white savior*. It is okay to point out the horrors of the past, although I know you prefer to look toward the future. But I wonder, just as we once only erected statues of white heroes, if we now overcompensate by erecting monuments only of black heroes, do we risk erasing the common cause of both black and white actors? Maybe we can put a bronze of abolitionist William Lloyd Garrison next to Sojourner Truth.

I can hear the criticism to this already—white people have had their day. White symbolism is everywhere, even in our capitalist system (according to the 1619 Project, capitalism was yet another product of slavery).[*] According to the Smithsonian's chart on "Aspects of White Culture," it even shows up in hard work, timeliness, and objectivity.[†]

But let's talk a little about this idea of saviorism. Yes, it's jargon, but like many slogans, it is responsible for our current obsession with all things racial. Here's the irony: in our bid to right historical wrongs, many have taken on the custodial duties that smack of saviorism. With tarnished halos, we tell young black children the bigotry of math, science, and even the law, dumbing the world down, so they don't have to compete.

Rankin was given no such coddling.

If we continue down this path, I fear we will look back on today with no heroes to emulate of any color. We will all accept the path of least

---

* For a response to this idea, see J. D. Richmond and W. F. Twyman, Jr., "The Alternative 1619 Reading Challenge: Day 3," *Truth in Between* (blog), *Medium,* April 14, 2021, medium. com/truth-in-between/the-alternative-1619-reading-challenge-day-3-69b856a22d4b.

† To read more, see J. D. Richmond and W. F. Twyman, Jr., "The Color of Culture," Counterweight, March 5, 2021, counterweightsupport.com/2021/03/05/the-color-of-culture/.

resistance—the mediocrity that our kindly custodians, or as Jonathan Rauch says, "kindly inquisitors,"* have forged to guard us against the cruelty of critical thinking.

Feeling snarky today,

Jen

---

* See Jonathan Rauch, *Kindly Inquisitors: The New Attacks on Free Thought*, expanded ed. (Chicago: University of Chicago Press, 2013).

Letter 50

Hi Jen,

It is a lovely Friday afternoon here in sunny San Diego. I just saw a hummingbird outside my deck above the treetops. The leaves are gently rustling in the autumn breeze. The sky is an endless blue. This is my frame of mind as I tiptoe once again into a dark part of our national past.

When George Shrewsbury died in 1875, he was living among black aldermen and judges and state legislators and congressmen. He probably foresaw continued elevation and prosperity for his family and friends in South Carolina. He could not have foreseen the Compromise of 1877 and the loss of all hope for Reconstruction. When Daniel Brown died in 1885, did he suspect the gathering clouds of white prejudice would snuff out the social relations he had with whites at the County Courthouse? Daniel could not read or write, and yet his will was witnessed by two white men of esteem in Chesterfield County, and I believe his doctor was white. Still, the page had begun to turn on Reconstruction. A part of me is glad that Daniel Brown didn't live to see the rise of Jim Crow. Of his children who survived infancy, at least four chose to pass for white and ten remained black. How would a parent navigate the realities of Jim Crow when they had beloved children on both sides of the color line? It is beyond me.

When Congressman Joseph Hayne Rainey died on August 3, 1887, the momentum of Jim Crow segregation was gathering speed throughout the country. One of the best books about Jim Crow is *The Strange*

Career of Jim Crow by C. Vann Woodward.* Woodward reminds us that the system of social segregation ran counter to the intimacy that whites and black house slaves knew during slavery. Separation of the slaves was impracticable. The system mandated interracial contact. W. E. B. Du-Bois wrote that when all the best blacks were domestic servants in the best of white families, there were bonds of intimacy, affection, and blood ties between the races.† This sounds much like the Daniel Brown and Twyman families. Of course, Woodward adds to Du Bois' perception by noting that most of these relationships were limited to a small percentage of slaves. Most field hands were not in close proximity with the best of white families.

This is a fascinating point Woodward makes. Jim Crow segregation was well established in the North before the institution made its way to the South. Blacks and whites in the antebellum South lived in close contact and knew each other intimately. When talking with my distant cousin Jim Smith, a 2x great-grandson of James Twyman (1781–1849), Jim would casually remark that relations between the white Twymans and the black Twymans reached back to the early 1800s. For generations, white and black Twymans lived in close proximity to one another. They probably knew one another as children, grew up together, played marbles together, and fished in creeks together. Of course, the context was one of white supremacy and black inferiority, but they were not strangers to one another.

Interracial associations and relations were fluid in the 1860s, 1870s, and 1880s, as Woodward sees it. There was nothing fanatical about race separation in the South before *Plessy v. Ferguson*, 163 U.S. 537 (1896), which upheld racial segregation laws. According to Woodward, two competing schools of thought vied for control between the Civil War and *Plessy*. One school was Conservatism. Under this school, whites understood blacks to be inferior, but they saw no need to publicly humiliate or segregate blacks. Only lower-class whites acted weird around blacks. Patricians were conservative in their dealings with blacks. After *Plessy*, many remembered the old days of friendship and intimate relations with

---

* C. Vann Woodward, *The Strange Career of Jim Crow* (New York: Oxford University Press, 2002).

† Ibid., 12.

blacks. Once again, my mind drifts back to Madison County, Virginia, and Albemarle County, Virginia, in the 1810s and 1820s. Coates and others would paint this place and time as one of constant, non-stop white male rape of black women. I have no doubt rapes took place. I also have no doubt that intimacy ran the spectrum in those days, just as they do in any age, and that relationships based on mutual attraction and interest occurred. How many men had genuine feelings for the cute, intelligent house servant? I'm looking at you, Thomas Jefferson. How many house servants fell for the handsome son of the master? These clandestine lovers—and yes, in some cases, this could very well be the most accurate description of the relationship—would not have kept written records. And so, we remember and recall the horrors and not the consensual passions and attractions down on the Twyman Farm. Well, that's my intuition. Life was nuanced and complex in those days because people are nuanced and complex in any age.

I oftentimes believe black Americans could accept their true multiracial past if they weren't brainwashed into thinking every mixed child born before the Civil War was only ever the product of rape—and never possibly the result of two individuals with emotional agency. And I don't know how one changes that deep-seated mindset. Any ideas? I fully believe slaves could and often did exercise some level of agency in their relationships with whites, and to uniformly argue otherwise, to me, denies their humanity.

Back to the genesis of Jim Crow, however . . .

Opposing the Conservatives were the Radicals. These guys believed blacks and poor whites shared a common oppressor. The idea was to forge multiracial alliances so as to overcome poverty and want.

So, why did Jim Crow emerge in the South? Woodward argues that these two forces—Conservatism and Radicalism—and a third force—Northern Liberalism—weakened at the same time. This weakening enabled the forces of fear, hatred, and fanaticism to rise to the surface. Having grown up in the South, I would go one step further and suggest it was the passing of the Conservative Generation *that had grown up together with blacks in the 1830s, 1840s, and 1850s* that released the hounds of Jim Crow. When the Conservative Generation began to die off in the 1870s and the 1880s, there was no one in white leadership who remembered a time of day-to-day interracial contact and association and relations and coexistence. That was the problem—the dying off of a generation predisposed against shaming and humiliating blacks.

Blacks became a scapegoat for the woes of all whites, North and South. The Old Conservatism slipped into Redemptionist appeals to Negrophobia. The federal troops were long gone, and fear and hatred became easier and easier to live out as an operating principle. This set the stage for *Plessy v. Ferguson* (1896).

The Octoroon Named Homer Adolph Plessy (1862–1925)

In 1890, the Louisiana State Legislature passed a separate car law, which required that whites and blacks sit in separate train cars. The measure was vigorously opposed by the Comité des Citoyens (Citizen's Committee), a civil rights group of blacks, whites, and Creoles.

As a matter of tactical strategy, Plessy agreed to violate Louisiana's Separate Car Law. It was hoped that Plessy's physical appearance as a white male would centerpiece the absurdity of racial segregation. On June 7, 1892, the thirty-year-old Plessy purchased a first-class ticket on the East Louisiana Railroad running between New Orleans and Covington. He sat in the whites-only passenger car, was arrested, and was released the next day on a $500 bond ($16,273.13 in purchasing power today).

Plessy became the appellant in the May 18, 1896, U.S. Supreme Court decision of *Plessy v. Ferguson*, which condoned "separate but equal facilities" in the United States. Plessy's civil disobedience marked one of the first legal challenges to the separation of races in the South following the Reconstruction period. Though he lost the case in 1896, the Court later upheld Plessy's Fourteenth Amendment arguments fifty-eight years later in *Brown v. Board of Education* (1954).

The ruling in *Plessy v. Ferguson* set into motion judicial blessing of segregation throughout all components of life in the South. Schools were segregated by race. Courtrooms were segregated by race. Department store waiting rooms were segregated by race. Public accommodations ranging from trains to buses and ferries and ships were segregated by race. Water fountains were segregated by race. Even cemeteries and morgues were segregated by race. The public humiliation and shame associated with race became institutionalized. Homer Plessy would return to obscurity. No photograph survives of Plessy.

Many of the separate institutions we see today, like Jack and Jill, Alpha Kappa Alpha, Alpha Phi Alpha, Delta Sigma Theta, Omega Phi Psi, the Boule, the National Bar Association, the National Medical Association, and other associations and groups too numerous to name, were born during the era of Jim Crow. Could it be that the lasting social isolation of blacks owes more to Jim Crow than the legacy of American slavery? Did blacks and whites know one another more at Oak Lawn in 1790 than in Ferguson, Missouri, in 2019?

I think so.

I don't really have a desire to dive into the innards of Jim Crow. It happened, and it would take a rebirth of the American Creed to put Jim Crow to bed.

I leave you with this thought: I was born in 1961 in Richmond, Virginia, the former capital of the Confederacy, and grew up in Chesterfield County, Virginia. I have no memories of any Jim Crow signs. I do have a memory of a *de facto* segregated school, Hickory Hill Elementary School, which I attended in first and second grade. I have the fondest memories of Hickory Hill Elementary. The seminal event in my life was the fall of 1969 when my world was desegregated.

The past should stay in the past,

Wink

Letter 51

Wink,

The Jim Crow era, in my mind, is almost a worse sin than American slavery. As horrible as it was, slavery was a global phenomenon and not confined to any continent or country. While that fact, of course, does not excuse its presence or existence in America, I'm less moved by rhetoric that paints slavery as the United States' original sin than by the institutionalization of Jim Crow policies after the promise of Reconstruction. Such an explicit repudiation of hard-won and long-overdue progress evokes stronger emotions in me.

Interestingly, it wasn't until the past five years or so that I considered whether this emotion was one of *guilt*. It was always one of sadness. It was also one of pride. No, not white pride. Rather, black pride. Or American pride. The pride doesn't emanate from Jim Crow but from the spirit of overcoming.

Born after the Civil Rights Movement, I was blissfully ignorant of Jim Crow in my early years. In all honesty, I really only began to study it in depth around 2016, when our country became more divided and segregated in the ways we've already discussed. Have I lived a sheltered life? Like many middle-class white Americans who never experienced racial bigotry, I have. My increasing awareness of the experiences of many black Americans only deepened my sadness.

While I don't buy into the idea of *guilt*, one thing I will say, as I've said before, is that this hyper-focus on race has forced an important conversation in a country where many people were, like me, blissfully and, in some cases, willfully ignorant. For me personally, it has expanded my empathy and my desire to connect. To learn and listen to stories different from my own. To understand.

Simultaneously, my pride in being witness to a country so determined to live into the ideals of freedom, liberty, and equality has expanded. To be a fellow American alongside the likes of black heroes who refused to sit idle in the face of discrimination, risking their lives to fight daily for these values, gives hope in the strength of our plurality. In many ways, it is the black and non-white experience that fuels my patriotism.

Of course, being white, I can only claim agency in such a movement from the sidelines. I can support and applaud but cannot lay claim to these successes. While my forefathers did fight for these ideals in both the American Revolution and Civil War, it is your ancestors who realized them in our modern society. How does that make you feel? Are you similarly imbued with a sense of awe and pride?

While middle-class white Americans were surely in a position to escape racial bigotry, the obsessive application of *guilt* and *privilege* has stalled what I considered was the coming of a new era of reconstruction—this time of a new American identity. I don't consider the penance of white *allies* groveling and tripping over themselves to bear the scarlet letter of racial prejudice as they relive their ancestral crimes a durable foundation for building a new community. The scaffolding of division layered upon division is sure to buckle under the weight. I wonder, if you were a white American, how do you think you would perceive the black American experience?

You asked me if black Americans could accept their true multiracial past if they weren't brainwashed into thinking that every mixed child born before the Civil War was the product of rape. I don't know if there is a way to change this mindset, but being able to connect and see the humanity in each other's eyes would be a step in the right direction. And when we do so and the color lines fade, and we go beyond this simple recognition to feeling love—whether simply the "agape" love of the soul or even the romantic "eros" kind of love—our hearts will influence our minds. I can think of no more durable foundation for recreating a common American community and identity.

Just recently, I read a piece on Beyoncé's ancestral search. The tagline for the piece reads, "Beyoncé's reconciliation of her ancestry reminds us that we live in danger of allowing narratives we didn't generate to tell our stories for us."* In doing her ancestral search, she found that she comes from a slave owner who fell in love with and married a slave. Not everyone will be able to determine if their mixed blood comes from rape or love, and I would wager that many could find instances of rape in their family tree, regardless of color. For example, did you know that Jesse Jackson was born out of rape? As was news anchor Faith Daniels. The list, sadly, is long. Balancing stories—whether stories of slavery with stories of uplift or stories of rape with stories of love—seems necessary in any review of history.

In order to fully embrace and account for our past, and to do so with an eye toward strengthening our plurality and multiracial future, we need to be wary of blanket narratives wrapping us up in an elusive hug of warm tribalism.

Wrapped in my own blankets and ready for bed.

Goodnight,

Jen

---

* Written by Caleb Gayle, "Why Beyoncé Exploring Her Ancestry Matters," *Guardian,* August 6, 2018, www.theguardian.com/commentisfree/2018/aug/06/beyonce-vogue-september-issue-slave owner-ancestry.

Letter 52

Hi Jen,

It is a beautiful Saturday morning. CNN Africa is on the television screen. My wife and my daughter have relieved me of having to attend a Alpha Kappa Alpha family interview this morning, but I've decided to attend in support of my daughter. The interview will take up to two hours. Then my daughter and wife are off to Children's Hospital for an afternoon of Jack and Jill volunteer work. Five hours of my daughter's day will be devoted to black-only institutions. It is ironic that we are writing about Jim Crow segregation while we, as a family, devote most of our day to black-only groups. Question: How does this advance understanding across the color line? Why is voluntary Jim Crow ignored by the larger society? I would like your opinion. My thoughts are no surprise.

How does a day like today with my daughter help us build together? These are the racial moments in real time today, not segregated train cars in New Orleans in 1892. I so often feel there is a disconnect between lived reality and what we hear and read about race in the public square. You sent me a hostile critique of the hug down in Texas between Brandt Jean—Botham Jean's brother—and his killer, police officer Amber Guyger.[*] And, yes, I share your sentiments—an opportunity to show forgive-

---

* See, for example, Hannah Knowles, "Amber Guyger Was Hugged by Her Victim's Brother and a Judge, Igniting a Debate about Forgiveness and Race," *Washington Post,* October 3, 2019, www.washingtonpost.com/nation/2019/10/03/judge-botham-jeans-brother-hugged-amber-guyger-igniting-debate-about-forgiveness-race/.

ness became just another racial moment. But why doesn't the *New York Times* air internal dissent and critique of hours invested in social isolation? In other words, why doesn't the *New York* Times publish sensitive stories of conflicting racial visions within black American families? This has more meaning for me and my family race-wise than some random black critique of some random hug following a random criminal conviction in Texas, a matter which is purely a family matter between a brother of a decedent and a convicted murderer. Why does the *New York Times* of the 1619 Project acclaim not review Jack and Jill and Alpha Kappa Alpha and debutante cotillions with a critical eye?

I am a positive person. So, while I understand the horrors of the past, we grow the most when we focus on the things we can change. I can't change what happened during Jim Crow, so why should I focus on it? Why not ignore it as I make my way into the future? Wouldn't that perspective be stronger evidence of mental resilience?

If I were a white American, how would I perceive the black American experience?

I would be saddened by past injustice and seek out stories of mental resilience and achievement. As an individualist, I would be attracted to blacks who are different in character and perspective. For example, I would be drawn to blacks from, say, Vermont or Montana because those stories would diverge from the norm and be of more interest to me. I would be weary of another *Blackness as Oppression* story. I might even subscribe to *Black Enterprise* magazine as a learning experience.

Question: Would I date black women?

Yes, I would be that type of white guy intrigued by difference.

Question: Would I marry a black woman?

It would depend on whether my mother hinged her love of me on my marrying inside the race. I would probably lack the courage to marry outside of my race. This assumes I had grown up in Chesterfield County, Virginia, as a white guy in the 1970s.

Question: Would I have experienced prejudice against blacks?

Yes. I'm sure I would have heard racist jokes in class and out in public. I would have felt a visceral connection with blacks as a result.

Question: Would the black experience have fueled my patriotism?

I don't think so. George Washington, Thomas Jefferson, and Patrick Henry would have fueled my patriotism. Odds are, I would have been a descendant of Confederate soldiers like several of my white friends. Robert E. Lee would have been revered in the pantheon of Southern heroes.

As a white guy, I would have been torn between living at home as a closet progressive or leaving for the sinful environs of Northern Virginia where blacks and whites actually visited one another in their homes.

So, that was my effort to imagine and view the landscape from a white American perspective.

Am I similarly imbued with a sense of awe and pride with ancestors who realized ideals in the American Revolution in our modern society? Hmmm. I am awed by family ancestors. Therein lies my pride. Perhaps there's a contradiction here, but I don't take pride in broader group accomplishments when I did nothing to earn group membership and I have no direct connection to those involved. Doesn't it seem odd to take pride in the achievements of distant others due only to shared race? I'm not a racist in that way. While I love black history and achievement, it is not out of awe and pride. It comes from my love of achievement, and achievement doesn't have a race. Doesn't that make sense? It is the colorless values and attitudes that matter to me. Those values and attitudes generate love and passion, not a sense of awe and pride.

Some people seem so anchored in group identity that any achievement of a group member imbues a sense of awe and pride. That isn't me.

Also, how are you defining ancestors? My second cousin seven times removed commanded the Continental Army. Another second cousin seven times removed introduced the Resolution for American Independence in 1776. My 5x great-grandfather had several family members who fought in the American Revolution. So, if you define ancestors as blood ties, my ancestors were front and center in the fight for these ideals in the American Revolution. Were you suggesting I have only black ancestors? Just asking. My ancestors include George Twyman III, George Twyman II, George Twyman I, Col. Richard Lee I, Peter Montague, Holy Roman Emperor Charlemagne, Rollo the Dane, William the Conqueror, Malcolm King of Scotland, Edward I "Longshanks" King of England,

and King Henry VIII. DNA doesn't discriminate between black and non-black ancestors. My DNA doesn't sidestep history.

I'm curious, what do you mean by accounting for the past? What does an accounting for the past look like? Putting aside the principle that mentally strong people don't dwell on the past, an accounting sounds suspiciously like reparations for American slavery. Let's use James Twyman (1781–1849) as a benchmark. In 1849, he left three slaves each the equivalent of $166,666 to start a new life and sustain themselves as freed people. Let's assume the typical descendant of American slavery has around 1,500 slave ancestors uncompensated for their labor. If we paid each descendant of American Slavery $166,666 for each uncompensated slave ancestor, that would mean we must pay 40 million Descendants of American Slavery a grand total of around 9 quadrillion dollars! That figure doesn't include the physical pain and suffering from rapes, floggings, castrations, and other forms of torture, or the emotional pain and suffering from the separations of slave mothers from slave children.

Dear Jen, we might as well close down the United States of America. A full and complete accounting for American slavery would open up a Pandora's Box leading to Rwanda, Bosnia, and Pol Pot in Cambodia. Question: Don't you see the danger of inflaming old, grievous grievances? It would never, ever, ever, never end.*

The best way to account for the past is to leave the past in the past. We need to hug one another, reach our peace with one another, and move on. And we need to date, marry, and have children together over generations. Otherwise, the social isolation in Jack and Jill will live on, and *the coming of a better time* will be delayed.

Living in the future, not the past,

Wink

P.S. You didn't engage my concerns about the rise and fall of generations over time. Question: Did you not see anything there from the perspective of shifting generations over time? I grew up on Star Trek and achieved success

---

* For a discussion about the bad consequences of collective demonization, see www.theamericanconservative.com/an-american-rwanda-courtesy-of-the-left/.

in the larger world. My daughter has been steered into race-conscious groups like Jack and Jill and Alpha Kappa Alpha. Isn't there a generational gap here? And, if so, doesn't it parallel the earlier generational gap between the Conservative Generation and the Jim Crow Generation or the New South Generation and the Age of Oppression/Lost Generation gap?

Letter 53

Wink,

Your response reminds me of something a comedian once said that I found interesting. I forget who. George Carlin, maybe? He was talking about what people mean when they say, "I'm proud to be an American." He laughed at this and crassly responded that being an American was just luck. Why should we be proud? Proud that the right sperm-egg combo just happened to occur in America doesn't imbue pride, he quipped. Or something like that.

We can love America and its values and feel lucky to have been born American, but is pride the right emotion? Perhaps even feeling lucky isn't right, either. Would values of freedom, liberty, and equality be so important to us if we had been born in China? Can we say that these values are more important than Confucian values of order and filial piety? Many Chinese are proud of their thousands of years old history and the belief that they are the birthplace of civilization. The Middle Kingdom.

And here we are.

We both value individual freedoms. We chaff at a life dictated and hemmed in with oppression, whether coming from governmental fiat or the dominant ideologies of a generation. To the extent that I am patriotic, it is to fundamental American values.

Perhaps a more accurate emotion than pride would be gratitude. But even then, my gratitude has been shaped by the values of my culture. That said, even in my travels and life in other countries with more dic-

229

tatorial paradigms, I see common themes in our humanity. The love of family and friends, the desire to live in relative security, and the craving to engage in activities that bring us joy—whether as a profession or a hobby. Given my experiences, I always felt our values provided a stronger foundation to realize at least the latter theme.

When I walk down the street and I see someone of a different ethnicity or race, I see an American. My first reaction is to assume that they are American. Not Chinese or African or Mexican. This diversity has also been the foundation of my "pride" and is unique. I am patriotic to the ideal of a plural community coming together in a shared community.

Do I take pride in a singular race, i.e., in black America's achievement? No, but like you, I value achievement, and to the extent that I think that is evident in black America's struggle, I have much respect. Respect for those notable characters who were able to lift entire communities.

I know you also have respect for your ancestors across the color line, from a Commander of the Continental Army to Congressman Rainey. I hear you when you say that you don't ascribe pride or respect to a group. I've had to sit with that realization for a while. It is so wise in its simplicity. And I see how the dogma we both are working to overturn has actually crept into my own mindset. I talk about valuing the individual, but I then talk about respect for a racial group's achievement and struggle.

Insofar as we are searching for a way to realize a common American identity, I respect the general struggles of a nation working to live true to its core principles. People of all colors have participated in this fight. This goes back to the idea that all Old Americans are descendants of American slavery regardless of our skin color. I continue to mull this idea over. Can we as a nation take responsibility for the past and combat the collectivization of resentments and grudges? You do so in your insistence on measuring a person, past or present, on their own merit, and not on their affiliation to any particular demographic group.

This is a noble endeavor. Despite my affection for individuality, we still operate in communities. Despite us being introverts, we still interact and collaborate with others. Groups are and always will be part of our landscape. I believe it is possible to be an individual in a community if we can dispense with all the labels and stereotypes that have created tribalism. Instead of communities, tribalism creates collectives. Collectives are not communities. Collectives, or communes in Mao's China, were public enterprises that purposefully swallowed individuality. Private life became public, and everything belonged to the commune.

I have a replica of a Chinese propaganda poster from circa 1944. It says, "All hearts and minds in the service of the people." "Serve the People" was the unofficial motto of the Chinese Communist Party, which helped it gain support, especially in the countryside, during the civil war. In an effort to create an *equitable* proletariat society, communes were introduced. Intellectuals, merchants, and officials were purged, killed, or re-educated in the Anti-Rightest Campaign (1957–1959) if they dared challenge the collective. Farmers joined collective farms to pool their resources, which led to one of the greatest famines in history under Mao's Great Leap Forward policy (1958–1962). In order to enforce the collective, especially in the cities, class struggle and struggle sessions became the norm during the Cultural Revolution (1966–1976). This was not the Beloved Community of Martin Luther King, Jr.

So, what do I mean by community? I guess I would say that a community is the overlap of humanity. We may belong to distinct communities—Jack and Jill, the Rotary Club, or an Alumni Association—that form for particular aims or have a certain identity. However, a true community is more like a Venn Diagram, where we can move fluidly between various groups with our humanity at the core, and at that core of humanity is pluralism.

I would even argue that "community" is the center of the "social contract." We come together for some social benefits that outweigh individual needs—efficient transactions, protection, etc. A community becomes a collective when a group identity becomes the foundation for collaboration, creating in-groups and out-groups. In China, the enforcement of a common peasant identity was devastating, and communities were torn apart. Is a community without collective tribalism possible? If we insist on pluralism within our communities, I believe so. I would go so far as to argue that this interplay, as tenuous as it may be, is what makes a society great, but great is not easy.

You have really touched on something here, with the idea of Old Americans as the foundation for community among individuals. The answer must be, in part, to see our individual selves in the individual selves of others in order to have a true reckoning. I still would argue that in our current cultural moment and the historical baggage that we continue to pack and unpack, sometimes under duress or threat from the collective, we are unable to take this leap.

One thing I see at work in younger generations is the destruction of the "imagined communities" that promoted a more national identity.* The proliferation of unique connections through social media has promoted tribal enclaves that erode larger meta-narratives on community and belonging. *Star Trek* and some of the iconic shows that defined your era and created an "imagined community" have been diluted with millions of voices vying for attention on YouTube and other platforms. Can we create a new community or common identity among all the noise? In an era of social isolation and tribal affiliation?

To see ourselves in each individual other, without the dictates of an authoritarian regime mandating forced identities, is a struggle that will define future generations. That will determine whether America as we know it survives and thrives or is another tragedy of history.

To *Star Trek: The Next Generation* and an Octoroon Nation . . .

In transit from Dubai to Toronto,

Jen

---

* Benedict Anderson, in his book *Imagined Communities: Reflection on the Origin and Spread of Nationalism* (London: Verso, 2006), discusses how we created a more unified community through national dialogues, even when our disparate communities were incredibly distinct, and hence this larger national community was, in essence, "imagined."

Letter 54

Hey Jen,

As I write this letter, I am watching the *Star Trek* episode "Court Martial" (season 1, episode 21), which I first saw as a six-year-old on Twyman Road. It was one of my favorite episodes. Captain Kirk faces trial for the death of a crewman. The most powerful person is Commodore Stone. He runs the legal proceedings and holds the power of life or death over Captain Kirk. No attention is called to Commodore Stone's skin color, which is as it should be. And this is true throughout the series.

In the 1960s, the American people decided segregation in public life was wrong. This consensus resulted in the Civil Rights Act of 1964, the Voting Rights Act of 1965, and the Fair Housing Act of 1968. Our country turned a corner as I lived on Twyman Road. I was the first generation in the South to live in the Age of Civil Rights.

As you know, I attended a *de facto* segregated public school in first and second grade (1967–1969). Technically, Chesterfield County public schools had enacted Freedom of Choice as of 1965, but no black parents of elementary kids chose to send their kids to effectively (if no longer officially) all-white schools. One can only imagine the hostility and name-calling that awaited any black child at such a school. Well, I don't have to imagine. I knew the hostility and name-calling well in the fall of 1969 at E. S. H. Greene Elementary School.

In the *Green v. New Kent County School Board* decision, 391 U.S. 430 (1968), the U.S. Supreme Court declared that public schools had an affirmative obligation to eradicate the vestiges of public school seg-regation. This meant the dismantling of freedom of choice, which had permitted parents to make racially identifiable choices. The Nixon ad-ministration's Department of Health, Education, and Welfare threatened the Chesterfield County School Board with the loss of federal funding if freedom of choice continued. The threat of a loss in federal funding con-vinced the school board to close my all-black elementary school, Hicko-ry Hill Elementary School.

As the 1968–1969 school year drew to a close, I knew nothing of this struggle in the larger world. I do remember my second-grade teacher, Mrs. Dorothy Taylor, saying things would be different next year. There was no sense of foreboding. My classmates and I felt more an uncon-cerned curiosity about what the future held. I actually give thanks that Mrs. Taylor did not alarm us. We were only seven years old. The last day of second grade was the last time I would ever attend an all-black school.

When I began the third grade in the fall of 1969, it was a rebirth for me and my classmates. Segregated schools were dismantled in the face of threatened loss of public funding from the federal Department of Health, Education, and Welfare. There were no longer black or white schools in the county. There were just schools. I was the only black kid in my all-white class,* and I had to accommodate myself to prejudice.

Greene Elementary School was a formerly all-white school a few miles from my home. I could no longer walk up the hill to school, which meant I had to ride the school bus. All my classmates were white, and my teacher was white. Was I prejudiced against my teacher and classmates? No, my mind doesn't work that way. Even at the age of eight, I took peo-ple as they were. However, some of my white classmates were decidedly prejudiced against blacks, including me. I was called the N-word and racial slurs every day. I have repressed many of those details. Perhaps one day I might undergo hypnosis or therapy in an attempt to recover from the full trauma. Then again, maybe not.

---

* Today, Greene Elementary School is 80.6 percent Hispanic, 16.3 percent black, and 1.9 percent white. The school is ranked 1,081 out of 1,096 Virginia elementa-ry schools, according to SchoolDigger.com. When I attended Greene, the student body was at least 98 percent white—possibly 99.8 percent white.

Every life has an inflection point, and Greene Elementary School is where I had my epiphany, which I will take the liberty of sharing again. One day, the harassment got to me. I sat down on the playground and thought about the situation. Why were these kids tormenting me? Skin color had nothing to do with intelligence. I had had strong teachers like Mrs. Walker and Mrs. Taylor in my past. I had strong uncles, always opinionated, and always enterprising, and all black. The most important people in my universe—Mom, Dad, Grandma, and Uncles William Womack, Robert Daniel Twyman, and James Scott Twyman—were all black. I had lived on Twyman Road, named after my family, and we were all black. There was no correlation at all between intelligence and skin color. And in that moment, it hit me: these kids were dumb. They didn't know better, and they were not intelligent. From that point on, I resolved to think of prejudiced people as unintelligent and thus not worthy of my soul, my spirit. That eight-year-old insight armored me for the years ahead and served me well. I could have turned toward resentment and hate and bitterness and self-destruction, but the womb of Twyman Road and Hickory Hill had steeled me well for the larger world. I was blessed.

The important point is that, as the nation was reborn in the 1960s at the level of federal legislation, I was reborn at the level of the classroom.

For me, Jim Crow in the classroom was dead. A whole new world with new horizons awaited me at E. S. H. Greene Elementary School.

They say the most important age for a kid is the age of eight. That was true for me.

In signing off, I told my wife a few moments ago that I feel like a grumpy old man. I do not want to feel that way, so I watch *Star Trek*, which reminds me of a better time or, at least, a time I understand. I don't understand a time when teenagers wear "stealing my identity" T-shirts at shopping malls.

*More reasons to remain in retirement
from race every day,*

Wink

Letter 55

Wink,

Local Chinese businesses often gain more attention and appear more sophisticated if they have an "international" flair. This was truer earlier in China's globalization when I was traveling throughout the country "riding the iron rooster" (aka trains). McDonald's iconic Golden Arches were just starting to make their debut in the early nineties. One winter day, as I stepped out of the Shanghai train station in search of a cheap meal, I caught sight of them. As I headed in that direction, I realized there was something off. The first upward stroke in the arch was missing, leaving it looking like a cursive N instead of an M. Perhaps a few bulbs had burned out. But as I got closer, I realized that, indeed, it was an N, as in Nancy's. It wasn't quite a copyright infringement, but the yellow half-M, red and white décor, and burger menu made it come close to an exact replica of our famous fast-food franchise.

Needless to say, I opted instead for noodles from a street vendor.

Later in my professional career, I was responsible for helping foreign companies navigate intellectual property (IP) theft in China. In Confucian ideology, imitation is the highest form of praise. You copy the strategies and methods of those you want to emulate. This cultural norm, coupled with a system that values relationships over contractual arrangements, underlies the high incidence of IP violations there.

These are the thoughts stirring in my head as I try to wrap my brain around "identity theft" or "stealing my identity." What does that even mean? Are we talking about cultural appropriation?

In a country like the United States, the idea of cultural appropriation seems silly. First, we are all mixed up here in this same "salad" together (you know, because "melting pot" is now a microaggression, as it assumes that we are all one, and thus "salad" is a better metaphor, because a salad's ingredients remain distinct while intermingling together—ha!). Second, I do believe that imitation is a form of praise. A lot of the American identity—to the extent that there is such an umbrella identity—is enhanced with a diverse array of contributions woven into our fabric. In fact, you often hear that black Americans are the most culturally influential people in the world today. Am I an identity thief when I pour a glass of wine and queue up my Louis Armstrong collection, or for having dreamt of naming my child after Ella Fitzgerald? Is my atonement as an identity thief to live in a musical wasteland?

This intermingling of cultures is exactly the reason that I believe so firmly in the American landscape. I have a great appreciation for this weave of a plurality of cultures. Perhaps it's even a sense of *pride*. There is strength in our differences.

Sadly, the problem with *Star Trek* and its planetary diversity is that it is a fantasy. In reality, we are worlds apart, and the distance continues to grow. For the nation to be reborn, or born anew, we should dabble in this fantasy to find an earthly connection in this intragalactic fiction.

As the visionary Captain Kirk says, "The prejudices people feel about each other disappear when they get to know each other."

To the future,

Jen

EPISTOLARY III

Letter 56

Dear Jen,

I could be wrong, but my wife has been mentioned at least twice in the *New York Times*. She was profiled in the Style Section when we were engaged to be married.* But her first appearance was as President of the Teen Group of the Brooklyn Chapter of Jack and Jill.

What is Jack and Jill, you might ask? And why would the *New York Times* take notice of my wife because she was President of the Teen Group of the Brooklyn Chapter of Jack and Jill? Jack and Jill is a marker of upper-class status in black America. Formed on January 24, 1938, by Marion Stubbs Thomas in Philadelphia, Pennsylvania, Jack and Jill was created officially "to provide social, cultural and educational opportunities for youth between the ages of 2 and 19." That is the official line. The unofficial story would be the wives of black lawyers and doctors wanted appropriate play opportunities for their children during a time of racial segregation as well as refined friends and playmates from good black families. Thomas and her fellow estimable moms were steering a space between white prejudice in the outside world and the distasteful conduct and behavior of some low-class and low-income black children. This was their mission in the world of 1938, and who can fault them?†

---

* See "Schuler Rainey, Capitol Aide, to Wed," *New York Times,* December 23, 1990, www.nytimes.com/1990/12/23/style/schuyler-rainey-capitol-aide-to-wed.html.

† Some mothers who had been denied membership in all-white organizations decided to create their own organization to benefit black children. If they had been let into those white organizations, there would have been no need to create black organizations. This same

Their most precious cargo in life was the children, the sons and daughters of the professional class of black people.

This inheritance from 1938 and Marion Stubbs Thomas has come down to my family through the generations. My grandmother-in-law was one of the founders of the Brooklyn Jack and Jill chapter. My mother-in-law grew up in Jack and Jill. My wife and her sisters were members as children, and as I mentioned, my wife was President of the Teen Group of the Brooklyn chapter (all teens were encouraged to hold officer positions at some point as part of their leadership development). And all my children, now adults, grew up in Jack and Jill. That is four generations within one American family.

I do not belong to Jack and Jill. I did not grow up in Jack and Jill. And so, my perspective on this inheritance comes from a certain distance.

Jen, when we moved from Alexandria, Virginia, to San Diego, California, I was heartened by many things. I fell in love with the Pacific Ocean and the views of Mexico from Coronado. I loved to see the dancing moonlight on the ocean waves. Swaying palm trees graced our new streets and home in San Diego. And there was a social toleration free of the sediment of social isolation that I had felt back in Alexandria. Consider that my wife and I had no white friends while we lived in Alexandria. After our move to San Diego, we had no black friends save for a handful of black law professors. Our closest and best friends were white, and race did not seem to matter one whit. Having grown up in the New South, I was enthralled with this easy, new way of being in the world. I was excited as well for my children, yet to be born.

Jack and Jill creeps up on you. To me, Jack and Jill had always been this amorous thing that some of my girlfriends shared in the background of their lives. I still remember the first time I ever heard the phrase "Jack and Jill." I was on a date with a woman named "Emily." We were flirting with one another, and she asked me a question that seemed as natural as, "Where do you go to school?" or "What church do you attend?" Emily asked me, "What Jack and Jill chapter do you belong to?" The question presumed Jack and Jill membership was a given. Well, at a primitive level, I felt flattered even if I didn't know what Jack and Jill was. Now that I think more about it, my close friend in college at the University

---

motivation applies to all the other black organizations mentioned earlier in this correspondence, such as black sororities, black fraternities, the National Bar Association, etc.

of Virginia had railed against Jack and Jill in passing. The rant had no context for me at the time. I just remember my friend seemed motivated in his resentment since his family may have applied for membership and been rejected. So, railing against Jack and Jill was a psychological defense mechanism that I vaguely recognized. I told Emily I was not a member of Jack and Jill.

In my answer, did my attractiveness to Emily lessen a degree? I will never know.

My next girlfriend, "Terri," was a proud member of Jack and Jill. She enjoyed her memories of the association, and I sensed a fair chunk of her black friends were Jack and Jill members as well. Jack and Jill was simply a part of her childhood background. It was almost like a country club membership, given the social prominence of her family. I have never been a joiner, and so Jack and Jill was simply another marker of Terri's comfortable perch at the top of the social heap in Black America.

And there was my wife, whom I met one Friday afternoon in an elevator in the Longworth House Office Building on Capitol Hill. After we started dating, she shared with me that she had been in Jack and Jill. But as before, I had no lived experience, no context, for what Jack and Jill membership meant. Was it like belonging to the Rotary Club? The Key Club? I didn't know, nor did I have anyone in my close circle to bring me up to speed. We married and the children came, and I assumed our trend line of having close white friends would continue for our children. All our few black friends were law professors married to white spouses. I was the one exception—the only black law professor in San Diego married to a black spouse.

One day, as I was passing a black colleague's office, I had a prophetic conversation. My colleague proudly showed me pictures of her son, who had no physical appearance of African ancestry. My colleague was married to a wonderful and great lawyer who happened to be white. For some reason long forgotten, a pause occurred in the conversation. My colleague remarked that I was the only black law professor married to a black person. She felt this would make a difference in my son's experience from her son's experience. I laughed as I could not see how having a black spouse would make any difference in the rearing of my son. My colleague chuckled knowingly and said, "You will see."

Years later, after Jack and Jill had taken full root in my home, I was at a wedding reception in Temecula, Riverside County, California. My wife's former boss had married a beautiful Yemeni Jewish woman. It was dark, and the drinks were flowing, and the dances grew sultrier with each passing hour. At our table was a lanky Beverly Hills doctor who had grown up among blacks in New Orleans. Although the doctor was white, he had many black mannerisms and danced with black swagger, if there is such a thing. He was a minor celebrity of sorts at the table as he was a doctor to famous athletes, including the now late Kobe Bryant. The doctor with swagger and I started to talk about marriages and relationships. And he made an interesting point that reminded me of what my black colleague had said years earlier—he had never appreciated how crucial the mother was in the cultural indoctrination within the home. He had married a Hispanic woman, and he was surprised at how heavily his wife had infused Latin culture into his children. And I immediately thought I had had no idea that the cultural aims of a mom (and grandma) could be so decisive in one's home.

I valued friendships and relationships for my children that reflected the larger world. I saw comfort in knowing all types of people to be an asset. Little did I know the aims of Jack and Jill would run contrary to my life's philosophy for my children.

Every Easter, my wife and I met a Jewish couple, Lisa and Ken, for Sunday brunch at a fancy hotel in La Jolla. We were friends because the wife was my law school colleague, and we got along well. We clicked at the level of temperament and personality. Our conversations were smooth and natural, so a friendship was the most natural thing to happen. My wife got along with the husband and wife as well. When we had our first child and our friends had their first child, our Sunday brunches grew to include diapers, bibs, and Cheerios. We were two young families learning about parenthood together. I was happy. We were happy.

On my eldest son's first Easter, grandmother asked to attend our Easter Sunday plans. We said sure, why not. Our family had a great time as usual. What I would learn years later was all was not as it appeared on the surface. I was not privy to the conversation but, as it was relayed to me, grandmother was appalled that her grandchildren were spending Easter Sunday Brunch with a Jewish couple. She declared out of my earshot that it was time for Jack and Jill. Having moved to San Diego from Brooklyn, New York, grandmother made good on her vow, although she would characterize her mission as "helping to facilitate the process." What did it all mean for me as my children grew up in Jack and Jill?

I hasten to add, in fairness, Jack and Jill is a group of black mothers. My wife would (with the utmost affection) tell me to butt out. She values the black experience and the centering of black heritage for the kids. I get that, but does one need to devote hours each week between the ages of nine and eighteen for the message to sink in? No, that is overkill and provides a cloaking device for what is really going on as I see it.

The real value of Jack and Jill is that it provides an instant network of upper-middle-class black people with a shared social experience. That's the real political value. When my wife and I hosted a graduation reception for our eldest son at the University of Arizona, the very first person to arrive was "Harriet," a local Jack and Jill mom living in Tucson. My wife knew Harriet well because she had taken our eldest son under her wing and made his path easier while in college. Harriet had a classic look that I recognized from my college days at the University of Virginia. She was light-skinned and smart with great poise. My wife shared with Harriet how I had my reservations about Jack and Jill, but that she believed the group had clear social advantages because black children need unique socialization. My wife was referring to the questions black kids inevitably get, such as about their hair, and the stereotypes they often hear, such as about black intelligence. Every black raised in a majority-white setting knows the odious comments: "I don't consider you black." "You speak well." "You are articulate." "You're different from other blacks." "That's a big word you're using."

I took no interest in Jack and Jill over the years. I was always welcome to attend functions and events. However, I am a natural-born introvert. Barnes and Noble and a *Star Trek* marathon are much more attractive to me. And besides, I had my philosophical misgivings with the aim of Jack and Jill going forward in time. The idea that professional black families *must* provide children some space where they are with other black children and families is dogma and presupposes a way of being in the world. None of the other black law professors in San Diego were Jack and Jill families, and their children turned out just fine.

I want to hear your thoughts and views on these rationales for Jack and Jill in the modern era. Is there harm in inherited networks and connections for black children of the upper-middle-class? Do inherited networks and connections serve the purpose of universal humanity or not? Must black children come together in Jack and Jill to be around others who look like them hours each week throughout elementary, middle, and high school?

Imagine you are a black graduate of Stanford undergrad and Harvard Medical School. You are married to a Jewish bond trader, and you live in Rancho Santa Fe, one of the most affluent neighborhoods in the United States. Maybe ten black people live in Rancho out of 3,117 total residents. So, that comes out to, oh, 0.3 percent black. Your older kids are always, always, the only black students in their private school classes at the Bishop's School in La Jolla. One day, your little five-year-old son says he is afraid to go into downtown San Diego because there are too many black people.

As a parent, do you drop whatever you are doing and apply for Jack and Jill membership pronto? Why or why not? Do you enroll in therapy? Do you consider moving to a more diverse place like Oakland, California, which is 25 percent black and more urban? What choices do you make for the best mental health of your son and for the greater purpose of dissolving racial boundaries?

These questions are loosely based on a real-life case. When I was growing up, there was a very affluent part of Midlothian in Chesterfield County called Salisbury. I believe two black families lived in the neighborhood. There was a wealthy black dentist who applied for membership in the all-white Salisbury Country Club. His application was rejected as he was not white. I recall, during his newspaper interview, that his young son was so unaccustomed to black people that he was afraid to go into downtown Richmond where there were too many black people.

Watching STAR TREK in San Diego,

Wink

Letter 57

Dear Wink,

In one of your first letters, you told me it was important to you that we could talk about race honestly and came close to giving me an ultimatum for our continued correspondence. Not quite, but close. Eager to keep our correspondence, I have been keeping up with your suggested readings, such as *Our Kind of People*. What I'm continually struck by is the gap between the prevailing discourse on race and your understanding of and experience with race. Your most recent letter provides a perfect example of what I mean.

According to the diversity training I've received and books on race I've absorbed, elitism implies whiteness. Oh, and evil. So, embracing your elitism flies in the face of current wisdom, as does the elitism you describe in the black Jack and Jill communities. Doesn't that strike you as odd? It is strange that in the current dialogue around race, we are being led to think that elitism is related to color—that black doctors, lawyers, entrepreneurs, and millionaires can't be "elitist"? It is assumed that black is both "good" and "oppressed." Prior to our latest obsession with race, I never thought of a color as "good." People are good or bad—the color palette is neutral in its morality. When I think of true oppression, however, there is no room for elitism. Elitism is inextricably linked to privilege. To be an oppressed elite seems like a contradiction. There is an incongruity between the two. Much of this likely stems from how narrowly "privilege" has been defined. By tying the idea of privilege to skin color, we forget about the hundreds of other types of privilege that ebb and flow and affect opportunities and outcomes over the course of a lifetime. With that understanding of privilege, then perhaps the contradiction disappears.

But back to the present discussion. I must admit I'd never heard of Jack and Jill until you first mentioned it. Your additional descriptions continue to reveal a new world to me. I reached out to several of my black friends to inquire of their Jack and Jill affiliations. Every one of them had heard about it, but none were members. Alpha Kappa Alpha, yes. Jack and Jill, no. Maybe my own solidly middle-class background has me carousing with solidly middle-class commonalities across the color line. While my family laughs at my affinity for convenience (I have an aversion to the inconvenient but seem to find it anyways, perhaps explaining my affections . . .), I cannot relate to elitism. I always gravitate to the salt-of-the-earth kinda folks. Those are *My Kind of People.*

It could be that my ignorance of Jack and Jill is chalked up to a lack of exposure, but I would bet if you asked most white people, they, too, would assume it simply is a nursery rhyme.

Having said that, let me get around to some of your queries and my own observations. First, I think you may be a little harsh on Jack and Jill. Our most precious cargo is our children, as you note. In the universal book of parenthood, trying to lead our children to the best possible outcomes is almost canonical. Finding positive role models to help our children navigate their coming of age seems natural, and in a country where the black American population sits at around 13 percent, I could see myself similarly steering my children into a Jack and Jill chapter under some circumstances.

Some of the fondest memories of my youth are of the group Indian Princesses. I'm sure that this name is now entirely taboo, but it came from a place of strength, and I loved being an Indian Princess. Unlike Brownies (I'm a Brownie dropout) or the Girl Scouts (I never made it that far), I found my place among the Indian Princesses. It was a "survival" group (no, not preppers or anything of the sort) consisting of dads and daughters, with our fathers teaching us how to camp, bird-watch, create tourniquets, use first-aid kits, and the like. It was about being in nature, and I guess it played on the stereotype that Native Americans are more closely aligned with our natural landscapes (I personally think this is a pretty cool stereotype, and we'd all be a little better off if we adopted it as our own, but you know . . . appropriation and all . . .).

Unlike Jack and Jill, Indian Princesses was open to all. No invitations were needed, and it wasn't a life-long commitment. In fact, I have never been a part of any organization that had such restrictions. A few of my friends were part of The Junior League, which had galas and "coming of age" cotillions. I don't think membership was exclusive, but it was perhaps a little more so than my Indian Princesses. My own family isn't really into pomp and circumstance outside of a few events honoring my dad's achievements in the Air Force.

Now to be sure, the need for Indian Princesses and Jack and Jill was heightened not only in 1938 when Jack and Jill was introduced but also in the 1970s when I attended my first Indian Princess meeting. Are we in a better place now, where we have eradicated racial prejudice and sexism, making these organizations obsolete? While we live in an age where gender is fluid, I still identify as a woman, much like, I assume, your wife identifies with blackness. We still must deal with a handful of bigots. This enhances the attraction of finding our *safe spaces*—places where we can find, develop, and empower ourselves. I'm personally not really big on this idea of *safe spaces*, but I do see how groups formed for particular reasons provide outlets for development that are of value as we learn to navigate the larger world.

As I think about my affection for this childhood group, I would absolutely consider it were I to have a daughter, assuming the word-police haven't canceled my beloved Indian Princesses. That said, I tried to get my son into Boy Scouts when he was younger, and we never made it far. The forced affiliation to other kids (not to mention the parents) where we didn't really click seemed phony. We both decided we'd prefer to dedicate that time to our friend networks, even though I did appreciate the structure it provided as I was managing single motherhood at the time.

Although we were Boy Scout dropouts, Indian Princesses was formative for me, even if the experience was temporary. It provided a launch pad for my life as a woman, created a great bond with my dad, and helped me to shed some of the more negative stereotypes of fragile femininity. It gave me a foundation for interacting in environments that are male-dominated, with self-awareness and confidence.

Outside of a necessary cadre of girlfriends, I don't feel the need to assign myself to female-only spaces. I love my sisters, but life is richer with a diverse posse.

Before I sign off, I want to address your request to imagine myself as a black Harvard-trained doctor married to a white Jewish bond trader. (This is very specific, Wink!) I have had two conversations recently with women in biracial relationships—a black woman married to a white man and a white woman married to a black man. In our media, we insist this is the norm. I challenge you to count biracial relationships in an hour of commercials. Yet, it is not yet really the norm, and for some reasons, I get why. The glue to a lot of relationships is shared experiences. Most white men my age will get my references to Saturday mornings watching *Land of the Lost* and the evil Sleestak. Although Sleestak fandom is not an ethnic or racial preference, in my unscientific polling of Sleestack affection, it does appear that this did attract a whiter audience. That said, my white husband has never watched *Land of the Lost*, and I have lost a certain reference with him, but his odd-ball New Orleans idioms keep our relationship fresh. And so, perhaps this glue is less like an adhesive and more something that simply greases the wheels, with common socio-economic and racial references acting as a lubricant.

Anyways . . .

Let's take the case of my new friend, Gabrielle (aka Gabs). Gabs is biracial but visually "presents" as black. Gabs married a white man, and their son has pale skin. So much so that in an antiracism exercise in a civics class that separated out the kids into white/oppressors and black/oppressed, his teachers insisted that he identify with the oppressors.[*] When he failed to label himself appropriately, he was told he would fail the course. After several attempts to negotiate with the teachers and school leadership, the family was forced to resort to a lawsuit.

After hearing her story and those of other biracial children, it dawned on me that biracial kids may be the ones who save us from a return of segregation. When children of biracial couples recognize that one of their beloved parents is singled out due to the color of their skin, some will push back. When darker-skinned parents realize their lighter-skinned kids are being shoehorned into negative stereotypes, some

---

[*] To hear more about Gabs, listen to the *Hold my Drink Podcast,* episode 38, "Education and Indoctrination," podcasts.apple.com/us/podcast/episode-38-education-indoctrination-gabs-clark/id1537516628?i=1000528937334.

will push back. There is no room for the dogma that insists that blackness is only and always about oppression. Kinship is not skin deep. These relationships that transcend color are antithetical to a dogma that insists on color as the most important attribute.

Under these circumstances, it would seem more appropriate to socialize their biracial children in groups that are multiracial, mirroring their family dynamics. And so, while I may put my hypothetical daughter in Indian Princesses, I don't know that I would subscribe to a group that is allegiant to only one race, in my imagined biracial scenario. Even though multiracial relationships are not as ubiquitous as our media likes to portray, I think they pave the way for a new consciousness that surpasses the binary categories so prevalent in the current antiracism movement.

In the thought experiment you propose, what would make my biracial son afraid of blackness? Is it the media's fallacious portrayal of black Americans as lower-class and poor? That would not sit well with me. I would lean toward multiracial organizations, but if my son were indeed afraid of blackness, I just don't know how I'd react. I would want him to know the strength of the half of his racial identity that he so fears. I would want to show him that blackness is not limited to the negative stereotypes that invoke fear. Maybe immersing him in all-black groups that provide positive black role models would be one solution. Like Indian Princesses, it would be a temporary solution. To overcome the walls of racial segregation, it would not be a place where I would commit extraordinary time. However, I could see it as a side trip on a larger journey to build character and self-awareness and to explore alternative worldviews and perspectives.

Likewise, were I to help him develop this part of his racial identity, I would similarly want him to understand his Jewish heritage. He may not have the same fear of his Jewish roots, and so my motivation would be slightly different in introducing him to this heritage, but I would want him to embrace his full self. And so, similarly, this would be a temporary exercise in an attempt to root him and help him embrace his diverse history. Providing that background is important but staying immersed in either world denies a universal humanity. That focus on a universal humanity is why I looked outside of my black bubble to marry a Jewish bond trader, after all. Do note, however, that you have me marrying someone of the same social class! I most likely met this beguiling Jewish trader hobnobbing with other professionals at a social event where we shared a love of pinot noir from the Willamette Valley, greasing the wheels of a conversation that lasted into the wee hours of the morning.

And this brings me to a question for you. Is it important to socialize our children into other social classes to alleviate this fear of the Other? Are elite black Americans less fearful of the inner city? When we equate blackness with poverty and crime, Jack and Jill offers an escape from these stereotypes, but do they work to eradicate the stereotypes? If the goal of Jack and Jill is to move beyond the stereotypes of the "ghetto," they may better serve the black community by bringing these elite opportunities into lower-income neighborhoods. If we work to lift these communities so everyone can realize their potential, it may threaten the exclusivity that makes Jack and Jill, and other elite organizations, so attractive. I would have to ask myself, as an elite black doctor married to an elite Jewish bond trader, do I want to preserve these institutions and traditions to maintain our position on the social ladder? Trying to twist my middle-class mindset into that scenario entails some mental gymnastics that are hard to perform. If children are our most precious cargo, is it wrong to want to give them the very best, even at the expense of maintaining a social hierarchy that continues to stratify and segregate across class and race?

If the Salisbury Country Club of the 1970s had an explicitly racist selection process, what are we to make of the selection process of Jack and Jill today?

Enjoying the diversity of the Jersey shore,

Jen

Letter 58

Dear Jen,

One of the most natural states of writing for me is authenticity. It is also a difficult and terrifying state of writing for me. Authenticity for me is like a runway at an airport. The path ahead is unavoidable and yet liftoff is fraught with anxiety, nonetheless. One suppresses the anxiety and commits one's soul in faith that flight will be sustainable.

I strive to align my actions with my core values and beliefs. Even in your first paragraph to me, it comes across that I desire to live in sync with my true self. However, as you picked up in our earliest correspondence, writing for me is about a deep dive into honesty: *"You told me it was important to you that we could talk about race honestly and came close to giving me an ultimatum for our continued correspondence."* You understood me well. For many years, I held my tongue and remained silent as more and more radical ideas were shopped in the marketplace of ideas. I censored myself as I felt what place did I have to write about blackness as the son of a small, conservative, Republican Southern suburb in the 1970s? The calamities of the black inner city seemed more urgent and worthy of discourse, so I censored myself in the interest of the larger mythology of blackness as a plight.

And what good did self-censorship serve? My wife assumed I shared her progressive activist mindset. My mother-in-law felt I must be disingenuous. In her world, all blacks are degrees of progressive activists.*

---

* My mother-in-law would not use the label "progressive activist." Instead, she would say

Self-censorship left a distorted view of me and other individuals in my home and the larger public square. I did not live by my own core values and beliefs—that if there are over 40 million black Americans, then that means there are over 40 million black American life stories, experiences, and perspectives, including my own. And because I and others have not aligned our actions with our core values and beliefs, the world has a distorted perception of black culture and consciousness. I am only one person, but as one person, I can align my actions with my core values and beliefs, and that alignment may make a difference. If nothing else, it may change the world a little among family and close friends.

So, what are my core values and beliefs in light of your letter to me?

I live for the uplift of black people. In my own life, I have adopted values and attitudes like ambition, self-confidence, curiosity, independence of thought, and deferred gratification that I believe lead to better life outcomes. I love black history and genuine stories of triumph over adversity—not grievance studies. I have thought nothing of going to the library at UC San Diego on Saturdays and Sundays and strolling through the stacks of black history books on the sixth floor. The stories of people who achieved against all odds rivet me. Toward this end, and despite a demanding full-time day job, I have found the time after work and on the weekends to research and publish essays and articles about George Boyer Vashon, the first black lawyer in Pittsburgh, Sadie Tanner Mossell Alexander, the first black female lawyer in Pennsylvania, John Mercer Langston, the first black lawyer in Ohio, and several other figures from our American history.* I may not be a progressive activist, but I live in a love of black history.

Who are my kind of people? My kind of people would be Jewish Soviet immigrant writers, like our friend Izabella Tabarovsky, holed up as a hermit in Jerusalem.† She is my kind of person. My kind of people

---

she opposes hierarchy among black people. All people have genius potential, and blacks should not accept the feeling of being less than others.

* Twyman, "A Career in Exile," 54–57; Wink Twyman, "Against All Odds," *Pennsylvania Lawyer* (July/August 2006): 39–42, www.pabar.org/members/PALawyer/julyaug06/AgainstAllOdds.pdf; and W. F. Twyman, Jr., "One Man and Many Obstacles," Counterweight, February 6, 2021, counterweightsupport.com/2021/02/06/one-man-and-many-obstacles/.

† One day, I read the words of a Jewish Soviet immigrant writer holed up as a hermit in Jerusalem. The writer was Izabella Tabarovsky, and her essay transfixed me (see "The American

would be distant cousins of all races enthralled with personal genealogy. Those are my kind of people. My kind of people would be my Tejana lawyer friend in San Antonio who believes books are her best friends. She is my kind of people. My kind of people would be my white rancher friend outside of Houston who shares my name and alienation from the legal profession. My kind of person would be a fellow introverted, intuitive, feeling writer troubled by prejudice and bigotry in Austin. That's my kind of person.

My prime directive in life is to engage the larger world. I seek out those who are different from me. When I went off to college, I wanted to learn about what else was out there in life beyond the all-black streets of my childhood. I chose the three smartest classmates I could find to be my roommates in my second and third year at the University of Virginia. Two of the guys were Jewish, one from New Jersey and the other from Long Island. The third guy was a certified math genius from Manassas, Virginia. The four of us lived in a walk-up on Brandon Avenue about a block from the rear of Cabell Hall. We were nerd central, and we all had a great time. We lived in studies and books and ideas. I could not have asked for better roommates. We were all on the same page regarding academic ambition. Race was irrelevant. It really, really was. I'm trying to remember if race ever came up among the four of us, but, no, it did not. This is one of many reasons why the modern quest for microaggressions remains vexing for me. Did the world turn crazy after 1982? We were forty years closer to American slavery, but we were focused on law school and graduate school admissions, not microaggressions.

I recoil when in the presence of tribalism. In my experience, trib-

---

Soviet Mentality: Collective Demonization Invades Our Culture," *Tablet Mag,* June 15, 2020, www.tabletmag.com/sections/news/articles/american-soviet-mentality). I was moved to reach out to this writer who articulated my unspoken fears: "As a writer, I read essays and articles every day. I only have Post-its on my laptop for ten essential sources to remind me of great truths about the human condition. Your essay, "The American Soviet Mentality: Collective Demonization Invades Our Culture," sits front and center on my keyboard. I have sensed for the past few years that the individual was being lost in the name of a greater collective good. I didn't have the words to articulate my fears and anxieties until I read your essay. I fear what you fear and consider it my duty as a writer to call out examples of collective demonization." I (and Jen) later had a conversation with her on the *Hold my Drink Podcast,* episode 28, "The American Soviet Mentality": podcasts.apple.com/us/podcast/episode-28-american-soviet-mentality-izabella-tabarovsky/id1537516628?i=1000520396445.

alism comes with an implicit bigotry against others. Bigots demonize entire groups. There is no truth to be found in this type of collective demonization because we are all individuals. Everyone has their own unique life story, experience, and perspective. When one comes together in a tribal group like Jack and Jill, one is implicitly rejecting non-blacks as not suitable for intimate relations. One is unconsciously carving out shared life experiences that non-blacks will not share. Non-blacks are collectively perceived as not trustworthy for doing the work of a healthy identity. The intentions may be noble and benevolent, but the results may be clannish and divisive.

Consider this illustration of what I am getting at: My daughter and "Melody" were neighbors and best friends in elementary school. They were inseparable. My daughter happened to be black, and Melody happened to be white. It did not matter in the age of innocence. Once grandma came to town, and my daughter was inducted into Jack and Jill, there developed this dynamic where my daughter had to explain why she had to attend Jack and Jill meetings. What was Jack and Jill? I still recall a Jack and Jill conference held in Arizona. Of course, my daughter invited Melody along for the ride. I wonder how Melody was received among the Jack and Jill types . . .

Now, let's apply my values and attitudes to some of your queries. Am I or my children afraid of blackness? Should your hypothetical biracial son be afraid?

Let's say a white female classmate warns your biracial son he must roll up the window when he is driving in the ghetto. Never forget to roll up your window. This would make your biracial son afraid of blackness.

An uncle shares the story of being mugged by two black male teenagers in downtown Philadelphia near the University of Pennsylvania campus. This mugging story would make your biracial son afraid of blackness. This unfortunate encounter of the criminal kind happened to me in the summer of 1984 while I lived in the Sammy fraternity house on the UPenn campus.* Because I see people as individuals, my worldview didn't change on race. However, I wrote off Philadelphia as a place I would ever live. Very sad, but I can't stomach criminal conduct.

---

* Sammy (Sigma Alpha Mu) is a Jewish fraternity. I was able to lock in the living arrangements for the summer since my law school housemate, Michael Fuchs, had been President of Sammy at the University of Pennsylvania.

Your biracial son sees a newscast of two black teenage girls who carjacked an Uber driver in downtown D.C. Your son watched in horror as the driver was thrown out of his vehicle, slammed against the pavement at high speed, and died.

Your cousins avoid downtown San Diego when they come to visit from the East Coast.

The black people on TV who live in downtown San Diego appear mean and angry all the time. Someone I know once made this comment to me, and I got it. I suppose things have changed now that Madison Avenue has presented us with a 30 percent black world in advertising and commercials filled with upper-middle-class and middle-class black people.

In providing my children with an elite worldview, do I alleviate their fear of blackness? This depends on how one defines blackness. If blackness is defined as mere skin color or phenotype, then, yes, Jack and Jill is what the doctor ordered. The elite worldview is beside the point in a way. It is simply time spent with other black people, more so than elitism *per se*, that makes the difference. And in my own life and the scenario of your hypothetical biracial son, you would be providing him with friends and acquaintances who share the same elite worldview. Everyone is on the same page, which facilitates bonding. However, if blackness is defined as something political or ideological, then your hypothetical biracial son will not find an elite worldview that aligns with blackness in this regard. Fear will be replaced with something more chronic over a lifetime—disaffection, alienation, misalignment. An elite worldview for your son results in misalignment with blackness as a political, dogmatic way of being in the world. It is like learning to live with colorblindness or a bunion on one's foot or chronic asthma. One accepts the imperfection in life and carries on.

There is no utopian way of being in the world. And this might be the greatest life lesson to teach our children, more so than Jack and Jill.

You ask if elite black Americans are less fearful of the inner city. It really depends upon the individual person. It would be impossible to generalize about elite black Americans and their fear or lack thereof vis-à-vis the inner city. I am sure if there are four million elite black Americans, there are four million black American fear-reactions to the inner city. It really, really depends upon the person and their generation and their upbringing.

A few years ago, a teenager who attended a private high school in California started to look at colleges on the East Coast. When the teenager landed in Baltimore, she and her brother drove through Baltimore to explore. By the time they returned from their driving tour of the harbor city, the teenager's eyes had been opened. She said Baltimore was "sketchier" than she had anticipated, but she didn't want to say anything more negative because she thought her parent might jump on her negative observations.

If there are over 40 million black Americans, there are over 40 million black American experiences, life stories, and perspectives on the world.

I grew up with a cow pasture in my backyard. I seek out small-town places like Mount Charleston outside of Las Vegas, Gaithersburg, Maryland, and Julian, California. These places are familiar to me. My late cousin Rosa Nell Grace sought out Santa Monica and Calabasas when visiting Los Angeles. She was attracted to celebrity and affluence. And I know an estimable Jack and Jill couple who religiously sought inner-city black neighborhoods when visiting San Diego. This couple viewed race as culture and culture as urban politics. All these people would fall comfortably within the Talented Tenth conception of the black elite.* And they all have different attractions and aversions to the inner city. It depends upon individual interests and preferences. There is no single black perception of the inner city.

One cannot rely upon caricatures and stereotypes.

You question whether Jack and Jill can eradicate stereotypes. I am sure Jack and Jill members are aware of stereotypes and work to eradicate them within the group. Stereotypes are offensive to all people, particularly people who come from great-grandparents who were all about uplift for the race. I would say eradicating stereotypes is in the DNA of Jack and Jill. We must define what stereotypes we are talking about, of course. I am talking about lack of discipline, low aim, laziness, dullness of mind, and low-impulse control as recognized racial stereotypes. In every way,

---

* The Talented Tenth is a term that designated a leadership class of black Americans in the early twentieth century. The term was created by white Northern philanthropists, then publicized by W. E. B. Du Bois in an influential essay of the same name, which he published in September 1903.

Jack and Jill eradicates these stereotypes, so that really isn't on the table as a concern.

However, there are other stereotypes we might not be as aware or conscious of. For example, is there a stereotype that blackness equals dogma? Is there a stereotype that blackness equals oppression and nothing else matters in life? Is there a stereotype that blackness means one must be a progressive activist? That one must live one's life in race today, race tomorrow, race forever? These are the stereotypes that concern me most, and I am not sure Jack and Jill is working to eradicate these stereotypes. I see no evidence of doing the work to eradicate these ways of being in the world.

Before I sign off for the evening, I want to address your final question on the differences between Jack and Jill and the Salisbury Country Club. The difference is material: Jack and Jill is about the racial uplift of black people, and the Salisbury Country Club was about the humiliation of black people. The elite selection with Jack and Jill is one part legacy, one part admission by sponsored invitation only. The elite selection with the Salisbury Country Club didn't confer inheritable legacy rights. The elite selection for Jack and Jill involves one national organization with 252 chapters organized by seven regions throughout the United States of America. The elite selection for the Salisbury Country Club was anchored in the Salisbury neighborhood. There are no affiliate chapters of the Salisbury Country Club throughout the country. The elite selection for Jack and Jill was born in 1938. The elite selection for the Salisbury Country Club began in 1963.

Jack and Jill uplifts black people. There is no overlap between the mission of Jack and Jill and the mission of the Salisbury Country Club. Maybe you were suggesting that Jack and Jill rejects mothers based on race. This is not technically true. The children of Reginald Lewis belonged to Jack and Jill even though Lewis was married to a Filipino lawyer. The daughter of George Lythcott belonged to Jack and Jill even though Mrs. Lythcott was white. I am aware (or I know) there are both mothers and fathers in Jack and Jill chapters across the country who are not black. So, try as I might, I can't agree that Jack and Jill is as mindlessly discriminatory as the Salisbury Country Club was in the 1960s and 1970s.

What Jack and Jill and the Salisbury Country Club have in common is elitism, a sense of high standards, and concern for the content of one's character. Where the Salisbury Country Club went wrong at its founding was in racializing virtue and character. No race has a lock on the highest of standards and the most virtuous of character. In *Old Money* by Nelson W. Aldrich, Jr., the writer bemoans, "Bigotry has been a continuous disaster for the Old Money class."* And yet the penetrating insight of *Old Money* is that the priorities and presumptions of the elite—as further demonstrated in *Our Kind of People*—do not belong to a "race." Reverence for ancestral habits, customs, and attitudes and a "vision of the good life" apply even more strongly to Jack and Jill than the Salisbury Country Club.

I still remember when I purchased *Old Money* back in 1988 at the shopping mall in Gaithersburg. Aldrich's sense of purpose and meaning has remained with me all these years, even as I have quarreled with my wife about Jack and Jill. For you see, Jen, retreating into all-black spaces bores me. I find such retreat tiresome and stagnant. What does excite me are the ways in which ancestral values, virtues, and vices are manifest not as the heritage of my race alone but as the legacy of particular families: families like mine, which began with some great act of courage in the year 1677 when a teenager left his home in Birchington, Kent, England for the New World. My family continues "on with a conscious sense of custom and obligation." Call it elitism if you will. I would call it reverence for the remnants of all the ancestors who course through my veins. I call it *pietas*.

When all is said and done, I learned more about myself after reading your letter. l learned that I may be too harsh on Jack and Jill, but that my motivations come pouring out of me from my core values and attitudes in life. I love engaging the larger world, and I wish these aims for my children. From my perspective, Jack and Jill centering black heritage is a cloaking device for an upper-middle-class social network and respectable, prescreened dating prospects. I'm an introvert, and I look within to understand the world and whether I align with the values and attitudes of others. I don't see the larger world as blackness now, blackness tomorrow, blackness forever. I see people first before I see blackness.

So, I better understand myself and this presence in my life called Jack

---

* Aldrich, *Old Money*, 278.

and Jill. I can appreciate its benefits for others but not so much for me.

Another Sunday afternoon in San Diego,

Wink

Letter 59

Wink,

I'm so frustrated right now I can barely write, and I'm afraid that what I do write will be emotionally driven. I lost my rational balance today. I haven't even been here in Baltimore for twenty-four hours.

Let me explain.

We flew in last night as part of a mission trip. This morning we went to a church in a low-income area. It was one of the most uplifting church experiences I've had in a very long time. The church was mixed, and there were even some homeless people who were not just part of the congregation but also involved in the communion, greeting and tithing. It was truly one of the most beautiful moments. The love. The acceptance. Race wasn't an issue. I was in my glory.

My son and I decided not to sit with our church group from Austin. We weren't there to mingle with the known, but the unknown. We sat in a pew with a young black mother. In front of us was a black woman who had just turned ninety. Behind us was a black family. The matriarch had a brother living in Budapest who had "gone native." He had received his PhD in education, moved to Hungary, learned Hungarian fluently, and fell in love with and married a Hungarian woman. Although she has since passed away, he continues to live and work in Hungary. What an amazing story. One black story out of 40 million.

The matriarch sitting behind me, his sister, was the most loving woman. She must've hugged me at least five times. After the time in our service when we "passed the peace" (which was a very moving time that took like ten minutes because everyone in that church wanted to talk to everyone else—homeless, families, black, white . . . no matter), this woman gave me and my son some hand sanitizer. I had to giggle inside. I'd take her germs any day. She told us over and over while holding my son's hand how important it was for our youth to have faith.

One of the young black acolytes sitting in the pulpit with the pastor got up at one point (Lutherans have a lot of opportunities for the congregation to speak and share) and said that she was sixteen and number one in her class. She also said that she loved hugs. I already knew that to be true after the bear hug she had shared with me while passing the peace.

It wasn't until the end of the service that the lady behind me told me the speaker was a homeless teen. Her mother was around but addicted, and she often didn't have a safe place to stay. I must've looked befuddled, and I asked our new friend, "You mean the young girl who said she was top of her class?" "Yes, yes, that young girl," my new friend confirmed. I was sure to get another bear hug from this amazing young lady before I left. She wasn't going to let the color of her skin or her circumstances define her. I stood in amazement and gratitude for being witness to her accomplishments, if only for a minute.

And I was so excited to come back and write to you. To tell you that in inner-city Baltimore, in a mixed church, I had NO racialized moments. That is, there was not a time when race mattered.

And then . . .

Back at our host church—a Presbyterian church in a wealthier area of town—a young white woman who runs the church programs was waiting for us upon our return. She was there to share a little of Baltimore's history—the past of slavery, forced segregation, and redlining, and the disparities that continue to define the city. After a brief history, she took us on a *racial* tour of Baltimore—that is, the entire purpose of the tour was to underline *racism* in the city. She showed us how neighborhoods turned literally from one street to another—from well-maintained brownstones to dilapidated projects. She asked us to notice the differences. One of the big things she asked us to notice was the trash.

It is a breezy day in Baltimore. In the wealthy neighborhoods, the breeze was caught up only in the swaying branches of the tree-lined streets. Travel to the next block and the wind, without the leaves to caress, tangled instead with plastic bags and rolling debris that tumbled past vacant and boarded houses. Her implication was subtle but so very clear. Trash is *racist*.

As politely as I could muster (and it took some engineering), I said, "I can't help but think there is a 'truth in between' here." I went on to say, "I recognize the services here may not be as thorough as in the neighborhoods lined with leafy trees, but could it also be that perhaps the people in these impoverished neighborhoods are careless with the maintenance of their communities? Of course, poverty can explain some of it—when finding a meal is the priority, trash is nary a nuisance—but I think that is only part of the story." She replied, "It's complicated."

I wanted to scream—great insight, Sherlock! So why are you simplifying it to a single story of *racism*?

We continued to weave in and out of pristine neighborhoods bordering low-income neighborhoods. All the way, our white guide continued her mantra: "We just crossed a boundary. What differences do you note?" Our all-white group ate it up, jumping with excitement at their oh-so-erudite observations: "There are broken windows here, and trees are growing out of the roofs." Cross another road, and there would be more excited observations: "This is a white neighborhood because the lawns are so manicured." Wait—what? Did someone take a census of this neighborhood? It didn't matter. It was *white*. Clean is *white*. (Hmmm . . . I don't think my non-white friends would appreciate this assumption.)

The guide made sure we noticed that in the poor neighborhoods, the supermarkets were Save A Lots. In a wealthier neighborhood, we saw a Whole Foods. At this point, it's getting ridiculous. Um, duh. This isn't about race. To echo Bill Clinton's advisor James Carville, "It's the economy stupid!" A Whole Foods would flop in poorer neighborhoods. Is Whole Foods *racist*? In a city like Baltimore, it is easy to see the correlation between race and socioeconomics, but correlation doesn't imply causation (as a wise friend of mine likes to say). We just love the "R-word" so much. We embrace it and all the power it imparts in its illustration of being the newly enlightened. Oh, the arrogance. The self-righteousness. I do believe the embrace originally came from a place of love and humanity but has since been hijacked by the "us vs. them" binary that is critical to maintaining one's place in the social justice hierarchy.

Soon I found I could hold my tongue no longer. We drove into a "white" neighborhood (you know, because the lawns were manicured, and they had their own security) that bordered another low-income "hood" on one side. The streets exiting this neighborhood to the hood were one way, making it hard for anyone to swing into the neighborhood from the poor side without going around the block. One of the kids asked why and this white pastor from another church said, wait for it . . . RACISM! My mouth opened before I could think better of it: "Racism, really? Not everything is racist. That word is so overused." My own pale-skinned pastor looked at me aghast. Sigh . . .

I preach about speaking civilly and with compassion and understanding. But I just couldn't take it any longer. I start the morning connecting in love and faith with people of various hues to end the day in a verbal scuffle with a white pastor. Sweet baby Jesus, give me strength.

There are definitely things happening here that smack of injustice. For example, the light rail only runs north–south. It doesn't go east–west, which would have it cross through the lower-income, primarily black neighborhoods. This lack of transportation diminishes opportunities— opportunities to find a job, opportunities to go to a better school, opportunities to enjoy neighborhoods without trash kissing your ankles as you saunter through the hood. I do think that we can tie some of the segregation we continue to see today to policies such as these that influence transportation infrastructure and past redlining policies that intentionally put additional barriers on the upward trajectory of those who are already wading through—literally and figuratively—the layers of trash that have been heaped upon them over centuries. And yet, today, Baltimore is a city with a black mayor, a black state's attorney, a black chief of police, a black congressman, and a black school superintendent. Surely, they embrace policies that would enable black and lower-income citizens to have more opportunities, right? And if or when they don't institute such policies, is the only possible reason racism? Without doing a deep dive into Baltimore's transportation politics, I assume, given the recent demographics of Baltimore's leadership, there is likely more nuance and complexity to the situation than simply *racism*.

Just another day in Baltimore . . .

Jen

Letter 60

Hey Jen,

You are right to feel frustrated. The genuine love you felt in the low-income church coexists with the hardline lens of raging caricatures and stereotypes you encountered on the bus. There are black upper-middle-class neighborhoods in Baltimore. Did you see those neighborhoods too, or were they not part of the narrative? Where do you think the black doctors and lawyers live? They must live somewhere. Where do you think the Jack and Jill denizens reside? They were not part of the tour, I suspect.

The big picture of Baltimore is more than the myopic lens you were treated to on your "racial" tour of Baltimore. I hate tier 1 consciousness, which you've referenced a few times, in which the complexity of life is ignored. As I understand the concept, tier 1 consciousness is rooted in dogmas. Those with tier 1 consciousness are unable to "comprehend any other side" of a way of understanding the world.* Tier 1 consciousness primes people for easy manipulation. Tier 1 consciousness is very tribal, and the Other is caricatured. In the world of tier 1 consciousness, one cannot conceive of nuance and complexity as integral to life. Life is lived in absolutes. Blacks are good and whites are bad.

There is a higher level of consciousness that I strive toward in my life. Above the herd of tier 1 consciousness is tier 2 consciousness, which

---

* To read more on tiered consciousness and thinking, see Michael Krieger, "Lost in the Political Wilderness," *Liberty Blitzkreig,* February 6, 2017, libertyblitzkrieg.com/2017/02/06/lost-in-the-political-wilderness/.

allows one to bring all of yesterday into a better tomorrow. Perhaps 5 percent of the population lives in this better way of being in the world. A person who has evolved to tier 2 consciousness is a threat to tier 1 consciousness for obvious reasons. A tier 2 consciousness would never denigrate Jordan Peterson on a public stage as "an angry white man," as tier 1 consciousness Michael Eric Dyson did in a famous public debate.* A tier 2 consciousness would include and integrate Peterson's vision as part of a greater authentic existence. A tier 2 consciousness would feel for others, not reach for racial rancor. The emphasis is on integrating all that has been into an interdependent, naturally flowing tomorrow.

I wager your young white female tour guide was fed a heavy dose of Ta-Nehisi Coates, Michael Eric Dyson, systemic-this and institutional-that in college and grad school. We are witnessing the results of a Lost Generation incapable of understanding real life and real love that you saw in the low-income church. You witnessed caricatures of black American experiences in real time.

The young white tour guide has been programmed to think like a robot, to conceive of black life as oppression *writ large* and *racism* morning, noon, and night. What is scary is that she has lost the insight to see people as individuals capable of picking up the trash. That's not *racism*. That's common sense. When did tossing trash into the street and not the trash can become *racism*?

I would not live in the City of Baltimore. Likes do not encounter likes in the public square. Upper-middle-class whites see mostly low-income blacks there. And so, blacks become caricatures to them. Caricatures! Things will not change until the average white encounters and knows the average black as an equal. Remember my upbringing? I saw whites as equals and lower-income.† It made a difference in understanding others

---

* See the clip at "Jordan Peterson Versus Michael Eric Dyson," *C-Span,* June 6, 2018, www.c-span.org/video/?c4733705/jordan-peterson-versus-michael-eric-dyson.

† Everyone on my boyhood street was black. There were whites who lived in the general area. Perhaps half of the whites lived in red brick homes a notch above the red brick homes on our street. But it wasn't a racial disparity thing since the all-black neighborhoods across the highway were comparable to the red brick homes in which the white families lived. There was also a significant contingent of whites who lived in wood-frame homes comparable to our homes. Finally, there were whites who lived in a trailer park on Jefferson Davis Highway. Their mobile homes were seen as less desirable. For these mobile-home dwellers, moving

as individuals first. Ask your young white tour guide about the Baltimore chapter of Jack and Jill. Ask her about the local chapter of Alpha Kappa Alpha and Alpha Phi Alpha. Ask her about black upper-middle-class neighborhoods in suburban Montgomery County. She will have no clue. She has been trained, educated, and programmed to see blacks as despondent and downtrodden. She is the *racist*. In fact, she is more *racist* than my white classmates in the 1970s, who accepted blacks as likes—as more or less the same. She lives in tier 1 consciousness about the world and that is a sad state of affairs for your tour guide.

This is a dangerous consciousness that has taken root among white educated folks. It must be rooted out for the good of society. Blacks will never advance if everything black is *racism*.

I am this close to banning the word *racism* from my vocabulary. The word has been corrupted. It is either meaningless or deliberate manipulation of emotions. Read *Politics and the English Language* by George Orwell. A prominent writer from the Libertarian tradition in England, Orwell wrote that overused words are chosen to mouth "the party line" or narrative. The concrete and specific give way to the abstract and the vague. "Political language . . . is designed to make lies sound truthful," Orwell wrote.* I have reached the point where the word *racism* has decayed into falsehood. Never use *racism* again. Urge your companions to spend a day free of the word *racism* for twenty-four hours. Q: Can they do it? It is interesting to me that no one at the lower-income church used the word *racism*. Why was that? No one divided into tribes at the lower-income church. Why is that?

Life is truth in between. Think about it. No narrative explains all of the truth. Life is too nuanced and complicated. That is the point of this correspondence between us.

To repeat myself, and it bears repeating, I would not live in a city like Baltimore. Since caricatures are embedded in the public consciousness, it would be impossible to live as an individual apart from group caricatures. I like living in places that are 3 to 8 percent black. This is what I

---

to our all-black street would have been a step up. When white neighbors moved onto my boyhood street, some of my neighbors said to me, "There goes the neighborhood." My black neighbors equated white neighbors with a decline in the neighborhood. They had no problem seeing white people as caricatures and stereotypes.

* George Orwell, *Politics and the English Language* (London: Penguin Press, 2013).

knew growing up in Middle America. Q: Did you find you were more resentful about race after your bus tour? This is the consequence of everything as *racism*. The mindset breeds resentment.

Ironically, one can also live life free of caricatures in a 100 percent black place. Where everyone is black, the individual comes forth. Perhaps this is the attraction and appeal of *safe spaces* like Jack and Jill and Historically Black Colleges and Universities and summer places like Highland Beach, Maryland, Sag Harbor on Long Island, and the Inkwell beach on Martha's Vineyard. On the other hand, is there greater pressure to conform to racial norms and mores in a 100 percent black space? It is an interesting question. Perhaps the driver is generational more than blackness *per se*.

And, yes, Jen, "white is clean" is *racist*. This tour guide is a lost soul. These group companions are lost souls. Once again, what about a tour of the leafy, affluent black neighborhoods for balance and context? I guess affluent blacks are outliers. If we could transport your tour guide back in time to Bellwood, Virginia, in 1975, she would have given a tour of black middle-class red brick homes and a white trailer park within the same mile or two. How would the tour guide's mind have made sense out of black achievement and white struggle side by side? Because this pattern was my lived experience, I find places like Baltimore distasteful.

Correlation does not equal causation. We must lift people from a tier 1 consciousness to a tier 2 consciousness—and fast.

Baltimore also created Supreme Court Justice Thurgood Marshall, entrepreneur Reginald Lewis, and the John H. Murphy, Sr., Afro-American newspaper family. What happened to that black Baltimore?

Baltimore Day 1,

Wink

Letter 61

Dear Jen,

After reading your Baltimore story, it reminded me of reading *Between the World and Me* by Ta-Nehisi Coates. My mother-in-law was excited when the book came out in 2015. She urged the family to read it together as an impromptu book club. I was loath to participate in a family reading of the book. From what little I knew of Coates, he fell within the Blame the Man camp, and I did not find this to be a constructive illumination of the truth. I doubted I would learn anything new. Call me crazy, but I like books that make me think. My mother-in-law persisted as she left at least one copy of the book at our home. Around the time of my daughter's birthday party that year, I decided to read the book. Maybe my instincts would be proven wrong.

The following are my impressions as communicated to my mother-in-law:

> So, I read the book quickly in one day for maximum impact. Coates is a gifted writer, particularly when employing poetic imagery and vivid verse. I found his description of Dr. Jones' investment in her deceased son, Prince Jones, to be very moving. I also connected with his self-propelled research at the Moorland-Spingarn Archives. I used those archives myself while researching my senior thesis at the University of Virginia. Coates was at his best for me when he illuminated experiences that I had experienced. Ultimately, for me, the book was not one I would read again, and here is why:

1. I was put off by his use of "body" as a motif throughout the book. The recurring use of body seemed like recycled verbiage I recognized from law review articles. I found the technique off-putting in, say, the *Yale Law Journal* or the *Harvard Law Review*, and I felt Coates wasn't saying anything new in his book. Indeed, the "body" references seem more and more contrived as the book carried on toward its 150-page close. To be honest, Coates's use of "body" seemed mildly pornographic until I read about ten pages into the book.

2. I like books that are positive. The aim of a memorable book for me is one that I return to again and again for insights into a life well-lived. For example, I have read *Titan: The Life of John D. Rockefeller, Sr.* multiple times since the book was published in 1998. I return to it again and again for a stunning story of outsized success in the face of grueling adversity. I like these kinds of stories. They reinvigorate me after a hard day at work. I feel like I am along for the ride as a small-town poor kid wills himself to success. Another book I love is *The Power of Positive Thinking* by Norman Vincent Peale. Peale writes about much I find compelling, particularly his idea that if you change your thoughts, you change your world. In my darkest hours in Las Vegas, I returned to this book again and again for spiritual strength.* This is the power of a great book for me. Right now, I'm on my third reading of *You Can You Will* by Rev. Joel Osteen. It is one of those books about having a positive mindset.

3. To put it mildly, Coates's world is a bleak doom-and-gloom world of murderous cops and vulnerable black bodies. Ahhh, nope. There is nothing uplifting here for me, with the exception of his good descriptions of Howard University and the upward mobility of Dr. Jones. Too much of the book reads like "The World According to Me." And that's cool. Coates is welcome to be as pessimistic and fatalistic as his heart desires about race, America, and the black body. I would rather read something else.

---

* From April 11, 1999, until the year 2004, I lived in Las Vegas, Nevada. Little in my life had prepared me for living among call girls, slot machines in grocery stores, smoke-filled casinos, oppressive heat for half of the year, and open celebration of academic underachievement. I spent over two hundred nights of my life at the Lady Luck Hotel and Casino on the Strip. I longed for academic life and found despair. The Summerlin Public Library gave me solace as a refuge from my home in San Diego. In the end, I read *The Power of Positive Thinking* by Norman Vincent Peale as an alcoholic might turn to drink and self-destruction. Let it be said I endured.

4. I couldn't relate to much of the book. I felt like I was reading a sensationalized tract designed to shock and horrify. For example, Coates talked about a classmate having a gun on a middle school playground and how this experience was so traumatizing. Not my experience. Not my life. I never saw guns in school. I might have heard guns in the distance, but do you know why? Hunters were shooting deer over in the cow pasture behind my house. Coates's experience in the streets of Baltimore has no overlap for me. Now, if Coates had written about desegregation in a Southern suburb, that's something I can relate to and would love to read. If Coates had written about overcoming stereotypes to win political office in a suburban junior high and high school, he would have my attention. Coates was writing for a different audience, either readers who grew up in cities and understood his challenges or folks who wanted to experience racial horror vicariously. Not my thing.

5. This leads me to my next point. There are over 40 million different black experiences in the United States. Each person has their own unique history and life story. Coates has a gift for telling his story, and that is great. I'm interested in hearing about other life stories that are more positive.

6. I didn't accept the Trayvon Martin and Michael Brown narratives. I saw those events as woefully blown out of proportion on the national stage. Once again, I accepted that Coates and his son saw these events as watershed moments. I didn't view them that way. I was more concerned about getting my boys into college and meeting time targets at work. Since I didn't share Coates's perspective, his narrative seemed to reinforce the same old "all cops are bad" song and dance.

7. In conclusion, Coates is a gifted writer. At times, I found his writing compelling and stirring. But for every one of those moments of connection, there were ten moments of disdain, dismay, disagreement, discord, and disengagement. I'm a dreamer like John Lennon. And really, Coates did not write his book for dreamers. He wrote his book for the forlorn.

Wink

Letter 62

Dear Wink,

I also read Coates's book. You say you were not his audience. The forlorn are his audience. I would also think that his audience is the elite. When I reference Coates among those like us—college-educated people interested in our history—most know his name. I don't consider myself elite *per se*, but if college education throws me into this category, then so be it.

Regardless, when I talk to my friends who hail more from the blue-collar ilk, the name Coates rings hollow across the color line. When you are more interested in the basics of life, you don't have time for such erudite pursuits around elite racial consciousness. And yet, it is this consciousness that has brought about spasms in the American experience that have reinvented segregation. As I sit in Baltimore, I can tell you that Coates's beautiful prose on the horrors of his hometown hasn't done much to clean up the streets.

One of the most shocking things in Baltimore is the ubiquity of abandoned buildings. I didn't get the opportunity to study the property laws or real estate prices here, but I do know there was a lot of "white flight" from inner-city communities (from hearing your stories, I would guess that there was a fair amount of black flight too, but that wouldn't fit Coates's or the white pastor's storyline and so it remains unnoted). I can only speculate that the property prices must've dipped so badly that keeping one's property entailed more costs than benefits. I've never been to a city with so many houses so forsaken.

And so, the city allows a lot of these plots to be razed, and land trusts have come in to create green spaces, much like the one where we have been working on our mission trip. Often, no one even knows who owns these spaces, and they are left fallow. Weeds climb the bordering buildings, and the rats find luxurious accommodations to build their families.

In one such area near our site is a beautiful mural. As we were told, this area had not long ago been visited by a local nonprofit. Without warning, a group of volunteers came rumbling into the neighborhood with trucks and gardening gear. They attacked this site with vim and vigor for a week, creating a beautiful gardening space for the community. Upon completion, they left, never to be seen again.

Our own white female gardener used this story to illustrate the *white savior* mentality that permeates the city. As she told it, these *saviors* came in without warning, without connecting with the community to see what they may want in the garden (I can't remember what it was they planted, but it was unappealing to the local appetite, we were told), and without the commitment to maintain the garden. It was simply a PR move—a sanctimonious attempt to rid themselves of the *guilt* of contributing to a societal disequilibrium.

I largely agree with our gardener's assessment. But I disagree with the language she used to wrap up her conclusions, complete with a bow of self-righteousness. First, does one need to be white to have such a savior complex? Heck, we were all a bunch of white folks from Austin. Should we have made the trip? As I've learned from you, there are numerous black service communities that may make similar calculations when deciding what projects to tackle in low-income neighborhoods. Second, this nonprofit was an environmental nonprofit. It wasn't a *white* nonprofit *per se*. Equating whiteness with contrived piety is perhaps not entirely wrong, but it's not entirely right either.

Terms like *white savior* are manufactured to create chaos instead of correction. When we insist on making everything black and white—literally and figuratively—we promote the discourse of discord and division, much like Coates. Words matter.

Signing off in Baltimore,

Jen

Letter 63

Jen,

Great insight. Nice nuance and complexity. As you may not know, my family did a little bit of "black flight" in 1970.

Once upon a time in the 1960s, there was a street in the Hickory Hill neighborhood of Chesterfield County, Virginia, where everyone was black and family. I might have mentioned it once or twice: Twyman Road. The region's only interstate highway, I-95, was two miles to the east alongside the James River. At that time, many black people in the South lived in rural or suburban areas like Twyman Road. Some black families had lived on family-owned property for generations, as was the case with my family on Twyman Road. Notably, we lived about two miles from the Richmond city limits, but our culture and psychology were suburban and had been for generations. We had no overlap with the City of Richmond in terms of taxation, real estate, or public school education. Under Dillon's Rule, counties in the state of Virginia were separate and independent entities from cities.

In 1970, two momentous events occurred that changed the character of Twyman Road. First, the City of Richmond annexed the Hickory Hill neighborhood, which constituted a 2 percent black enclave in a 98 percent white part of Chesterfield County. We were now city residents, and my mom was seized with anxiety. Our Twyman family had been a suburban family since Daniel Brown's purchase of over 350 acres in Hickory Hill in the 1870s. We did not see ourselves as city people. My mom watched the nightly local news out of Richmond, but being from the country in Southside Virginia, she felt no connection to urban life. She had two brothers who had moved to Baltimore, and I'm sure mom got a heavy dose of "Baltimore lore" from her siblings Nathaniel and Raleigh Womack. Mom was a very frugal woman, and the idea of paying higher city taxes was a nonstarter.

Second, a federal district court decision was imminent any day in *Bradley v. School Board of City of Richmond*, 317 F. Supp. 555 (E.D. Va 1970). I remember watching the news coverage about the case on our black-and-white TV set and the coming specter of cross-town busing in the city. My mom and Uncle Robert Daniel Twyman opposed busing for their children into the heart of Richmond. The public schools were better in the county.

And so, the clock was ticking as control of my elementary school, Greene, would be turned over to the city in the fall of 1970. I remember frantic drives to visit homes with my dad behind the steering wheel. My mom was on a mission, and her mission was to move to the county before school started that fall. It was all a blur to me, house after house after house. I was eight years old, and my mom would say, "The taxes are lower in the county" and "The schools are better in the county." The direction of my life was going to change. Would I attend city schools or county schools in the fall?

Meanwhile, my cousin M. Ralph Page was the lead attorney on the Bradley school case seeking busing for the city of Richmond. Lawyer Ralph Page attended my family church and lived across Terminal Avenue from my grandma Rosa Twyman Jackson. Maybe lawyer Page had given my mom a heads-up—i.e., it is time to get out of Dodge and now! I don't know, but I know one thing—the universe was not going to deny Lourine Womack Twyman her mission of moving out to the county. We were just like other families doing the same thing in the spring and summer of 1970. Was it racial? No, it was seeking out familiar places to raise children. It was lower taxes and better schools.

On July 21, 1970, my parents signed a deed on a red brick home in the suburbs. All of the neighbors were two-parent households who wanted the suburban experience for their children. And we all got it.

After my mom slipped us away from the city, she relaxed and met her new neighbors on Jean Drive. Cows would occasionally escape from the cow pasture and rampage through everyone's backyard. On August 17, 1970, Federal Judge Robert Merhige opened the door for cross-town busing in Richmond. I entered my neighborhood county school a few days later at Bellwood Elementary Annex with a great fourth-grade teacher, Helen Friend, who taught us about slavery in our Virginia history textbooks. Our teacher was black, our school was a formerly all-black school, and our class was 92 percent white, which reflected the neighborhood demographics. While a student at the University of Virginia, I read the U.S. Census and observed that 90 percent of the black families in our general area were two-parent households. Mom had chosen our future well.

So, families left and, as a city street, Twyman Road began to decline. Annexation, lower taxes in the county, and better public schools in the county drew families away from Twyman Road to the suburbs. This was black flight, for lack of a better word. And it happened in 1970.[*]

Did we contribute to the chaos in low-income, inner-city Richmond, Virginia? I have an affinity for so-called white flight because many, if not most, of my classmates were in the same boat as our Twyman family. We celebrated uproariously when the U.S. Supreme Court rejected metropolitan-wide public school busing in 1974. Our parents had moved us out to the county, and we were settled in our schools. We had lived under a cloud of uncertainty for several years. We loved our junior high school, and no one wanted to have to be bused across the county and the city to a strange, distant school. Because Richmond is so heavily black, suburban blacks may have felt a reluctance to say these things in public. Fidelity to the race and all. And to think my cousin was the lead lawyer on the Richmond public school desegregation case. 1970 was a rip in space and time for us. Adults had months to make decisions that would ripple through the years.

Words matter, yes, indeed. I cited *Politics and the English Language* (1946) by George Orwell. Read it when you're back home and have time.

Wink

---

[*] For the story of a black woman in the Richmond area impacted by changes in the 1960s and 1970s before moving out to the suburbs, see Scott C. Davis, *The World of Patience Gromes* (Cune, 2000).

Letter 64

Dear Jen,

Sometimes, race just pops up without warning.

One day, I was having lunch with a young superstar in the biotech industry. I had this idea about relationship excellence as a way to enhance professional advancement in the workplace. Basically, the idea was that black Americans are only half of one percent of the world's population. If blacks limited themselves to relationships *only* with other blacks, how could one hope to compete in corporate America? One had to develop relationships with the other 99.5 percent of the world's population to have the best chance of gaining social capital. The idea seemed reasonable to me. And so, I had sought out young black professionals who were living relationship excellence. I did some research and discovered this rising black star. She seemed perfect for my research. She was vice president of a significant biotechnology firm. And she had been profiled in a recent article about rising black businesspeople under the age of thirty-five.

We met for lunch in Carmel Valley, a biotechnology corridor outside of downtown San Diego. The restaurant was upper-end and very posh. I easily envisioned venture capitalists meeting with startup entrepreneurs at several of the tables. As I grew to know my lunch guest, I learned that she was from the Deep South and had attended a Historically Black College. Her high school had been 30 to 40 percent black. We were on the same page in every way when it came to relationship excellence as a constructive force multiplier for career success.

It was time for dessert.

I looked over the menu and was torn between ordering some fruit offering or a chocolate treat. I asked my influential vice president what she was considering. "I would like to order the watermelon, but I refuse to do so." I asked her why. "Well, you know, I can't be seen eating watermelon in a restaurant." It was a very small thing but telling as well. I was in the presence of a mover and shaker who probably ranked among the most promising young black professionals in America. And yet she was imprisoned by racial taboos. She could not be herself and order what she wanted to order because of racial stereotypes. I teased her and said it wouldn't be that bad. No one is looking. No one cares. As God is my witness, she could not bring herself to order what she desired to have for dessert because of race.

If we lifted a layer from my vice president's outer veneer, we would find a frightened little girl who still fears prejudiced caricatures of black people. Her entire will is devoted to confronting stereotypes about black people. I get it. I know the type. I am that way myself. It was my upbringing in Virginia. And yet here we were in an opulent setting, miles from the endless Pacific Ocean, and racial stereotypes were controlling our simple desire to order watermelon.

She never ordered the watermelon. I did and enjoyed myself.

Wink

Letter 65

Wink,

My friends had finally made the trek to visit me in China. We were young and poor, and finding the resources to travel across the world took a gargantuan effort and much foresight on their part. Somehow, they had scraped together their tips from their transitional restaurant jobs and eked out enough to join me on a backpacking adventure.

Our first dinner together, we all sat around the typical round table in a Shanghai alley, with a Lazy Susan in the center. This was the Chinese way. We ordered an array of food, the dishes vying for space on the revolving center console. Chopsticks ready, I was eager to dig in when one of my jet-lagged friends grabbed a dish off the Lazy Susan and situated it on the placemat directly in front of her.

"Hey, pass that along so we can all get some," I quipped, trying to sound lighthearted since it was clear she had no intention of sharing. I was hoping that as she saw the dishes spinning around, she would get the picture—eating in China is not an individual exercise. To my dismay, she said she had ordered this one dish for herself and proceeded to have me ask the waitress in Chinese for salt and a fork.

It is somewhat taboo to ask for salt in China, as it suggests that the food lacks flavor (a grave insult). And why not at least try the chopsticks, right? Might as well get in some practice among friends. I was disappointed in this single-minded determination to continue with her American food etiquette, but I let it go as we had many more trip logistics to concern us. Still, her rigidity in not breaking from a cultural habit to venture into the new and unknown nagged at me.

There are times in China when we would long for home just enough to break down and get a Big Mac. Curiously, I think I've eaten American fast food overseas more than I ever have in the United States. I can't really call it comfort food, as it is the last thing that I would find comforting if I were on my home turf. However, if there is such a thing as *white* or maybe just American food, it would be the McDonald's #1 combo: Big Mac, fries, and a Coke (no wonder French gastronomists look down their noses at American food).

Once when my mom was visiting me in Beijing, a Chinese professor I know there invited us out to dinner. He wanted to show off how hip he was to American ways, so we found ourselves at a Hooters. That was the first and, to date, last time I've ever been to a Hooters. Let me just say . . . the vibe at the Hooters in Beijing was much different from what I had expected. And the food? Let's just say the culture shock was the most entertaining part of the evening.

Whenever I travel in India, my Indian friends always, without consulting me, tell the waiters to put less spice in my food. "I'm Texan," I decry, trying to mask my annoyance with humor. It is assumed that pale-skinned folk can't take the heat. Clearly, they have never seen my dad and me in a pepper-eating contest. Admittedly, he usually wins, but it is at his own expense the next day.

These are the food memories that waft through my mind as I read your watermelon story. I know the stereotypes around watermelon, fried chicken, and grape soda, but I can't figure out why they're stereotypes and why they matter. When we travel to the Deep South, I often go in search of local cuisine, which includes grits and, my favorite, collard greens. When in Charleston, we are always sure to make reservations at a restaurant serving Gullah cuisine. From reading up a bit on the cuisine and watching travel and cooking shows (Anthony Bourdain, you are so missed), I know that it often uses simple staples that were plentiful in the region. I will take Gullah food over grilled cheese any day (are grilled cheese sandwiches *white*?).

But I still don't know how a food becomes stereotypically *black*. I had to do a little research here. One site claims that watermelon and fried chicken were both plentiful and cheap, but also food that you could eat with your hands and therefore "dirty." No table manners are necessary.*

Another source informs me that after slavery was abolished, watermelon was a popular crop that free black people ate and sold, and it became a symbol of freedom. Apparently, watermelon is also associated with laziness insofar as it's easy to grow, and you must sit down to eat it. This same source suggests that the watermelon has become a potent symbol of "white people's fear of the emancipated black body."† Whatever that means!

Do most black people know the history of watermelon? This history is certainly new to me, and it is disgraceful how in a quest for dominance, food was twisted into another hierarchical symbol. Or is it just a negative, ahistorical trope, and therefore high-profile black executives, like your acquaintance, do not want to be associated with something considered low class?

As I try to put myself in the shoes of your lunch companion, I'm torn with these new revelations. There are many negative depictions throughout history that have reified the watermelon trope, including paintings and pictures in local papers with caricatures of black people enjoying watermelon. Although my family doesn't come from the Deep South (most Texans don't consider themselves Southerners . . . we're Texans, dammit!), I can tell you that we enjoy watermelon at almost all summer celebrations, and no one in my family ever suggested that the fruit was tied to skin color. Instead, we comment on the crop and rank the sweetness and color.

If I grew up in a place where I had been exposed to these old images, I could see how I might, even unconsciously, be resistant to unveiling my love of the fruit in a swanky joint in San Diego. I can only speak for myself, but I would venture to say that many white Americans who do not have ties to the Deep South or who are part of a younger generation where those images have faded into nonexistence outside of obscure books in a university library, have no idea of the symbolism.

---

* See Gene Demby, "Where Did That Fried Chicken Stereotype Come From?" *NPR*, May 22, 2013, www.npr.org/sections/codeswitch/2013/05/22/186087397/where-did-that-fried-chicken-stereotype-come-from.

† See William R. Black, "How Watermelons Became a Racist Trope," *Atlantic*, December 8, 2014, www.theatlantic.com/national/archive/2014/12/how-watermelons-became-a-racist-trope/383529/.

Perhaps that is why IKEA found itself in hot water after introducing watermelon and fried chicken on its menu in celebration of Juneteenth.* I'm guessing that whoever made this fateful decision was unaware of the insult. After my research, I understand the insult, but I gravely doubt that any corporation, whose primary objective is to keep their cash registers humming, would have knowingly made such a snafu. Ah, but you know what they say these days, intention doesn't matter . . . Repent, repent, repent.

It is possible that even many black people wouldn't have recognized the insult, or at least not have felt so outraged, if it wasn't for our constant Hunt for Racism. If the media hadn't brought it to my attention, it would have totally escaped my notice, but then again, my skin color isn't associated with the fruit. In some ways, I think we need to "own" these silly stereotypes. Be the VP who eats watermelon. Take back the power of these caricatures. We allow them to continue to have weight. You do more to crush them when you laugh at them instead of recoiling from them. Dave Chappelle does this well in his famous chicken routine.†

One of the best ways to counter hate is with laughter. We need to be like Wunsiedel, Germany. Wunsiedel, the burial ground of Hitler's deputy, Rudolf Hess, is a popular place for Nazi marches. The townspeople tried to dissuade these visitors through a variety of aggressive tactics before they tried "humorous subversion" to great effect.‡

And you know what? If my friend wants to eat her bowl of over-salted noodles all by herself with a fork, so be it. Or perhaps, instead of trying to change her, I could've used a little humor at the expense of American mores. Or maybe I could've even approached her with curiosity instead of judgment.

No matter how equal or just the world might become, stereotypes will always exist. It is part of human nature to make quick judgments,

---

* See "IKEA Slammed for Serving Friend Chicken, Watermelon to Honor Juneteenth," *WGN9,* June 23, 2021, wgntv.com/news/ikea-slammed-for-serving-fried-chicken-watermelon-to-honor-juneteenth/.

† You can see a clip of Dave Chapelle's routine at "Dave Chappelle Chicken," YouTube video, uploaded by Classon24, February 5, 2007, www.youtube.com/watch?v=wJ4B7G8Rw3Q.

‡ See Moises Valesquez-Manoff, "How to Make Fun of Nazis," *New York Times,* August 17, 2017, www.nytimes.com/2017/08/17/opinion/how-to-make-fun-of-nazis.html.

what Daniel Kahneman calls "thinking fast," which often results in these mental shortcuts.* However, we can decide to flip these stereotypes if we laugh a little.

I leave you with one final thought, or memory. In my diversity-training class, one of the questions on the *white privilege* quiz was something like this: I can easily find the food I like in my grocery store. If you can easily find the food you like, you just might be *privileged*. The trainer told us that he couldn't find the fixings for his collard green recipe in most stores.

I always thought this was a silly statement. Most successful stores cater to their customers and carry the food that those in the community prefer. We once had to consult with Wal-Marts operating in China, where they failed this basic sales strategy, which severely limited their growth. Needless to say, now a Wal-Mart in Chengdu carries different delicacies and merchandise than one in Shanghai. This isn't prejudice—it's just economics. I know when I'm looking for Tajin to make my Mexican micheladas, I must go to the Fiesta grocery store instead of my local HEB, a popular Texas grocery chain. It's a pain in the butt, but I make a mean michelada.

I wonder, if all stores started to regularly carry watermelon and fried chicken, or grits and collard greens, to address this disparity, would there be calls to ban these prejudiced overtures? How about sushi? Oh, the appropriation! Damned if you do, damned if you don't. When we look for prejudice everywhere, we find it, or sometimes we even create it. After my research, I do understand your lunch partner's concerns and was frustrated with the history I found. I think the only solution to overcome this history and the hijacking of the watermelon is to take back control of pernicious clichés with confidence and a smile.

I'm glad you ordered the watermelon.

Jen

---

* Daniel Kahneman, *Thinking Fast and Slow* (New York: Farrar, Straus and Giroux, 2013).

Letter 66

Dear Wink,

When I attended the diversity-training class here in Austin, I had already written a lot about race, but I lacked first-hand experience with this kind of training.* Our trainer handed out a "white privilege" exercise sheet with questions based on Peggy McIntosh's famous essay "White Privilege: Unpacking the Invisible Knapsack," which outlines fifty examples of how white people benefit from the hidden privileges of being white.† The exercise constructed contrived "affinity groups" based on suppositions, caricatures, and stereotypes. I came to the training looking for authenticity. Instead, I found artifice. The white privilege exercise asked us to evaluate how strongly we agreed with statements such as, *I can turn on the television or open the paper and see people of my race widely and positively represented.*

Forget race. You know what arguably the most underrepresented demographic on TV is? Women over fifty.‡

---

* To read more correspondence on race, visit the *Truth in Between* page on *Medium,* medium.com/truth-in-between/letters-a-correspondence/home.

† For more on this, see Peggy McIntosh, "White Privilege: Unpacking the Invisible Knapsack," *Peace and Freedom Magazine* (July/August 1989): 10–12, available at nationalseedproject.org/Key-SEED-Texts/white-privilege-unpacking-the-invisible-knapsack.

‡ Eric Deggans, "More Evidence TV Doesn't Reflect Real Life Diversity," *NPR,* December 4, 2020, www.npr.org/2020/12/04/942574850/more-evidence-tv-doesnt-reflect-real-life-diversity.

Another one of the statements we were asked to consider was, *I can criticize our government and talk about how much I fear its policies and behavior without being seen as a racial outsider.*

Criticizing the government is a multiracial pastime. Half the country criticized the Trump administration day in and day out, and now the other half will criticize the Biden administration. Think about the number of monuments and symbols of the American past that have been illegally destroyed over the past few years with few repercussions, including those featuring abolitionists.* In the case of Trump, the only people who might rightly have been considered "racial outsiders" were those racial minorities who openly prasied him! Fear of the U.S. government does not seem paramount among non-white or even white people these days. It is a somewhat racially agnostic affair.

And yet, as a white woman living in Austin, I am afraid to be honest about what governmental policies and behaviors mean to me. I fear the disdain of family and friends, the loss of employment opportunities, and backlash from the woke, and I believe that my personal life experiences count for nothing in their minds. I cannot openly criticize current events or talk about how much I fear proposed policies without being seen as a racial outsider. Although I cannot today offer proof that I have experienced discrimination, I will say that several employers who seemed interested in my experience later gave me the cold shoulder. Of course, they wouldn't say it is because of things I might have written, but I can't help but wonder. This is particularly true given that my area of expertise—geopolitics, intelligence, and Asia—is not entirely common in Middle America, so when I get passed over for something rare but squarely in my wheelhouse in Austin, Texas, without even a letter of consideration, my mind can't help but consider the implications of my public persona and writings. I don't know. Maybe I'm just oversensitive and underqualified . . . all possible explanations as well, but I remain curious, nonetheless.

Anyways, after finishing the "white privilege" exercise, participants were told, very dramatically, to line up without speaking in order of our scores, which were held like placards across our chests. After years of

---

* For example, see Rob Tornoe, "Photos of Defaced Statue of Philly Abolitionist Matthias Baldwin Go Viral," *Philadelphia Inquirer,* June 12, 2020, www.inquirer.com/news/philadelphia-protests-matthias-baldwin-statue-abolitionist-twitter-photos-20200612.html.

studying the Chinese Cultural Revolution, which was premised on public struggle sessions and shaming, this felt oddly familiar. People were then segregated into "affinity groups" based on their scores. I was marched off with a group of other pale faces, similarly tainted by *privilege*. Approximately 80 percent of the participants were white. The handful of people of color in attendance assembled at tables with those of a similar shade.

I was forced into a group with whom I felt little personal affinity. Our trainer instructed us to characterize whiteness. My fellow pale-skinned group members worked hard to surpass each other in descriptions of the evils of our race, ranging from rape and violence to capitalism and civility (classified as sinful). Even time is measured differently for black and white people, we were told. According to the facilitator, black people "bend" toward white society when punctual (an unsupported claim that even the Smithsonian recently made in its chart on "whiteness," which they took down following extensive criticism of its fallacious propositions and stereotypes.*)

When the facilitator asked for divergent viewpoints, I raised my hand. Several of the previous white speakers had tearfully signaled their sorrow at their *privilege*. I questioned some of their stereotypes and assumptions, especially the idea that all relationships and interactions are based solely on race and power. This did not go down well.

After the recitation of our "white sins," the facilitator—a darker-skinned, half-black, half-German gentleman in Kente cloth and African jewelry—highlighted several other racial differences. For example, he claimed that only black people like rap. When a black person turns down her rap music, she is bending to white society. If a white person likes rap, it's cultural appropriation. The facilitator played John Denver for the white folks, assuming that that is the kind of music we like. (Truth be told, I'm a big fan of Denver's "Country Roads," which was on a loop in a bar on a small island in Thailand where I spent some time, and we never failed to belt it out night after night as we reminisced on our travels over Mai-Tais. But when I'm pushing through a grueling workout, DMX's "Ruff Ryders' Anthem" sees me through.)

---

* To read more, see Valerie Richardson, "African American Museum Removes 'Whiteness' Chart over Claims of Backhanded Racism," *Washington Times,* July 17, 2020, www.washingtontimes.com/news/2020/jul/17/smithsonian-african-american-museum-remove-whitene/.

One of the statements we were expected to agree with in the "white privilege" exercise was *I am never asked to speak for all of the people of my racial group*. Yet many people in the training did just that. *Blacks do this; whites do that. Blacks like this; whites like that.* Everything was expressed in this tedious monochrome. Everything was about segregation and safe spaces.

The justice promoted by these affinity groups, as Irshad Manji has remarked, is more like "just-us"—a *just-us* that has devolved into empty slogans and caricatures. You are against us, or you are with us. Rich, varied histories are reduced to a single narrative of oppression.

This *just-us* is the new *Plessy v. Ferguson*, an enforced distance and disconnection based on dogmatic essentialist ideas about race.[*] Diversity trainers would view us only in black and white. Isn't that how racists see the world?

Jen

---

* W. F. Twyman, Jr., "The New Plessy," *Truth in Between* (blog), *Medium,* October 10, 2020, medium.com/truth-in-between/the-new-plessy-40edf6088aa9.

Letter 67

Jen,

Ironically, diversity training in the United States creates the opposite of genuine affinity between Americans. In the real world, two individuals may have nothing to talk about until they grow to know one another, as we have. We have both learned more about who we are by talking to one another. A deep acceptance of one another has developed, which comes from our common interests and our common desire to improve ideas about race in America. None of this would be notable—save for the fact that we come from two different ethnic groups, a fact that seems to mean everything to diversity trainers.

Growing up, my social world was all black. I attended the all-black Ebenezer African Methodist Episcopal (AME) church, founded by my paternal great-great-grandfather Daniel Brown around 1871. Only black barbers cut my hair, and only black teachers and classmates surrounded me until the third grade. And as I've shared, 1969 was a pivotal year for my classmates and me. It was our Rubicon. It was our finest hour. We were now attending schools no longer segregated by race. Turning segregated buildings into a home for all. Where are the great novels, the great works of literature for my generation? These were epic times, heroic moments for little kids. I never see myself on the silver screen or in novels.

The first time someone told me that my conscious affinity should be based on race was in the seventh grade of junior high school. A new black student, a transplant from a City of Richmond public school, noticed that black students were fairly evenly dispersed throughout the common areas at lunchtimes. Kids sat with friends based on common interests such as sports or intellectual jockeying. At the time, there were thirty-seven black students out of a student body of roughly one thousand. The new black student came to my junior high school from an inner-city public school system that was 82 percent black.

I was surprised by his suggestion that black students should sit with other black students. After trying this out for a couple of days, I got bored. I was in the intellectual group and missed the conversations with those who had an affinity for student council politics. There was no reason to continue eating at the black table.

That was my first, but not my last, experience with affinity groups.

In college, I joined the Black Students Association. The group seemed easy to join and allowed me to do some tutoring at the Luther P. Jackson house and gain important extracurricular experience that I could cite on my law school applications. I enjoyed tutoring students in writing and hanging around notables like Larry Wilder, son of future Virginia Governor L. Douglas Wilder. I never felt that I had to suppress my own ideas or opinions. In the early 1980s, the culture and consciousness of black affinity groups were such that one could disagree without being viewed as disagreeable.

In law school, I joined the Black Law Students Association just because it seemed like the thing to do. Was there an affinity among us? Yes, since we were all driven by uplift among the black Harvard Law School community. However, I found myself with two Jewish roommates, living in a two-story wood frame house in a pleasant 1 percent black neighborhood in Arlington, Massachusetts. As with my roommate experience at the University of Virginia, an affinity developed that had no bearing on race. Arlington reminded me of my hometown.

After law school, the next black affinity group I joined was the Congressional Black Associates (CBA), a junior league counterpoint to the Congressional Black Caucus. I was working on Capitol Hill for a member of Congress. The CBA enabled me to show my solidarity with other black congressional staffers and expand my circle of friends on Capitol Hill.

And finally, upon moving to San Diego, I became involved in the Earl B. Gilliam Bar Association. I was motivated primarily by the need to increase the number of black judges on the bench, to provide steward-ship of the neighborhood law school held at a local black church, and to promote activism that would increase the number of dollars flowing into black businesses.

Then, in the 1990s and 2000s, as Critical Race Theory (CRT) in-creasingly captured the interest of black law professors, my empathy for affinity groups waned. The advent of CRT meant disagreement was sup-pressed and repressed. While I was open to racial affinity groups, these groups still had to align with my intellectual interests. Otherwise, mem-bership was just dishonesty. Now, *affinity groups* stifle dissent and intel-lectual curiosity and place an unwarranted emphasis on policing thought as opposed to hunting for truth.

I'll give an early example: I attended a conference for law professors of color in Boulder, Colorado, in the mid-1990s. I was working as a law professor at the time. In one session, thirty minority professors were dis-cussing the Civil Rights Movement and Critical Race Theory. I felt that they were failing to acknowledge the wide range of black thought in the 1960s. I raised my hand and suggested that the Negro college presidents of the 1960s were often conservative and leery of political activism, as they wanted to protect black institutions from unintended consequenc-es. (In the 1950s and 1960s, black people used the term "Negro" as an expression of racial pride—see Dr. Martin Luther King, Jr.'s "I Have A Dream" speech.) The room fell silent, and people glared at me as if I had released a foul odor—just because I had mentioned a historical truth that contradicted CRT. This was one of many such occasions. Eventually, the gap between ideology and reality became too great for me to swear fidelity to any group based on race.

This gap has become even more evident in contemporary diversity training.

So, let's choose civil disobedience. Let's choose genuine affinity. Clearly, we have plenty to talk about.

Wink

Letter 68

Dear Wink,

I like to think of myself as an intellectual, but I have a confession to make; I would rather read Stephen King any day over the work of, say, Ernest Hemingway. In high school, rather than reading *The Great Gatsby* or *Jane Eyre* in my AP English class, I would buy the CliffsNotes that would enable me to write my assignments passably. Truth be told, in retrospect, I'm a little ashamed that I didn't take these literary giants more seriously. Great literature is a window into our culture that ultimately promotes critical thinking and dialogue. But I'm a dreamer, and the fantasy worlds of C. S. Lewis and J. K. Rowling are where my mind would wander with the centaur and the elusive unicorn.

This somewhat anti-intellectual mindset changed for me in college when I was introduced to "scar literature." That's what they call the thousands of books written after the Chinese Cultural Revolution that depict the heinous crimes against humanity under Mao Zedong. I devoured these books in my China studies. The horrors and the torments were so unreal; if only they were fantasy, but alas . . . sometimes truth really is stranger than fiction.

In Mao's effort to completely destroy any vestiges of the "old culture" and replace it with his egalitarian, communist vision, Mao established the Red Guards—a corps of ordinary young citizens committed to rooting out any hints of bourgeoisie influence (1966–1976).

The first targets of the Cultural Revolution consisted mainly of the wealthy and former landlords whose property had been stripped in Mao's land-reform campaigns shortly after he came to power (1949). Targets soon broadened to include anyone who had ancestors who had been landlords or wealthy. Then came the intellectuals, who had already been cowed into silence following the Anti-Rightest Campaign (1957–1959), which cracked down on those who had accepted the invitation to speak openly about the Chinese Communist Party during the Hundred Flowers Campaign (1956), and the teachers. Those who had taught English (very bougie) were condemned and shamed, among so many others. If you used to teach or even work in any capacity under the previous Guomindang government, you had to be very careful how you navigated this new landscape. All individuals with previous ties to the *old* ways were hunted as *imperialist running dogs*.

Schools and universities were closed. Young Red Guards ruled the streets and began to grab power from local governments, setting up their own Revolutionary Committees. Different Red Guard corps would compete to see who was the most *red*, often turning in family members and friends under false pretenses in public displays of loyalty to the Great Leader. And then the competition turned in on itself, and competing red brigades would rise and fall with just a few words. No one was safe. Even Mao had little power over the resulting chaos. According to best estimates, upward of 20 million people were killed and 100 million were persecuted.

Perhaps the saying is true that history tends to repeat itself when we don't learn the lessons of our past. Lately, I've seen people from both the left and the right cite Pastor Martin Niemoller's poem about the role of silent complicity in the rise of Nazism when discussing the current socio-political climate in the United States:

> First they came for the Communists
> And I did not speak out
> Because I was not a Communist
> Then they came for the Socialists
> And I did not speak out
> Because I was not a Socialist
> Then they came for the trade unionists
> And I did not speak out
> Because I was not a trade unionist

Then they came for the Jews
And I did not speak out
Because I was not a Jew
Then they came for me
And there was no one left
To speak out for me

The left calls upon Niemoller to reference the rise and rhetoric of the extreme right, the rolling back of legislation protecting the environment, transgender people, and abortion, and, as many claim, the use of misogynist and racist language that does not embolden the "better angels of our nature." In turn, the right applies this poem when criticizing the left's selective application of freedom of speech, enforcement of uniformity in information and thought, and patrolling of language to ensure compliance with new terminology, as seen most often in what is called *cancel culture.*[*]

I guess there is some common ground between those on the left and right who invoke the same shibboleth to proselytize to their bases. It is right for all of us, regardless of ideology, to be afraid. Who's next?

The other recent invocation to explain the culture wars has been Orwellian. As proclaimed in *1984*:

> Every record has been destroyed or falsified, every book rewritten, every picture has been repainted, every statue and street building has been renamed, every date has been altered. And the process is continuing day by day and minute by minute. History has stopped. Nothing exists except an endless present in which the Party is always right.
>
> Don't you see that the whole aim of Newspeak is to narrow the range of thought? In the end we shall make thoughtcrime literally impossible, because there will be no words in which to express it.
>
> And if all others accepted the lie which the Party imposed—if all records told the same tale—then the lie passed into history and became truth.

With all the swirling information in mainstream media and opinion masquerading as fact in social media, truth has been devalued. Instead,

---

* Zachary Evans and John Loftus, "The Cancel Counter: Thousands Sign Petition to Remove Walt Whitman Statue from Rutgers," *National Review,* June 19, 2020, www.nationalreview.com/news/the-cancel-counter/.

we elevate narratives that buttress our own party's claim to power and position in the ensuing culture war, sacrificing verity on the altar of a purported moral authority.

The competition for setting the parameters on truth has become an all-out battle in a new Cultural Revolution.

The revolution seemed to have started with Confederate statues and the renaming of buildings and streets with Confederate names. I was okay with that, as you already know. After all, many of these statues were erected during the Jim Crow era, not after the Civil War, in what amounted to a snub at civil rights. We should be careful not to erase history (lest we forget), but these statues could be relegated to a history museum. Fine by me.

But we will never get away from our slaveholder past. We can't erase history. Nor does it seem that we want to as we increase the educational resources available to review this history. (The 1619 Project in schools is a good example.)

And yet, we have started to censor history that is uncomfortable or in any way exhibits the inequities of the past. *Gone with the Wind.* Gone.[*] Nancy Green, aka Aunt Jemima, was born a slave and became a powerful advocate for equal rights. Gone.[†] *Paw Patrol*, a cartoon show with a German shepherd police character that depicted police in a positive light. Gone.[‡] *Live PD*, a popular show that followed police live on patrol (isn't some level of public transparency a good thing . . . ?). Gone.[§]

There have been discussions on whether or not to remove the Washington Monument and Jefferson Memorial in Washington, D.C. Anything that memorializes those who participated in slavery, including the

---

[*] Frank Pallotta, "'Gone with the Wind' Pulled from HBO Max until It Can Return with 'Historical Context,'" *CNN*, June 10, 2020, www.cnn.com/2020/06/10/media/gone-with-the-wind-hbo-max/index.html.

[†] Ben Kesslen, "Aunt Jemima Brand to Change Name, Remove Image That Quaker Says Is 'Based on a Racial Stereotype,'" *NBC News*, June 17, 2020, www.nbcnews.com/news/us-news/aunt-jemima-brand-will-change-name-remove-image-quaker-says-n1231260.

[‡] Amanda Hess, "The Protests Come for 'Paw Patrol,'" *New York Times*, June 10, 2020, www.nytimes.com/2020/06/10/arts/television/protests-fictional-cops.html.

[§] Nellie Andreeva, "'Live PD' Canceled by A&E Amid Ongoing Protests Against Police Brutality," *Deadline*, June 10, 2020, deadline.com/2020/06/live-pd-canceled-ae-protests-against-police-brutality-george-floyd-1202956175/.

Founding Fathers, should be written out of history. Stating that their ideas of freedom belong to everyone and that the slow march of history is finally allowing their principles to be fully realized is a dangerous exercise, especially if one is white. As is questioning the dogma of antiracism unless you want to be labeled a *racist.*

And *privileged.* And *fragile.* And . . .

And maybe these things all could be true, or not, but engaging in critical dialogue and discussion to assess the truth succumbs to the circular argument that any questioning of the dogma confirms *racism, privilege,* and *fragility* (this is particularly true in the popularized and flawed reasoning in Robin D'Angelo's *White Fragility*). Critical thought is silenced. As author Saul Bellow laments in *There Is Simply Too Much to Think About,* "Their taste for packaged opinion stemmed from their desire to be approved by their peers. The right sort of thinking makes social intercourse smoother. The wrong sort exposes you to the accusations of insensitivity, misogyny, and perhaps worst of all, racism."

Those who dare to question the opinion of the masses are canceled and sometimes fired.* Examples in the past few years include a professor from UCLA who was placed on leave for not canceling an exam after the George Floyd protests erupted.† The calls for a professor at the University of Chicago to be fired as the editor of the *Journal of Political Economy* for criticizing the BLM movement.‡ The data scientist who was fired from his job for tweeting an article from an African American scholar that questioned the efficacy of the riots.§ The call to fire a *New York Times* writer for daring to mention the "civil war" within the paper among

---

* Uri Harris, "How Activists Took Control of a University: The Case Study of Evergreen State," *Quillette,* December 18, 2017, quillette.com/2017/12/18/activists-took-control-university-case-study-evergreen-state/.

† "UCLA Professor on Leave After Students Blast Response to Request to Postpone Final Exam as 'Woefully Racist,'" *CBS Los Angeles,* June 10, 2020, losangeles.cbslocal.com/2020/06/10/ucla-professor-on-leave-gordon-klein/.

‡ Gregg Re, "Paul Krugman, Professors Seek Top Economist's Removal from Influential Job for Criticizing Black Lives Matter," *FOX News,* June 3, 2021, www.foxnews.com/politics/paul-krugman-professors-demand-top-economist-lose-his-job-for-criticizing-black-lives-matter.

§ See Lee Fang (@lhfang), *Twitter,* June 11, 2020, twitter.com/lhfang/status/1271166899666079744?lang=en.

progressives, sparking collective outrage.* The Oklahoma State football coach who was forced to apologize for a T-shirt he wore with the logo of a conservative news outlet that has criticized BLM.† The New Orleans Saints quarterback who was also forced to apologize for his comments in support of standing for the American flag.‡ And the stepmother of Garrett Rolfe, the officer charged in the death of Rayshard Brooks, who lost her job as a result of her family ties—guilt by association.§

Not willing to speak publicly and openly for fear of such an outcome, a Berkeley professor penned an anonymous letter of concern—concern that the current discussions around race actually strip agency from black Americans, which in many ways ensures that a new form of mental slavery continues, wrapped in cloaks and conical hats of groupthink.¶ AmeriKKKa indeed. We often hear that *white silence = violence*. In truth, contrarian opinions that could empower black lives over and above empty slogans and ultimately lessen violence get silenced.

Ah, to be a contrarian. Debate is as democratic an ideal as liberty or freedom. It is only in debate and discussion, and not always so civil, that our country was founded. Yes, yes. Founded for the white man. But those ideals and our contrarian nature have expanded and continue to expand, giving rise to powerful voices across the color spectrum. In order to keep the momentum, we cannot silence or censor the discomfort. I care too

---

* Tabarovsky, "American Soviet Mentality." See also the *Hold my Drink Podcast,* episode 28, "The American Soviet Mentality."

† Andrea Adleson, "Oklahoma State's Mike Gundy Apologizes of 'Pain, Discomfort' Caused," *ESPN,* June 16, 2020, www.espn.com/college-football/story/_/id/29319943/oklahoma-state-mike-gundy-apologizes-pain-discomfort-caused.

‡ Ben Morse, "Drew Brees Issues Apology for 'Insenstive' Comments," *CNN,* June 4, 2020, www.cnn.com/2020/06/04/sport/drew-brees-apology-nfl-spt-intl/index.html.

§ Mollie Mansfield, "'NO LONGER FELT COMFORTABLE' Melissa Rolfe, Stepmom of Cop Who Shot Rayshard Brooks, Fired from Mortgage Company's HR Dept for 'Hostile' Environment," *Sun,* June 19, 2020, www.the-sun.com/news/1010085/melissa-rolfe-stepmom-rayshard-brooks-fired-mortgage-company/.

¶ Wilfred Reilly (@wil_da_beast630), *Twitter,* June 12, 2020, twitter.com/wil_da_beast630/status/1271301272491171840?ref_src=twsrc%5Etfw%7Ctwcamp%5Etweetembed%7Ctwterm%5E1271301272491171840&ref_url=https%3A%2F%2Fwww.zerohedge.com%2Fpolitical%2Fanonymous-berkeley-professor-shreds-blm-injustice-narrative-damning-stats-and-logic.

much about getting this right—liberty and justice for all—to be silent on a worrisome and recognizable trend. A trend that has us careening toward our own Cultural Revolution premised on the destruction of the old instead of the construction of the new. Intent on collective victimization instead of individual uplift. Intent on silencing dissent instead of inviting constructive engagement and disagreement.

As former U.S. Vice President Hubert H. Humphrey said, "Freedom is hammered out on the anvil of discussion, dissent and debate."

But what does an old, dead white man know?

Cultural Revolution, baby. Who's next?

To the coming of a better time,

Jen

Letter 69

Dear Jen,

I'm listening to "Mandolin Rain" by Bruce Hornsby and the Range. This song has become my go-to song for uplift and peaceful feelings. Did you know that Hornsby grew up in Virginia? He attended the University of Richmond for a year, and his big brother was at the University of Virginia before me, and they would perform together there. Hornsby is white, but something deeper binds me to the man and his music. There is something about having grown up in Virginia that binds me to other Virginian men of a certain age, regardless of race.

When Hornsby and I grew up, reminders of the Confederacy were ubiquitous. There was a statue of a Confederate soldier standing tall at the County Courthouse. As a kid, I would ride my bicycle up Jefferson Davis Highway to Fort Darling at Drewy's Bluff. Fort Darling was a Confederate encampment that had prevented Union warships from storming up the James River to capture the Capital of the Confederacy. I recall a field trip to the White House of the Confederacy. And the statue of my fourth cousin three times removed, Robert E. Lee, stood on Monument Avenue. I had classmates and friends whose ancestors fought under Bobby Lee's command.

This was part of my growing up. It was a part of everyone's growing up in and around Richmond in the 1960s and the 1970s.

How do I feel about the Cultural Revolution, starting with Confederate statutes and the renaming of buildings and streets with Confederate names? It seems so Taliban to me. The history we have is the history we have. Why don't we spend those energies showcasing activism or encouraging intelligent nieces and nephews to be ambitious and self-confident in life? Why not focus on rebuilding *Black Enterprise* magazine to a North Star once again for the best enterprise and aspiration? Why this low-brow hunt for offending Confederate statues? Do these things really matter in terms of greater achievement?

I often wonder if black people of my age and older really focus on these things to the exclusion of higher education, deferred gratification, and institution building. Destroying monuments feels fake to me. I get far more of a good feeling looking at the black-and-white picture of Manning Funeral and Cremation Services, a solid third-generation black business serving families since 1941. Defacing the Robert E. Lee statue on Monument Avenue in downtown Richmond, Virginia? That leaves me empty and feels like young white woke kids are attempting to save black people, and it seems phony.

They are also coming for a street name that has been a part of my memory and my dad's memory for probably a century. When we said "Jeff Davis" or "Jefferson Davis Highway," the street name was devoid of rebel meaning. The words were just a familiar name, a reference point grandma would have used to drive to a distant cousin's home. Isn't it odd to think that black people might reconceptualize names to imbue them with a different sense and meaning? In other words, the black people I grew up around had the fortitude and mental strength to imbue words with their own meaning. My people were "based."* But I understand the mob's need to cleanse the name of the President of the Confederacy from a public state highway. The name honors a traitor to the United States of America and needlessly offends in the modern day and age. I'm not going to be fighting to save the name.

Regarding the rest, I'm not advocating for Confederate memorials, the statue of Cousin Bobby notwithstanding ... But I am advocating for a legal process—a serious deliberation before removing names and destroying public art and replacing them with God knows what. I saw this statue on Monument Avenue in Richmond, Virginia, that remind-

---

* The hip-hop philosopher Lil B, in a 2010 *Complex* magazine interview, defined "based" as "Being yourself. Not being scared of what people think about you. Not being afraid to do what you wanna do." This describes the descendants of Daniel Brown well.

ed me of the predator from the movie *Predator*. Why create a statue of a dreadlocked predator-looking dude that most generations of black Richmonders would have found embarrassing? Why not a monument to black individuals of achievement and resilience? It seems the lowest common denominator is glorified.

So, we disagree on this point. You are fine with the destruction of the Confederate past in all its public manifestations. I see how these street names and statues just became backdrops for lived life, and their destruction destroys relics of black life—black life just in the sense that these places and things were markers for life and suggested an integration of our racial past in Central Virginia. What is more emblematic of the New South in the 1970s than a little black kid riding his bicycle up Jeff Davis Highway to see a Confederate fort on the James River and his white friend, a descendant of a Confederate soldier, attending a black church for Sunday service with the Key Club? I am reminded of Forrest Gump attending a black church in Greenbow, Alabama. There are echoes of the television show *In the Heat of the Night* set in Sparta, Mississippi, where a black detective had a picture of Dr. Martin Luther King, Jr., on his wall and the police chief had a picture of Robert E. Lee on his wall—a united police force and no sidestepping of history. Fort Lee was just a military base, nothing more. To know one another is to have an integrated past. To destroy the past just breeds resentment and grudges and distance between blacks and whites.

Am I making sense as I suggest something is lost *in black memory* when Confederate statues and street names are removed? Isn't it ridiculous to attempt to erase the Confederacy from the South? Our energies are better spent *erecting* monuments and street names throughout the South to Walter White, John Hope, John Mercer Langston, Governor P. B. S. Pinchback, Jean Toomer, Senator Blanche K. Bruce, George Shrewsbury, James Mitchell, Oliver Hill, Thurgood Marshall, Spottswood Robinson, etc., etc.

Even better, let's shame smart, poor teenagers into choosing the Governor's School for the Gifted or a private boarding school over an underperforming public school. That's the long game John Mercer Langston, Oliver Hill, and the founding father of Manning Funeral and Cremation Services would have applauded.

My cousin, Nathan Twyman, likes that I resist understanding the human condition through filters created by someone else. I feel the forces at work behind the removal of Confederate statues and street names are a resurrection of McCarthyism.

What do I mean?

Beginning in roughly 1950, there was a strong drive to ferret and censor communist thought in the United States. A series of loyalty reviews were instituted so as to ensure no wrong-thinking communists infiltrated the highest level of government. The aim was good, but, as with all things, the good aspirations were weaponized into something more sinister, into communist-hunting investigations. Now, to my mind, part of what makes America great is the ability to disagree without being disagreeable. We need the freedom to express our thoughts, come win, lose, or draw.

The more I read about the ups and downs of our recent cultural landscape, the more echoes I hear of the McCarthy era. You might recall the Salem witch trials and mass hysteria about witchcraft. We can laugh about it now, but at the time, everyone in Salem, Massachusetts, lived in fear of being pointed out as a witch. There was no reasoning with the accusatory mob, which must have scared the beejesus out of everyone in town, from the governor down to the lowest indentured servant and slave. It was the unthinking fear that echoed again in public during the McCarthy era.

The mere accusation of being a communist was crushing. It is difficult to know the exact number of victims, but more than three hundred actors, authors, and directors were blacklisted due to the mere suspicion of being a communist or a communist sympathizer. Among the talented people effectively "blacklisted" or "canceled" were Lucille Ball, Leonard Bernstein, Charlie Chaplin, W. E. B. DuBois, Langston Hughes, Lena Horne, Arthur Miller, Paul Robeson, and Orson Welles. If these rich and powerful people could be blacklisted and put out of work, what hope was there for the lowly government clerk?

And so, Americans lived in uneasy fear between 1950 and 1954.

As you intimated, professors who should be some of the bravest folks on the planet are cowed into silence (but I thought *white silence = violence*? I'm so confused). Professors who think wrong thoughts in the face of slogans like *Black Lives Matter*, *white fragility*, and *systemic racism* are silenced in an odd Orwellian twist. Silence for thee but not for me!

As I review the McCarthy era of suppression, I can easily lift the most eloquent voices of reason and clear thinking into our time. President Truman said, "In a free country, we punish men for the crimes they commit, but never for the opinions they have." Those words should be offered today in the public square. Maybe I will do so.

In defining McCarthyism for the ages, Truman described the movement as "The corruption of truth . . . the use of the big lie . . . the rise to power of the demagogue who lives on untruth. . . It is the spreading of fear and the destruction of faith in every level of society." Does this describe the stranglehold of Black Lives Matter and woke doctrine today? I think it might. (Digression and not relevant to anything, but my three children are distant cousins of President Harry S. Truman.)

Imagine if we had a public leader with the vision and courage to speak against character assassinations and proclaim for the ages that the basic principles of Americanism are the right to criticize, the right to hold unpopular beliefs, the right to protest, and the right of independent thought. See Senator Margaret Chase Smith (R-Maine) in her speech "Declaration of Conscience."[*]

The need for leadership in the wake of the resurrection of McCarthyism is compelling. My cousin Elizabeth Twyman Anderson recently expressed a desire for someone to articulate a Sense of America. I tried to do so two weeks ago in a private communication, but I don't have the chops.

Perhaps we should look to our past. How did real patriots who cared about their country speak out against McCarthyism? The record is fertile with positions and statements that speak to a Sense of America.

For example, we can just as easily apply news reporter Elmer Davis's words about McCarthyism to the excesses of antiracism: "a general attack not only on schools and colleges and libraries, on teachers and textbooks, but on all people who think and write . . . in short, on the freedom of the mind."[†]

Let's also tap into the judicial wisdom of U.S. Supreme Court Justice

---

[*] "Not Afraid to Call Selfish Political Opportunism What It Is," Emersonkent.com, www.emersonkent.com/speeches/declaration_of_conscience.htm.

[†] Richard M. Fried, *Nightmare in Red: The McCarthy Era in Perspective* (New York: Oxford University Press, 1990), 29.

304 • LETTERS IN BLACK AND WHITE

William O. Douglas as he penned his powerful dissent against McCarthyism: "Guilt by association is repugnant to our society. . . . What happens under this law is typical of what happens in a police state. Teachers are under constant surveillance; their pasts are combed for signs of disloyalty; their utterances are watched for clues to dangerous thoughts."[*]

That's the judicial leadership needed in today's world of a weaponized Black Lives Matter.

Where is the broadcast journalist with the integrity and courage of Edward R. Morrow to speak what needs to be said on the airwaves: "We must not confuse dissent with disloyalty. We must always remember that accusation is not proof, and that conviction depends upon evidence and due process of law. We will not walk in fear, one of another. We will not be driven by fear into an age of unreason if we dig deep in our history and our doctrine and remember that we are not descended from fearful men."[†]

I don't know about you, but brave men run in my family, and they would be sickened by cowardice. George Twyman I, George Twyman II, George Twyman III, Richard Henry Lee, Robert E. Lee, landowner Daniel Brown, landowner Robert Daniel Brown, James Twyman (1781–1849), James Scott Twyman, Robert Daniel Twyman—all men of character who cared more about tomorrow than today. Where are public figures who speak to destiny today?

In closing, I write you out of an undying faith in the coming of a better time. The resurrection of McCarthyism will come to an end when the woke overplay their hand and public opinion turns increasingly negative. We are not there yet, but if victims of cancel culture start to sue and win damages, that might break the fever of the mob—modern-day pursuers of witches and communist sympathizers.

To the coming of a better time,

Wink

---

[*] Albert Fried, *McCarthyism, The Great American Red Scare: A Documentary History* (New York: Oxford University Press, 1996), 114.

[†] "See It Now: A Report on Senator Joseph R. McCarthy (transcript)," *CBS-TV,* March 9, 1954 (archived from the original on November 10, 2015).

Letter 70

Dear Jen,

Let me start this letter with a quote from George Orwell's book, *1984*: "Don't you see that the whole aim of Newspeak is to narrow the range of thought? In the end we shall make thoughtcrime literally impossible, because there will be no words in which to express it."

It has been said that democracy dies in darkness.

It is equally true that free speech suffocates as slogans constrict the free exchange of ideas and thoughts in the public square. Frederick Douglass knew this suffocation of speech in his abolition work: "To suppress free speech is a double wrong. It violates the rights of the hearer as well as those of the speaker."[*]

We must be aware of the insidious way that slogans and slogan words are weaponized. They are often used in an attempt to diminish the rights of the hearer and the speaker, including the critical inquiry necessary to keep the beacon of liberalism alight. Pithy and simple, a slogan is a cleverly crafted word or phrase, oftentimes three words to five words in length, which evokes an emotional response in the listener and the reader. The phrase is sufficiently vague and ambiguous so that any objection places the discerning listener and reader on the defensive as lacking compassion and empathy. Why would anyone oppose *Power to the People*? Who could oppose *Black Lives Matter* in good faith? *No Justice No Peace* sounds reasonable. *Check Your Privilege* is a trite, mean-

---

* Frederick Douglass, *A Plea for Free Speech in Boston*, 1860.

ingless phrase in that all individuals can dredge up some dimension of privilege. *White Silence Is Violence* is self-evident, right? *Let a Hundred Flowers Bloom* was a wonderful Chinese slogan (until, as you note, those who accepted the invitation to speak were identified and denounced or worse). Those who create slogans are deliberate in their machinations, channeling the thoughts of others toward a desired end. Slogans are not the consequence of a search for meaning, for purpose. Slogans are the intentional creations of a hunt for power and dominance.

And so, when one reads powerful essays backed by powerful interests, as with the *New York Times'* 1619 Project, on the need to "reframe American history," what does this mean? No reasonable person would dismiss black history as American history, rich with a myriad of stories, both of tragedy and triumph.

The 1619 Project is a wonderful work of literature to the extent it creates a vivid, continuous dream in the mind of the reader. (The best stories set off a vivid and continuous dream, to paraphrase novelist John Gardner.) Stories unfold of the horrors of America's checkered past. The psychological wound from the past is kept alive, but for what purpose? Are we letting the horrors of the past distort our judgment in the present for political gain and profit? In this regard, the 1619 Project functions like a mega-slogan. We are left with the question—is this all to the story of American history? Is black American life only a living embodiment of past American slavery? Does blackness equal American slavery and nothing more? For those who call upon the above-mentioned slogans, the answers to these questions are often self-evident truths.

Each individual black American has their unique life story, experience, and perspective—not to mention personality. Those who shout slogans and slogan words like *power*, *oppression*, and *racism* distort the reality of lived life on the ground. It is as if *Blackness Is All About Oppression. Nothing Else Matters.*

Slogans distort reality.

Our thoughts are shut down when we can only talk about events using pre-approved jargon. Misalignment between words and reality is ever present in a world governed by slogans. A sloganeering writer has an ideological agenda and seeks to impose the use of catchy lingo to assert power and dominance over the reader. The use of language as a weapon of power and dominance may fit under the rules of engagement for free speech, but be warned, anyone who can only see the world via slogans and propaganda is complicit in narrowing our range of thought.

The slogans and slogan words dumbing us down have become overused.* They are drained of meaning. They all lend themselves to different political and ideological definitions, depending upon the whim of the slogan word enforcer. None of these words are nuanced or complex. None of these words are narrowly tailored so as to capture the richness of reality. And, in all fairness, the proponents of these words do not care so much about the nuance and complexity of life. The idea is to bully others into using approved slogan words as a way of understanding the world.

And this bullying simply will not do for me. Nor will bullying do for anyone who cares about freedom of speech, the marketplace of ideas, or concern for a robust exchange of thoughts.

At the heart of the individual is the freedom to choose one's words for communicating and understanding one's place in the world. The world is complex; life is messy. There are over seven billion sentient souls who see the world through their own individual eyes each and every day. Why would it stand to reason that one slogan word would describe all of reality for over seven billion people? The idea is nonsense. What one person might understand as "oppression" another person might understand as a "manifestation of personality" or a "character flaw." It is an individual's human right to decide for oneself how one wishes to see the world.

Slogan words do not welcome this basic human right. Slogan words seek to suffocate the individual's ability to breathe in the world for him or herself. And so, we ask, is there genuine free speech when slogan worlds suffocate the airways of truth?

It is far better to describe the world using three hundred thousand English words than thirty slogan words.

Slogan words reward limited thought. And limited thought has never led to greater freedom and prosperity. Limited thought is the father of repression and the assassin of creativity. As a matter of societal advancement, we should beware of those who would limit thought via the stranglehold of slogans.

---

* Izabella Tabarovsky makes this argument in "What My Soviet Life Has Taught Me About Censorship and Why It Makes Us Dumb," *Areo Magazine,* May 21, 2021, areomagazine.com/2021/05/21/why-censorship-makes-us-dumb-in-soviet-russia-then-and-in-america-today/.

There was a study done to determine whether the number of words heard by children between birth and the age of three made a difference in lifetime academic success. As one would expect, the study found that, yes, it was a good investment to read as many words as possible to babies. Doesn't it stand to reason that the same principle would apply to a country? The more words that are exchanged in the public square, the richer that country's intellectual development, which is to everyone's benefit. Simply put, a country that suffers under the suffocating blanket of slogan words is a country that will regress in its ability to think and reason, to comprehend and to understand the nuance and complexity that is life. The truths in between.

Is there any upside to the widespread adoption of slogan words?

For the conformist, there is much to be said for a set menu of acceptable slogan words. Say *privilege* and *white supremacy*, and one is in the club. The slogan card has been accepted at the faculty lounge and the diversity-training session. Life is easier when all experience can be boiled down to thirty slogan words. Less stress on the cerebellum, you know.

For the resentful and holder of grudges, it is a Golden Age when the tables are turned upside down. They have a straightforward no-work and no-effort opportunity to be made whole. Resources and positions for profit and gain are there for the taking. Want that corner office? Set up a colleague as a *racist*, and the colleague is out the door. The corner office is yours, just like in the Soviet Union of yore. Faithful professions to Mao Zedong's "Little Red Book" can secure advancement.

For the lover of power and dominance, slogan words on behalf of the powerless offer the garb of benevolence. One can shout slogans at "mostly peaceful" protests and enjoy the fruits of one's sloganeering in multimillion-dollar homes. Who will be the wiser? The powerless remain powerless, but it was never about the powerless, was it? It was about the power grab.

The widespread adoption of slogans rewards the inauthentic over the authentic, the ill-fitting word over the truthful word, and the lust for power and dominance over the search for meaning and purpose.

As Soviet dissident Aleksandr Solzhenitsyn reminds us, "You can resolve to live your life with integrity. Let your credo be this: Let the lie come into the world, let it even triumph. But not through me. The simple step of a courageous individual is not to take part in the lie."

Words matter. Choose wisely.

Everyone has a family, and every family is susceptible to slogan words. Once I was in a car traveling home from a pleasant family outing. A relative recounted how, as a babysitter, she passed by a Blue Lives Matter rally. She told the little ones in her charge that those people were *white supremacists*. I was stirred to raise my voice since I reject collective demonization.*

I said it was wrong to stereotype people. Left unsaid was the law enforcement identity of my father-in-law, a proud New York City Police Department officer for years. The relative in question said I did not understand. These people who supported Blue Lives Matter were white supremacists through and through. The conversation deteriorated as the relative became more and more emotional. We stopped speaking to one another for a full week after that incident. I prevented the lie from coming into the world through me, but at what cost? I once asked Professor Wilfred Reilly how to reconcile conflicting visions of race within a black American family. He did not have an answer that satisfied me.

Perhaps, Jen, you will have an answer that will satisfy me.

Wink

---

* Tabarovsky, "The American Soviet Mentality."

Letter 71

Dear Wink,

I greatly appreciate your Solzhenitsyn quote. Not only have we co-opted words, but also symbols.

Let me expand upon your thoughts on slogans by giving a personal story on symbols. This story relates to your experience with the Blue Lives Matter discussion.

I was getting comfortable in my home office when the yelling started. It sounded like it was right outside my door, but everything sounds loud in our community, a popular walking neighborhood. The sounds of the neighborhood are typically ones of carefree carousing. Couples laughing. Dogs barking. Bicycle bells ringing. All often punctuated with the sound of a woodpecker or, more commonly, the coo of a dove. This staccato interruption was an exception, but I was busy and chalked it up as an anomaly and carried on.

A few minutes later and just as I was about to start recording a podcast interview, I heard yelling again. This simply wouldn't do for a recording. Now I had to investigate. I went to the front window to find a white hatchback screeching away as a woman yelled from the car, "People are dying!" That was curious, but there is a mental hospital not too far away and, every now and again, a patient breaches its walls, usually without keys to a car, but I was on a deadline and didn't have time to give it any more attention.

Allow me to rewind for a second before continuing this story. Back in

July 2016, there was an ambush that killed five police officers and wounded nine others in Dallas. On that day, my husband, as you know, a law enforcement officer (LEO) himself, bought a thin blue line flag to honor the fallen.* We have had it hung outside our house, next to our American flag, since then. At this time, under President Obama, the flag was innocuous. A symbol of support as well as respect for fallen LEOs.

Over the past few years, this symbolism shifted.

Almost overnight, the original symbolism was hijacked—by those on both sides of the political spectrum. The extreme right sees it as a symbol of support for the 2017–2021 presidential administration, and the extreme left fashion it as the new "Stars and Bars" (i.e., Confederate flag) and thus a symbol of *racism*. It was a tense four years for our flag. She was stolen (and replaced). She was dumped in our fishpond. She was slashed down her middle. But she remained.

What started as a symbol of respect and mourning for five police officers in Dallas turned into a political symbol. The meaning of the flag did not change for my husband at first, but as the public square turned its anger toward the police, my husband became hardened. Here was a man who, for half of his thirty years of service and counting, protected the streets and the people of a large and violent Southern metropolis—mostly those who had more melanin than himself. He has been stabbed, shot at, and run over, and yet he continues to serve. I will never forget the evening that this man, who is not well-versed in emotion, a drink or two working its way through his stocky frame, said with watery eyes he couldn't understand how the people he vowed to protect now liken him to the vile Ku Klux Klan.

It was like the world turned around and dumped on his lifetime of service in a poorly maintained public restroom where the scat of humanity clogs the drain. He didn't know how to not make it personal. And so, like the rest of the world, he became increasingly angry. The angrier he got, the more the symbol of the flag morphed into one of defiance.

We don't agree on a lot, including the flag. Often our own discussions reflect the heated moment of our current national discourse. But like the flag, we remained. I even had to take a breather after the George Floyd

---

* Manny Fernandez, Richard Perez-Pena, and Jonah Engel Bromwich, "Five Dallas Officers Were Killed as Payback, Police Chief Says," *New York Times,* July 8, 2016, www.nytimes.com/2016/07/09/us/dallas-police-shooting.html.

murder when I suggested that perhaps the flag could use a rest from decorating our porch. I packed up my bags for a mental health holiday and a week with a girlfriend. The perceived betrayal that I saw reflected in his eyes was too much. It was like his one safe harbor was just bulldozed, and I had joined the demolition team.

A few years after the Dallas shooting, but still not to our current bluster, our house was chosen to be featured in our historic neighborhood's annual home tour. We accepted the invitation, but with the caveat that we wouldn't take down our flags. Trump still sat in office, and the flag was by this time overly politicized, but it still hadn't reached the level of stigma that it holds today. The home tour curators shrugged their shoulders, not seeing an issue.

The day of the tour came. Although docents dotted our house to show visitors around, I chose to hang out. I only left for a short time to visit some of the other homes, but my timing was off. While away, *she* came. Accosting the unsuspecting docents, she condemned them for spreading fear in our neighborhood. "I live here too," she proclaimed. Living in a community with a LEO was frightening to her.

It was so frightening to this young, affluent white woman that she decided to lodge a complaint with our neighborhood association, asking for an apology for putting our home on the tour.

And now I circle back to the screaming banshee outside. As professed, I had chalked her up as an escaped mental patient. The next morning, as I headed across my lawn for the first time in twenty-four hours for a highly anticipated brunch, I noticed a collection of trash inside our fence. Trash pick-up was just the day before, and sometimes the wind blows debris that misses its mark into our corner lot. But there was a bit more than normal, so instead of ignoring it until later, I decided to address it immediately. In addition to a collection of cups, an empty wrapper lay under the flag. Picking it up, I noticed it was an empty bag of pork rinds. I normally wouldn't think anything of this either, but aren't pork and police somehow synonymous in some circles?

After our varied flag trespasses, we had installed security cameras for our own safety (never mind that we slept with a fire extinguisher next to our bed and that my husband had to vary his routes home after the George Floyd murder, so those canvassing his office wouldn't discover his personal abode). After a little investigation, we identified the litterer. Now the pieces started to fall into place. Our suspect, as caught on camera, was also the screamer. As I had been sitting inside prepping for a podcast interview with the Executive Director of the Californians for Equal Rights Foundation, we had been attacked for how we expressed our fundamental rights.

Let me get real here for a second. I get it. As a firm proponent of (classical) liberalism, I promote free speech and protest. You can yell at me and my house all day long. You do you. If I was outside, I would've invited this woman into conversation, much like I invited the anonymous home tour protestor into conversation through the association.

But I can't help but wonder, if I had been sitting on the porch as I am now, would this woman have had the courage to scream profanities at my house? Was this a safe space for expressing her daily angst, screaming at a structure? Is this how we dialogue these days?

From the video, she clearly recorded herself and her rant. I use that word deliberately—when you throw trash and scream falsities into the air, that qualifies as a rant. To be fair, people are indeed dying. In 2019 police killed 11 unarmed black men and one female.[*] In the same year, 48 police were killed on duty.[†] And I won't even go into the rising rates of homicide and violent crimes. But one thing is certain: the insanity of the rhetoric that has taken over the country—including tropes about *racist* cops—will only lead to more deaths. And yet, this young woman's virtuous social media post will hold more weight in her circle of true believers than the carefully curated numbers of scholars like Wilfred Reilly, who has an unnatural passion for crunching data.[‡]

All the while, someone, somewhere, is vulnerable and calling my husband for help. As the dominant anti-police narrative increasingly drives good people away from the profession,[§] will anyone be there to help in

---

[*] "999 people Were Shot and Killed by Police in 2019," *Washington Post,* www.washingtonpost.com/graphics/2019/national/police-shootings-2019/ (updated August 10, 2020).

[†] See "FBI Releases 2019 Statistics on Law Enforcement Officers Killed in the Line of Duty," press release, FBI National Press Office, May 4, 2020, www.fbi.gov/news/pressrel/press-releases/fbi-releases-2019-statistics-on-law-enforcement-officers-killed-in-the-line-of-duty.

[‡] Wilfred Reilly, *Taboo: 10 Facts You Can't Talk About* (Washington, D.C.: Regnery Publishing, 2020).

[§] Steve Volk, "The Enemy Within," *Rolling Stone,* May 12, 2021, www.rollingstone.com/cul-

time?

Calling out abuses in any organization with authority is necessary. Doing so is foundational to our democracy even. We must persist in this pursuit. But how we do it matters if we are to keep our social contract intact.

Demonizing and hijacking language or symbols doesn't bring us closer to this ideal. The littering of empty pork rind bags doesn't build empathy. Yelling into the void for your own audience doesn't build bridges. And a family member telling young children that people who support the police are *white supremacists* perpetuates the lie. Are there some people who support the police who are also white supremacists? Perhaps so. Perhaps so. However, this binary tier 1 thinking doesn't bring us closer to the complexity of life that defines us. We aren't actors in a black-and-white TV drama. We're living life in full color.

And so, the flag, with all her knife wounds, remains. Not as a symbol of hate, but instead, and for me, as an invitation for conversation. In defense of freedom of speech, both unhinged rants and uncomfortable truths must be addressed if we are to walk forward into the future as neighbors.

I don't know if this is an answer that satisfies you. Like you, I had to take a break from the family drama. In the end, I came home. For the most part, I just keep a lot of my thoughts bottled up in my head and preserve them here in my letters to you. I invite people into conversation but have put limits on the conversations at home to keep the peace. In fact, the other day, my husband and I made a pact, somewhat in jest but with a kernel of truth—we would only talk about food, money, and sex. Now, whenever we mention something outside of those three topics, we laugh and remind ourselves that we are treading on the taboo.

Is this living authentically? I don't have an answer either. I guess that is why we write.

To the coming of a better time,

Jen

Letter 72

Jen,

My friend Dan and I were talking outside of the law school library at the University of San Diego (USD). Our years of comfortable friendship allow effortless conversations about the mysteries of the universe. On this particular day before the pandemic, we were talking about the meaning of a black person being related to President George Washington. The connection seemed pregnant with meaning, but neither Dan nor I, try as we might on the grassy USD campus, could connect the dots for the purpose of a common American future.

I still remember the light bulb moment for Dan.

Dan remarked that while he and I never had any problems talking about race, he always worried about saying something in a public forum that a black person might take offense to. This was partly due to experiences he'd had in which someone found fault with something he had said, leading him both to apologize and to be more uncomfortable about future discussions. The fault-finding that seems to occur in every utterance about race troubled Dan, especially since he never had any ill intent or made any intentionally malicious comments. Having shared his concerns, Dan suddenly widened his eyes as if he'd found an obvious solution to the problem and said, "Why don't the two of us talk about race before the Harvard Club of San Diego?" I admit I was not excited about the idea. Once upon a time and years ago, back when I was eager to advocate for positions in support of race-based affirmative action, I would find myself on many panels. But my experience with the Black History Month panel at UC San Diego had soured me on the idea of panel discussions, as it seemed many minds today are closed on the subject of race. And I had better things to do with my time than to be ignored and dismissed.

However, Dan was an old friend of over fifteen years. We had broken bread together over the years. Our wives knew each other. Our children had played together at the Lawrence Welk Resort on holiday. We were both middle-aged guys who had graduated from Harvard Law School in 1986. Fate had taken us to San Diego and the same downtown area. My wife and I had invested thousands of dollars in a "Dan startup," but we won't talk about that little matter. So, I agreed to the idea more out of affection for Dan than any burning desire to share my thoughts and opinions before the august Harvard Club of San Diego.

The next thing that happened shocked me to my racial core.

Dan pitched the idea of our two-man road show on race to the Harvard Club. I expected a polite and dutiful, "Oh, that's nice. Well, we always appreciate new ideas. Let's schedule you down for such and such a time." I was very wrong about the Club. I'm going to let Dan explain in his own words what happened:

> I proposed our two-man talk-about-race show to the SD Harvard Club board. I was surprised and a bit saddened by the reaction: about 1/3 cautious support, and 1/3 silent, and the rest actively expressing fear of doing anything so controversial. We have no black directors but have one Latino (a prominent local attorney) and one Indian. Both were supportive but skeptical and counseled caution. . . One director (white) came up to me after, she's about 30, and shared her fear of breaking ranks with African American dogmas.

When I read the word dogma, I felt as Galileo must have felt centuries ago. They wouldn't dare host an event in which people didn't speak on script. My life experience and truth be damned! Dan and I have a good friendship because we don't do dogma. We are friends. Dogma is why people can't talk honestly and openly about race.

I raised a thought experiment with Dan. Suppose two guys wanted to talk about religion in America. One guy was Protestant, and the other guy was a dissident Jewish intellectual like Philip Roth or Saul Bellow. Would the Club members be loath to hear out a Jewish intellectual who offered a different perspective on religion? I don't think so. So, why must a black

American difference of opinion and thought be shut down? It troubles me. I do not welcome anti-intellectualism and dogma from the Harvard Club of San Diego.

Dan explained to me the cowardice of the Club members:

> They were just scared. The fear was palpable. Those who spoke up supported the idea in the abstract but in the concrete, it confronted them, and they didn't know what to do about it. Fear can be paralyzing. There wasn't reason for fight, but there was reason for flight. I'm always saddened to see people I like, care about and respect crumble like that, and those who aren't crumbling couching their lack of support for the idea with expressions of pragmatism.

This fidelity to dogma was a watershed moment for me. I do not swear allegiance to dogma. I have sworn allegiance to the Flag of the United States of America many, many times in my life but never allegiance to racial dogma.

My first instinct was to retire from blackness. Dogma doesn't work for me. Does dogma work for you?

Before you answer that question, let me say I learned in the third grade to equate prejudice with ignorance and stupidity. It is dumb for this woman on the Board of the Harvard Club of San Diego to view all black Americans through a prism of rigid dogma. I grew up in the 1970s in small-town Virginia, and prejudice was an old friend. I never, ever had a teacher or administrator or classmate refuse to hear my views. They might have disagreed with me, but the operating norm and more was for one to disagree without being disagreeable. There is a new world out there, Jen, that has passed me by, and I feel like a stranger in my own country sometimes.

We are rendered blind and dumb by Dogma,

Wink

P.S. I actually knew someone who attended Ku Klux Klan meetings around the block from me growing up. I convinced him it was a bad idea and would haunt him for the rest of his life. He lives somewhere in Central Virginia today. He had a strange gig of chasing ghosts and ruminating about Confederate battlefields. If anyone should be reviled today, it should be this dude attending Klan meetings as an eighth grader, not your husband.

Letter 73

Dear Wink,

I think, in many ways, we have provided each other, through our letters, a respite from the infiltration of dogma into our personal lives. How nice it is to speak to someone without the suffocation of dogma.

The other day I was telling Charles Love, the author of *Race Crazy*, the story of how I complimented the hair of a black woman in church, and for the rest of the day, I had this nagging internal dialogue of whether I had committed a microaggression against her. You know this story, because I texted you immediately for your feedback. I told Charles this too. He laughed at our relationship and called you my "black filter."

I must be honest, though; you are a bad filter! You don't do dogma, and so what may offend one person, you see without the fog of race. I know one of your family members says you are a bad black role model, in part because of this reason. Ironically, it is your refusal to be shoehorned into a racial category that has earned you the Archie Bunker epithet in your household. You don't do race, and so now you're characterized as a cranky, bigoted, old white curmudgeon. How can that be so? Isn't your racial agnosticism a better way of being in the world?

Dogma is everywhere.

The dogma in my family has less to do with race and more with politics and the good versus evil that has permeated both sides of the political debate.

Not too long ago, I found myself on the receiving end of my progressive ex-husband's rant about the Trump administration. A self-pro-claimed progressive who believes in social reform through government action, he yelled over the phone, excoriating Southerners and the ad-ministration. After being with him for fifteen years before parting ways, I'm used to the passion. I don't say anything, even when, later in the conversation, he retells a story of an obnoxious New Yorker. "You bash the South; you bash the North—there is no in-between," I think. I sigh internally but continue to keep quiet during this outburst. I didn't call to talk politics; we had something more important to discuss . . . our son.

Meanwhile, as he continues to rant in his wildly intelligent manner, he catches the ear of my husband. As I hang up with him, I then get an earful of reverse political dogma. In many ways, there is no in-between for me either. I went from an extremely progressive musician to an ex-tremely conservative law enforcement officer in my choice of compan-ions. Oy vey.

Well, as my grandpa used to say to me after his retirement, "At least you're not bored." Understatement of my life.

I'm a little like a chameleon, I guess. It's not that I'm a waffler, al-though I can be. I just have always lived a little in the *in-between*. I ap-preciate good arguments, and I think there is often value on both sides. And honestly, I think most of us, at our core, have similar dreams, hopes, and aspirations even when our ideologies diverge. Throughout our own conversation, I've become more convinced of this truth, and I see how you've persuaded me to look at issues around race in a different light. We may not always agree, but I can still appreciate your views.

As you always remind me, you are but one person. One in 40,000,000 or so black Americans. Be that as it is, you have given me yet one more perspective that allows me to better assess the world and to understand a new way of being in community across our racial differences. Our letters have become the foundation for a newfound empathy and understand-ing. For developing my consciousness beyond the binary.

It is this binary and tier 1 consciousness that we've discussed that worries me. The rising tensions throughout our country over the past decade have caused me grave concern. How can we not see humanity in the Other? This tension, in particular, has impacted our racial relation-ships across the country as we increasingly segregate based on the color of our skin.

As you know, every morning I get a curated list of *Medium* articles in my inbox. You and I usually share the most inane ones for a morning laugh, or sometimes cry—remember the very serious article on racist dogs?* That had us between humor and alarm in our correspondence.

On most mornings, I don't have the energy to cull through all the vitriol to find meaningful essays. This one morning, I happened upon a particularly thoughtful article on white and black friendship. I thought maybe someone had finally broken the code to being in an authentic friendship—we found fellow *travelers*! However, as it turned out, the author, a young black woman, lamented that her blackness was in question among her friends of similar shades for developing a friendship with a white woman. Sure enough, someone felt compelled to leave a comment that all white people were evil, and these evil white people wanted us (the entire human race, I assume) to remain forever divided.

Hmmmm . . . will a message of friendship resonate in this atmosphere that insists that we revile our brothers and sisters due to ancestral sins?

There are so many things wrong with such a blanket statement on the morality of skin color and its relationship to ancestral ties. I don't even know where to begin. Sighing, I went on to read another article that looked as if it might have some promise. It started out as a critique of the TV show *#blackAF*. I was hoping that it would be a critique of the tensions in our society that the media seems hell-bent to advertise, exacerbate, and even create.

Another sigh, alas . . .

It was a critique of one of the character's light skin color and the colorism that permeates black culture. The author of the critique even decided to dissect the word *fair* (apparently, this woman spends some time as an armchair linguist when not turning over rocks in the constant hunt for racism). According to her argument, the word fair, which means "attractive" and "light-skinned" as well as "just," is all a ploy of white people to establish a hierarchy and the *white means right* mantra. Apparently,

---

* For the article, see Louna Délicieux, "Racism Is White People's Dog," *Medium,* February 13, 2020, medium.com/@delicieux.louna/racism-is-white-peoples-dog-eb351375e789. For Wink's thoughts on this and related articles, see W. F. Twyman, Jr., "To the Coming of a Better Time," *Truth in Between* (blog), *Medium,* November 23, 2020, medium.com/truth-in-between/to-the-coming-of-a-better-time-11fcc5f11cdc.

until we all learn a new "more equitable" language, we will continue to be pawns to subliminal racist messages coded in the English language.

I'm no linguist, nor do I pretend to be one, but a few immediate queries started bouncing around in my (fair-haired) head. First, the English language was indeed started by a bunch of white people. So, there may be references in the language, back in the day before multiculturalism was even a consideration, that casually equated their idea of beauty with what is *good*. Not being a linguist, I would guess that this may hold true in other languages, too, but I cannot and will not spend much time researching this theory. I'll leave that to the professionals.

The author goes on to comment that darkness, or blackness, has connotations to evil in the English language. And so, black people will always be oppressed; indeed, it is even baked into how we communicate.

In most cultures where I have exposure, light—as in daylight—is often seen as *good*. It is in the dark—as in nighttime—that the evil monsters step out from the shadows. This is a theme in children's stories that I've seen around the globe. This has nothing to do with skin color; rather, the cover of darkness allows for more sinister activities.

I don't know why I decided to run down this rabbit hole, but down, down, down I went. And so, I decided to look up the etymology of the word black. According to one source, it came from the root *bhel*, which meant to shine, flash, or burn, as well as *blaec*, which means absorbing all light. Nothing evil here. What about the word ebony? It comes from *ebenos*, Greek for the ebony tree, which has a dark hardwood known for its durability.

I really liked the root of the word black, meaning to shine. And dark ebony wood is highly valued.

And yet, we insist on parsing and selecting language to fit into the racial dogma that has infected our minds and holds true diversity in chains. If the aim of Critical Race Theory (CRT) is to dissect power, even to its most elementary forms found in language and communication, it must maintain a commitment to critical inquiry even within its own theoretical boundaries. Without such introspection, the allegiance to truth rings hollow, and we all tumble headlong down the rabbit hole of competing disinformation masquerading as verity.

A commitment to diversity necessitates that we resist dogma and embrace critical thought, constructive disagreement, and, most importantly, friendship, as we search for the seeds of humanity within all of us. The seeds of humanity not bound to the limited and superficial jargon crudely wielded to identify and separate us. The seeds of humanity defying race. Arguably, that is what we have done here. We have allowed ourselves to be vulnerable and to be wrong. We have approached each other in our common humanity with curiosity and humility instead of judgment and hate. You've given me the space to grow and consider different views even when you pushed back on some of my language and a simplistic, racially laced tier 1 consciousness.

Language is always funny to me. I watch in amusement as we twist and turn it to conform to our wills, which are oh-so capricious. We choose what words are good and what words are bad, and we are constantly changing our language-legislation and word-policing to fit popular narratives and trends. Life would, after all, be rather dull if we couldn't find colorful and passionate expressions. Ahhhh . . . lest we be bored! But to be *fair*, when I use the word *black*, I often do so to describe "shining" strengths, amazing "durability," and a fondness for the shade of night that promises dreams of a better tomorrow.

It is for this reason that, despite our differences, we came together in search of the stories of strength and community that are so often lacking from our current national dialogue.

Earlier in our conversation, we discussed the idea that Theodore Weld's *American Slavery as It Is* should be mandatory reading. A horrifying account of some of the most brutal crimes against humanity. Today, I've been listening to Isabel Wilkerson's *Caste*. Like Weld, she does a brilliant job of outlining the absolute depravity of our past. As I listened to her book while exercising, AirPods in my ears as I pushed through my next mile, I found her stories so powerful that I almost lost my footing and came perilously close to being the latest gym casualty.

Our world is currently in a debate on CRT in K–12 education. I think this is a misguided exercise. We should teach the histories presented in *Caste*, but much like our alternative reading guide for the 1619 Project essays,[*] they need to be coupled with the stories you share in your letters of agency and resilience. My greatest fear is that we are teaching division.

---

[*] You can find our alternative reading guide for the 1619 Project essays on the *Truth in Between* page on *Medium* at medium.com/truth-in-between/supplemental-reading-guide-for-the-1619-project-essays-74d8265cfcad.

That we are teaching victimization. I have no fear of teaching the truth, but our truths these days seem dedicated to stories of resentments and grudges and are missing the other truths of tenacity and determination. Without these other truths, we see a whole generation committed to the idea, as your family member says, that *Blackness Is All About Oppression and Nothing Else Matters*. What would John Mercer Langston say?

I end my letter with the latest story of how dogma has directly affected my community and even led to the loss of a friendship.

After the murder of George Floyd, when the world was scrambling with how to address *racism*, and 21-day racial reading guides proliferated in the public square, I suggested to my Rotary Club that we start our own reading group.* Our two black members and about five of our white members were eager to get involved.

I never hid my concerns with some of the twisted or one-sided perspectives that were being heralded in our national dialogue. My friends even shared with me how much they appreciated my deep dives into the national conversation.

This lasted until one person found out that I didn't believe in CRT as the correct method for addressing our lingering discriminations. It all started with my invitation to a speaker who promoted common humanity and dignity over the racial segregation often promoted in practices that applaud CRT. I was never shy to push back against single narratives of oppression. This stance should have suggested my concern with the infiltration of dogma across the country, but I had also never directly referenced CRT until this point.

Somehow this debate over CRT has become the latest wedge in our polarization. Saying you are against CRT is seen, in some circles, as nothing more than a right-wing talking point. For many like me, however, questions about CRT do not underline a commitment to the "right" but rather a deep desire to get at root issues that keep us separated, and I worry CRT invokes separation and discrimination as the only way to make amends for our past.

At any rate, my stated preference for human dignity over CRT apparently contained some implicit and insidious message to my friend that

---

* You can find our alternative 21-day racial reading guide on the *Truth in Between* page on *Medium* at medium.com/truth-in-between/the-alternative-21-day-racial-reading-challenge-44ce5c45b71a.

signaled my own covert bigotry. Despite my previous actions to spark discussions on racial healing within the club, and numerous attempts to take our heated conversation off text and into a call or, better yet, a coffee, my friend refused to give me the space to converse. Our truncated notes only served to entrench a tier 1 consciousness. I don't think it would be a stretch to suggest texts and tweets may be a foundational factor in our current cultural disconnect.

I was told I was dishonest and not trustworthy and that our friendship had come to an end.

My husband, who in my opinion can often be quite bigoted—although he, as a law enforcement officer, would say his intolerance is directed only at criminals, regardless of race—couldn't help but laugh at my misfortune. He started to call me, in jest, *a little racist*. (He often tries to diffuse tension with humor.) When I retorted snarkily that it was he who was the bigot, he responded, "Maybe so, but I have never had a black person call me a *racist* . . . you just took it up a notch." This dialogue was all said in warped humor, but there was still a kernel of truth. Now, to be fair, my former friend never explicitly called me a *racist*. It is my assumption that she must have thought as much, given she was willing to end our friendship over a disagreement about CRT. Or maybe in today's climate, she simply couldn't bear any connection with someone who was against CRT, given the associations. Both alternatives highlight the trap of simplistic and tribal thinking that seems to hold many of us captive and prevent any kind of meaningful conversation.

How do we deal with ideas that are no longer niche intellectual theories but that have become accepted dogma in much of our media and government? What happens when this dogma comes to roost in our own friendships and homes? As I said at the start, for me, you are my respite. Writing to you is my act of civil disobedience. If I cannot change the world, I can change myself. I can reach across the differences not only with you but also with the others in my family who are a few shades darker than myself. In you and in them, I find a plurality that is, truly, more than skin deep.

Your suggestion that I explore my own family tree has been life-changing and life-affirming.

I only hope our words might one day inspire others into authentic conversation, even if not in places like the Harvard Club of San Diego.

To the coming of a better time . . .

Your friend and forever pen pal,

Jen

Letter 74

Dear Jen,

It has been nice to speak with someone without the suffocation of dog-ma. Nearly all Americans traffic in slogan words and caricatures and stereotypes, falsehoods, and delusions when it comes to race. In my sub-urban, conservative, and Southern small town, I expressed myself fully and completely growing up. Do you know I always tried to ask the most questions in every class? Consider that I was the only black student in nearly all my classes. I was driven by curiosity and competitiveness. And I offered my thoughts freely and without fear of censorship. I never, ever had a teacher or classmate refuse to hear me because my views might de-viate from dogma. Never happened in my youth anywhere in the shadow of Confederate imagery.

How many times in presumably more progressive San Diego have I encountered dogma in my own home in this century? Let me count the ways.

We can start with hair since you mentioned your own hair story. I was once watching this therapist on YouTube. God knows why. The ther-apist was a light-skinned black therapist who I found to be intelligent, clear, and firm in her thoughts. For some reason, I focused on her hair and the marvelous things she did with her hair over the course of several videos. I was mildly enthralled. I mentioned to my wife that I found the woman's hair interesting.

My wife turned hostile. "How could I say that? She's a professional!

You should focus on what she is saying, not her hair." Sorry, I thought to myself, but I don't do dogma in my own home at night. I liked the therapist's evolving hairstyles, and I was certainly going to say so *in my own home!* And when did it become a thing to not notice and appreciate interesting hairstyles?

Or, how about the time I observed one night that 9 out of 10 television advertisements contained black actors? This seems laughably unrealistic to me since San Diego is 6 percent black, California is 6 percent black, and the United States of America is 13 percent black. My wife did not believe me. I found this disbelief incredible since she watches television every night. She literally rewound the DVR and watched all nine advertisements to confirm my observations. Only a dogmatic mind blind to reality would not have caught on that blacks are wildly overrepresented in television advertisements. That is a racial moment, a close encounter with dogma.

Dogma can mar an otherwise pleasant family moment.

One summer, both of my sons were home from college for my wife's birthday. It was a special moment, and she requested that we all rent a specialty bicycle (double Surrey) near the beach on Coronado. We have enjoyed special outings on Coronado since we moved to San Diego in 1992. Coronado is a resort city blessed with wide sandy beaches and divine views of the ocean's horizon. Coronado is not large. The population is approximately 24,697, and I like it that way. To get to Coronado, we travel across the spectacular Coronado Bridge, one of the highlights of the California coast. I always soak in the breathtaking views of Mexico, Point Loma, and the water's edge where our country slips into the Pacific Ocean. Not that it matters, but the median home price there is $1.8 million, and the population is 6.8 percent African American.

We checked out rental family bikes from the Hotel Del Coronado, and we were on our way!

And it was a lot of fun. One son pedaled up front while my daughter complained in the back. My eldest son kept horsing around chasing our bike. Mom was enjoying the company of her children. It was a pleasant day all the way around as we rode up along the beach toward North Island. My eldest son had the idea that we turn right and go inland through some of the quiet neighborhoods. We did, and we laughed and joked the entire time. I think my wife was as happy as I had ever seen her.

We slowed up in front of a typical house. Out of the blue and with no context or warning, my wife said, "Don't slow up. We're black, and they might think we're casing their place." With this remark, my wife turned what was otherwise a carefree, family moment on a sunny afternoon into some race-fear moment. I hate that. No one was thinking about race. There was no need to think about race. No Oppressor made my wife utter a racial fear. No long-dead slaveholder programmed my wife to succumb to catastrophic thinking on this peaceful, fun-filled moment with our adult children.

This is the raw tragedy of a mind where all is about race, where the boogeyman lies in wait around the next bend. The slaver is long dead, but the mind refuses to let go of racial fear.

Let's queue up the next example of suffocating dogma.

I am minding my own business after a hard day at work. To relax and to feel I am not alone in a dogmatic world, I pulled up a wonderful podcast featuring Professor Glenn Loury and a young black liberal/leftist interviewer. My wife comes into the room and says with utter contempt, "I leave you to your anti-black stuff." In my wife's world, Glenn Loury is anti-black. How open-minded. I don't even reply to these microaggressions anymore.

On another occasion, when I first learned that my wife sometimes refers to me as "Archie Bunker" with her friends, I took exception and asked for an explanation, an argument, some marshaling of facts and logic that would show I am indeed channeling a blue-collar WASP bigot from the 1970s in Queens, New York. I did not expect reasoned discourse, and my wife did not disappoint. She flat-out declared, "You were never of the culture, and you will never be of the culture!" To not be of the culture was the kill shot in my wife's estimation.*

Race Is All About Culture. Blackness Is All About Oppression. Nothing Else Matters.

---

* My wife offers this clarification after reading this passage: "My calling you 'Archie Bunker' was as much about my perception of your political/societal views as it was about you fighting change—you've always fought change, in everything. You want things to stay the same. For example, you used to hate every change in Charlottesville and the buildup of the road we would take to get to Charlottesville from Alexandria, Route 29. I saw it as natural progress. You hated it and wanted it to stay the same. In many ways, this desire is natural, but most of us must reconcile ourselves to change."

Some time ago, a relative forged an uncle's will, causing a cousin, the rightful heir, to lose everything. I did all that I could to right the wrong. Eventually, the crime was exposed, and my cousin was able to come into his rightful inheritance. Even so, I never talked to the criminal cousin again. Years later, I felt the offense as if it had occurred yesterday.

One morning while having breakfast with my daughter, I asked my daughter for her opinion: How might I let go of this old grudge? With teenage insight, she said, "Don't dwell on it. Move on. That'll do it." I took note and forgave my relative at that moment. The resentment dissipated.

Around that time, I wanted to hang on our wall at home a portrait of General George Washington kneeling in prayer at Valley Forge. I am a second cousin, seven times removed, of the first president, and I understood myself at that time as a black American.

The image inspired me.

My daughter, however, erupted in outrage. All she could see was a slaveholder.

"He won the American Revolution," I said.

"I don't care," my daughter replied.

"He was the greatest president ever," I rejoined.

"I'm only related to Washington because he raped someone," she said.

I flatly said there was no evidence whatsoever Washington had laid a violent hand on any of our slave ancestors.

Nuance and complexity eluded my daughter. President Washington might grace our currency, adorn the National Mall, and hang on the walls of the White House, but no, not the wall of our home. In this matter, slaveholding alone mattered to my intelligent daughter.

The greatest threat to a healthy black culture and consciousness today is an inability to see beyond slaveholding.

When we carry resentments in our hearts over generations, these resentments hurt us. Dwelling on slaveholding creates a desire to get back at others, to lash out. One feels entitled to destroy institutions due to the original sin of slavery.

Our ancestors would want us to move on and live our lives to the fullest today. We dishonor our ancestors if we bring trials and tribulations from their times into our times. We disrespect our ancestors with limited and negative thinking, while living in the greatest country ever.

My daughter was not persuaded, and the portrait of Washington remains curled up in our supply room.

Here's one racial moment for the road: A cousin lectures a relative and another young cousin about how he wasn't given the appropriate credit for his work compared to his white colleagues at a major firm. Of course, the story is racial from top to bottom. Any nonracial understanding of the cousin's job experience is verboten.

So, yes, it has been nice to speak with someone without the suffocation of dogma.

Am I a "black filter"?

Even you caught the inanity in that statement. I am an anti-dogma man. I have a contrarian personality. What are we doing as a society when obedience to dogma is prized over deep understanding, when black and white is praised over the gray of existence? And while we drink our self-deceptions away at night, we lose the respect of our spouses and children and grandchildren.

I don't filter life through the prism of race. And this insistence on who I am has come at great cost. Did you know that a relative has threatened to change her last name if she runs for office one day because of what I say and write? And she made the threat because she craves belonging, being popular so much. Those threats wound me deep inside as I love my relative and my family name.

Have I committed such terrible crimes that my own flesh and blood must disown our family name? It creates anxiety within me, and still, I write truths that need to be said. I am a human filter. I am a personality filter. I am a highly sensitive filter. I live above the temporal need to be popular with other black people. A member of my family, in anger, has accused me of being on the racial spectrum. Am I on the spectrum as I face powerful dogmatic forces to toe the racial line?

Consider the madness of the crowds regarding the George Floyd incident in Minnesota. The crowd was enraged over the senseless killing of a human being on video. The passing of any life is a tragedy, even if one is a convicted felon. Murder is murder. It is important for me to write those words as the name of George Floyd alone evokes, for some people, visceral and primal emotions, the unbridled passions of Black Rage. For some, *Blackness Is Oppression. Nothing Else Matters.* Some considered burning, looting, and murder the proper and appropriate response to uncalled-for death. I think there is never a good excuse for rioting, but I get it that they were extremely angry.

But I don't have much else to say about George Floyd as an individual. Was he a good ancestor like Daniel Brown? Did George Floyd bring more joy and beauty and laughter into the world? Did Floyd build lasting institutions for his grandchildren's grandchildren? The aim of a good life is to be a good ancestor. I am going to resist the temptation to say more about the life of Floyd. All deaths are tragic, but not all lives are lived in black enterprise and black achievement. I choose to remember George Vashon, not George Floyd so much.

Am I a bad role model for black people?

As you aptly point out, one of my young relatives has said I am a poor role model for black people. I question racial faith at every turn. I don't like racial segregation. I do not call for the blood of all white people in my essays and articles. I don't code-switch. I strive to be the same person, regardless of the racial setting. I don't do faddish black idioms and jargon and slang. I don't have time to keep up with the latest ways to exclude others.

And for these reasons, my family member has cast me out from the universe of people to be heard and seen. My rightful place, in her judgment, is to be ignored and dismissed.

And my family members are not alone. As we've discussed, 76 percent of black Americans consider being black extremely important or very important to one's sense of self.* I am in the decided minority as I live my life in another realm altogether, a bubble, as my beloved cousin Toni Twyman would say.

We've lived through a pandemic. People are passing away, and still, people cling to race as extremely important or very important to one's

---

* Pew Research Study, "Blacks Are More Likely Than Other Groups to See Their Race or Ethnicity as Central to Their Identity," May 2, 2019, www.pewresearch.org/social-trends/psdt_03-25-19_race_update-01. For painful reading, see also James D. Johnson and Leslie Ashburn-Nardo, "Testing the 'Black Code'": Does Having White Close Friends Elicit Identity Denial and Decreased Empathy from Black In-Group Members?" *Social Psychological and Personality Science,* August 8, 2013. The authors of this study quote L. Marcus, "The Black Code: Why Obama Stills Owns the Black Vote," *American Thinker* (July 2011): "Relationships with whites *must* be kept at arm's length maintaining a silent us against them mindset. Blacks who appear too friendly and comfortable around whites are viewed with suspicions; their blackness in question."

sense of self. I don't know, Jen. Maybe my relative is right.

And if my family member is right, what does that mean about the world we must live in? Well, it means ambitious young black people will be close-minded to anything but race. Race will explain all. *Blackness Is Oppression. Nothing Else Matters.* We will see increased acceptance of segregation in the form of safe spaces and inclusion. Whites and blacks will know each other less and less well. Pressure and stress will accelerate in mixed-race families. Children will have to choose one identity over another and implicitly view one parent as evil and one parent as good. Black colleges will receive more money and support. Black fraternities and sororities will capture more and more of the souls of black folks. Suspicion of one another will increase. Trust will decrease.

For the 24 percent of black Americans who are not on board with the new Jim Crow, there will be increased repression within families and homes. Disaffection between the generations will compound. Ironically, the young will care less and less about authentic black history rooted in triumph over adversity. Black history will be Emmitt Till and Tulsa and lynching. The Great Leaders of Nikole Hannah-Jones and Kimberlé Crenshaw will shove black men to the sidelines in the struggle for power and dominance. Black achievement will decline as achievement and ambition are caricatured as racist and white.

A descent into a Dark Age is foreseeable.

Wink

Letter 75

Dear Wink,

I can relate to the dogmatic application of race in my own family—the black-and-white mindset. We talk about retiring from race, and I think that is a beautiful concept. Our friend, Dr. Sheena Mason of the Theory of Racelessness, would approve. And yet, our own family ties keep us mired in race day in and day out, despite our best efforts. Together, you and I, we dabble in the Blessed Society. Perhaps we have created a blessed spark in our own writing, but when we shut down our computers to engage the world around us, the spark dims in the haze of a reality determined to inflame racial division.

We started our conversation before the pandemic and before the death of George Floyd. Even before these two global earthquakes, we witnessed the growing divisions based on race. Divisions that were amplified after these two events.

At the beginning of the pandemic, I thought this travesty might make our words moot. That it might bring about a "kumbaya" moment as we all learn to see ourselves in the suffering of others. That lasted about a minute, didn't it? The death of Floyd burned any fledgling kumbaya to ash. In our new world of forced separation, the tribe became even more alluring and all too easy to access in our online realities.

Sebastian Junger noted in his book *Tribe* that "the one thing that might be said for societal collapse is that—for a while at least—everyone is equal."* Junger, a former war correspondent, references his research and time in the field under "normal" warfare and/or collapse. There was nothing "normal" about the pandemic. It's not that we haven't seen pandemics in our history—although you and I haven't lived through one until now—but this pandemic entered into an Internet era that allowed us to sink into further tribal enclaves in our online realities. And as this reality became the norm, the death of Floyd supercharged the trend.

During the pandemic, I binged on the TV show *The Walking Dead*. I know it is not as erudite as your beloved *Star Trek*, but it kept me entertained. Being human, the survivors of a zombie apocalypse band together into different tribes, and the tribes have their own conflicts even as they fight off the zombie threat. Despite the tribal element, what I find so attractive is that the zombie threat has erased hierarchies based on race or sex. There is no room for such petty social structures. Can you fight, and can you survive? If so, you're pretty much in.

I have a girl-crush on the lead female character, Michonne. She's a sword-wielding heroine, with more melanin than myself, who lost her son in the early days of the apocalypse and finds herself in a new tribe where she becomes the wife and mother of a white man and his daughter. Black, Latino, and Asian characters all fight alongside white brethren and carve out a life together despite all the odds, operating in solidarity for the common good.

Sometimes, I find myself almost daydreaming about such a society. Do we need a zombie apocalypse to get us to this place? Or intergalactic warfare?

Junger comes to many of the same conclusions played out in *The Walking Dead*. For example, there are no depressed people in zombie-land, and similarly, studies have shown depression to decrease in times of war. Depression seems to be more of a modern malady that is particularly aggressive during times of peace. When people are active in their communities and feel that they are of value, depression lessens measurably. Sadly, in our modern era, with so many conveniences and without active combat within or near our borders, we've diminished the bonds of community. We just don't *need* to come together any longer, and we choose to remain safe in our online harbors.

* Sebastian Junger, *Tribe: On Homecoming and Belonging* (New York: Hatchette Book Group, May 2016), 43.

In these *safe spaces,* we flatten our individuality to find belonging in a group. In a world of forced isolation, this group identity becomes more and more vital to our survival, or at least for our mental well-being and as a recourse from physical isolation.

In my dream world (the one minus the zombies), I see this country as a quilt. Yes, there are different squares with their own pattern and colors, and yet we are all woven together, and together we actually produce something magnificent. Can we see ourselves in the quilt as just Americans, as our colors blend? The black, white, yellow, brown are all distinct but are part of something bigger. The pandemic created nightmares out of my dream world, as the quilt frays.

Since our founding, our weave has always been a bit tenuous, and recent events make me wonder if the damage is irreparable. I try to temper this pessimism with the imagination of fellow dissidents like Sheena Mason. Or like Angel Eduardo, who suggests a way out of the impasse between being colorblind and seeing color everywhere by being "color-blah."*

If 76 percent of black Americans feel that race is incredibly important, there is still the 24 percent. That's enough to create a tipping point. Enough for us to begin the movement to become truly "raceless" or, at the very least, "color-blah."

We may lose some battles among the ranks, even in our own families, but this is the long game. We write not only for ourselves but also for the Next Generation, and our children's children. For the imagination of a Blessed Society.

Jen

---

* *Hold my Drink Podcast,* episode 45, "On Being Color-Blah," with Angel Eduardo podcasts. apple.com/us/podcast/episode-45-on-being-color-blah-angel-eduardo/id1537516628?i =1000534067181.

Letter 76

Dear Jen,

How many days do any of us have left? When we began this correspondence, my sister was a living presence in my life. Now, she has passed on. And so have distant cousins Essie Robinson and Jeremiad Womack and double cousin Kent Womack, who was 95 years old, and Floyd Wright, who was 98 years old when he left us. I miss my Great Aunt Hannah Lewis, who passed away at the age of one hundred. We should be honest while we still have time left to be honest. People are passing away. Eternity waits for no man or woman.

After I wrote these words, my beloved cousin Rosa Nell Grace passed away in Richmond, Virginia. Rosa was the soul of our extended family, and she delighted in our podcast interviews with cousins James F. and Nathan Twyman.[*]

We have said much about race. With every stroke of the keyboard, you and I have striven to be ourselves in the face of family and friends who, as I see it, are content to live unexamined lives. Living in a divided world will not send us straight to heaven. Can someone tell me why we live in a delusional world? Why do we pretend we're 100 percent of African descent when we are not? Why do we mouth slogan words and perform Oppression Art for strangers? Why do we obsess over random criminals who meet a tragic end and not our own flesh and blood who make poor choices in life? When judgment comes for us, it will not be

---

[*] For a childhood image of Rosa Nell Grace, see Twyman, *On the Road to Oak Lawn*, 47.

the white cop who shoots us but the middle school teachers who flunk us out of school because we chose not to study. I miss my mom and my first-grade teacher Lucille Walker, who did not tolerate nonsense in the classroom.

Can I get a witness? as the old timers might have said at church.

Izabella Tabarovsky has written about the American Soviet mentality as a cautionary tale. Collective demonization of others might feel good as just desserts. But like all resentments and grudges, there is a downside to vilification based on group membership. I do not pretend to write with the grace and authority of our friend Izabella, so I will allow the words of Izabella to resonate throughout the soul of this conclusion:

> All of us who came out of the Soviet system bear scars of the practice of unanimous condemnation, whether we ourselves had been targets or participants in it or not. It is partly why Soviet immigrants are often so averse to any expressions of collectivism: We have seen its ugliest expressions in our own lives and our friends' and families' lives. It is impossible to read the chastising remarks of Soviet writers, for whom [Boris] Pasternak had been a friend and a mentor, without a sense of deep shame. Shame over the perfidy and lack of decency on display. Shame at the misrepresentations and perversions of truth. Shame at the virtue shaming and the closing of rank. Shame over the momentary and, we now know, fleeting triumph of mediocrity over talent.[*]

I miss truth in the public square.

The truth is, every day in the United States of America, we live among closed minds. We live in a hateful world where George Washington is reviled as a slave owner and not revered as a man of epic character and courage and bravery on the battlefield. As a lawyer from Tucson, Arizona, once told me over lunch, he would not think of slaveholding when thinking of our first president. Owning slaves might be number ten or twelve on the list. Forgive me for my emotion, Jen, but black and white men died for us, our American Independence, under Washington's command on battlefields forgotten—Brooklyn, Murray Hill, Trenton, Princeton, Valley Forge. But living in a hateful world of misrepresentations and perversions of truth is how the close-minded roll.

I know an intelligent, well-educated black woman who is a descen-

---

[*] Tabarovsky, "The American Soviet Mentality."

dant of Robert Telfer (1780–1861). Telfer was married to a white woman, but he fell in love with a free black woman named Mary James. They became lovers, and he had six children with her. Telfer was a Scottish immigrant who resisted slavery and attested to at least one daughter's freedom to the best of my knowledge. I do not know about the other children. But his legal oath for at least one daughter was a powerful affirmation of affection and affinity. Telfer is a noble ancestor, but the black woman I know refuses to recognize or acknowledge Robert Telfer as a 4x great-grandfather because he is white. Isn't refusal to accept genetic truth a sign of a closed mind? I know another black woman, less educated, who refuses to reach out to white Twymans. Another case of a closed mind that we will never hear about on the nightly news. No one calls this type of close-mindedness to account. Life is too short for me to be blind to all those who flow in my veins. I want to know, and I want to know for my uncles and aunts who never knew in their lifetimes. These men we studied in history books are blood kin. Who knew?

It is the cold heart I find most disturbing and troubling. I grew to know a distant white cousin. We were destined to meet when he was next in San Diego, but he died before Christmas Day. I was sad and prayed for his soul. I shared the sad passing with a member of my family, and there was nothing—no empathy, no caring, no recognition of a common humanity. Some people are so tribal that they feel nothing when whites die. I feel when anyone passes before their time.

Sadly, we never know how many days we have left.

When judgment comes for you, who will mourn . . .

And so, I pray every day that we will move the dial toward something better, toward a higher consciousness about race. We don't have to live in a hateful world. We can live in a world where everything in our past is integrated into our sense of self. We can be white and see ourselves in distant black cousins, as you have, Jen. We can be black and see ourselves in distant white cousins. We can strive to be one under a single flag, not a black or a white flag or a brown flag but one flag that is a manifestation of us. No race has leave to reject our Founding Fathers and the flag our ancestors of all races fought under. To take offense at the flag of Yorktown shows an ignorance of real history.

If one takes the long perspective, we are living in the better times our grandparents' grandparents dreamed of.

We are at a moral and spiritual place where we can see ourselves in each other, and this is only possible because, at our best, we are one nation. We could not exist as full and complete Americans without the Other. A shift in consciousness from "us vs. them" to "out of many, one" is the best way forward toward a division-free country. This is the best thing that will ever happen to the United States of America, and, when we write the life story of America a hundred years hence, historians will say this turn in consciousness was the best thing that ever happened to the heirs of those men of character in Philadelphia in 1776.

When we began our communication, you and I used the clumsy term "Octoroon Nation" to describe this feeling for something better. The word "Octoroon" has grown into disfavor in recent times as a sign of hyper-stigma due to partial black descent. In our innocence, we wanted to repurpose the word, cleanse it of stigma, and bring it into the world as something new. We did not judge partial black descent. We aimed higher toward a consciousness where all parts of our past were integrated into a coherent whole. And we prayed over the years that a higher consciousness about race would better inform a Sense of America, a sense of us, a manifesto of us.

I see a crossroads up ahead. There's nowhere to hide as we approach the coming times.

What does a higher consciousness of race mean? It means Jennifer Richmond may reach out to her flesh-and-blood cousins who are black Americans, and she will feel warmth and acceptance and embrace. Divisions of race dissolve away.

And we pray . . .

A higher consciousness of race means Wink could ask out a girl named Julie on a date in high school, and her dad would say "yes" or "no" based on the content of the young man's character, not the color of his skin.

A higher consciousness of race means Jen is not afraid to write about black history since black history is her American history. And it means Wink's daughter accepts a portrait of distant second-cousin George Washington in the Twyman home because she can see beyond slaveholding.

A higher consciousness means Wink can forgive his aging dad for the "acting white" slur half a century ago.

A higher consciousness means we live in acceptance of all that has transpired in the past with the perspective of our limited time on this Earth. As my beloved cousin Abraham Lincoln Day, Jr., has said, "We all have an expiration date."[*]

How many days do we have left to get it all right?

And we pray . . .

One day, it all came together for me, Jen. Judgment came for me in a sense. The Harvard Club of San Diego refused to allow me and my long-time friend, Dan Wolf, to talk about race because I might deviate from dogma.[†] I may be many things, but, at my core, I respect myself as the son of Lourine Womack Twyman and Winkfield Franklin Twyman, Sr. No man or woman tells me what to believe or what to think or what to say. At that moment, I decided blackness was not working for me. I would rather be me than spout dogma as blackness.

I retired from blackness.

There is a long, long tradition in the New World (and the Old World, for that matter) of people striving for authenticity. At some point, the search for authenticity requires one to redefine oneself so that the match between the inner self and the outer identity is a better fit. In 1860, my wife's ancestors in Fauquier County, Virginia, filed a legal petition to no longer be recognized as Negroes.[‡] Her ancestors decided to stop living a lie and be recognized for who they were inside. And the Circuit Court granted the petition in 1866.

During the Civil War, P. B. S. Pinchback was warned by his sister to

---

[*] Cousin Abe and I are fourth cousins four times removed of President Abraham Lincoln through Lincoln's maternal line and the Lee family. The chromosomes of Washington and Lee and Lincoln make us whole as Old Americans. The study of genetics could be perceived as the greatest tool ever for creating a sense of a unified American identity. Individuals like my daughter who see themselves only as black Americans are mixed race genetically speaking.

[†] It is beyond ironic that Harvard's motto for two centuries has been *Veritas*, which means truth in English. Perhaps the search for truth today really means the search for dogma at Harvard. Indeed, viewpoint diversity no longer seems to exist at Harvard. See Renu Mukherjee, "Without a 'Diversity' Leg to Stand On," *City Journal*, October 12, 2022, www.city-journal.org/affirmative-action-and-viewpoint-diversity-at-harvard.

[‡] A copy of the petition (dated January 26, 1861) and the certificate granting the petition (dated February 27, 1866) are in Wink's possession.

be true to himself. She urged him not to follow the colored race but to be the white man he was inside. Pinchback rejected that plea and went on to become the first black governor of a U.S. state. And I applaud his decision, but his decision resonated through his daughter and grandson, Jean Toomer. Toomer invested a lifetime into understanding himself before concluding he was of many races and an American when all was said and done. Of course, the larger world couldn't understand a nuanced, complex understanding of one's self, but that was on the larger world, not Toomer.

In 1967 when Jean Toomer passed away, I was of no race. I had no conception of race. I was too young to understand race, and no one made me aware of race. I lived in an all-black world. I watched *Star Trek*, *Gunsmoke*, *The Beverly Hillbillies*, and *Petticoat Junction*. Nearly all of the characters were white, but it didn't register with me that I should care. Even when I became aware of blackness, hey, that was me, and I loved me, so it was all cool.

A few years ago, I read about the artist Adrian Piper. She was born in New York City to an upper-middle-class, light-skinned black family. While studying at Harvard, she encountered a white professor who questioned her blackness. This incident was one of many as she ran into racial stereotype after stereotype in her career. As an artist, she was on top of her game, but she felt boxed in by stereotypes. I could relate to her tired battles with dogma, the way one must be and present oneself. One day, Piper said, chuck it! She packed up her bags, moved to Berlin, Germany, and retired from her blackness on September 20, 2012. Reading about her retirement is what first gave me the idea. Unlike Piper, I would never be confused for white, but retirement? Anyone could retire from an ill-fitting consciousness if one had the courage.

Nudging me further toward retirement was the inspiration I have drawn from Thomas Chatterton Williams. He has retired from his blackness, and I found myself wanting to have his freedom, to experience his freedom from the weight of racial doctrine, racial dogma.

But judgment day for me ultimately was being caricatured and placed into a racial box by a white liberal board member of the Harvard Club of San Diego. I'm a human, first and foremost. Blackness tells you nothing about my essence, my soul. That might not be true for my mother-in-law or my wife, but my truth is my truth. And so, I decided that the black thing wasn't working out for me. It was time to move on and be judged for who I am on the inside. I have retired from blackness and no longer wish to be boxed inside of racial doctrine, racial dogma.

And we pray . . .

It was all so tiresome. I don't do dogma with my friends. I do friendship. I grew weary of having my authentic, genuine childhood seen as atypical among other black Americans. Wouldn't you grow weary too?

I was tired of a black spouse and grandma committed to the cultural indoctrination of my children in black separatist organizations like Jack and Jill and all the rest. I do not lean into offense. I do not wake up offended in the morning or look for reasons to be offended throughout the day. I am happiest engaging in the larger world of people, books, and shows like *Star Trek*.

I can't take woke black intellectuals like Coates and Kendi seriously. I just can't. My eyes roll. I am an agreeable, open-minded, and conscientious person. I am not close-minded to my white ancestors and cousins. I am not hardwired to hate white people. I view Historically Black Colleges and Universities today as a sad step backward and corrosive of genuine friendships across the color line.

The black thing wasn't working out for me. I remain estranged. At least, I didn't choose divorce from blackness. I chose retirement.

There is a coming of a better time straight ahead. Young children will grow weary of being taught *Blackness Is Oppression. Nothing Else Matters.* Little kids will resent being taught *Whiteness Is Oppression. Nothing Else Matters.*

There will be a Golden Age in Culture and Consciousness beyond the horizon's edge, where we again value purpose and meaning over power and dominance. We may not live to see it, but I know our children's children will desire a better world, a better way of being in the world.

See you at the crossroads.

Wink

Conclusion: To the Next Generation

Dear Reader,

Why should you care about authentic conversation and correspondence?

For us, the answer is clear: We want to do what we can as individuals to stem the festering division in the United States born out of a dispiriting racial past and to move beyond the caricatures and stereotypes in the public square of ideas. People love oppressed blacks, and this love haunts our present. We also desire connection—pure and simple. Together, we know our national soul can be set free from limited thinking. *American slavery from the 1790s doesn't define any black American's future today.* This refrain should be loud and clear. No other country in world history has so expanded liberty and freedom. We waged a bloody Civil War to breathe new life into an old aspiration: *We hold these truths to be self-evident, that all men are created equal.* We create our tomorrow with our vision today.

We lean into life as individuals not because we are blind to racial disparities in the land. Media platforms and corporate diversity trainings remind us unrelentingly that black life expectancy is not white life expectancy, that black educational attainment is not white educational attainment, and that black wealth is not white wealth. We know, people, we know. Our own life experiences tell us this. But we also know that along with slogans of despair come self-loathing and despondency, resentment, and learned helplessness. This is not a recipe for a flourishing culture and consciousness. This also does not mean we deny or avoid history. To the contrary, this means discussing history—all history. There are important lessons in history to be absorbed and internalized, but sadly, in today's current milieu, we never encounter or learn those vital lessons.

We delight not only in celebrating stories of triumph over adversity and the power of the individual spirit but also in bringing people and ideas together, whether it be distant black and white cousins across the color line or opposing positions about reparations for American slavery. Our emblematic signature is disagreement without being disagreeable, a trait missing in our public discourse. We all need to focus more on the things we have in common despite our differences, racial or otherwise.

As with much about the human condition, some of the best and most salient ideas and messages about race can be found in the world of fiction—in this case, where no man has gone before. On September 8, 1966, the original science-fiction series *Star Trek* aired its first episode, "The Man Trap." The last episode, "The Turnabout Intruder," aired on June 3, 1969. For three years, the viewing public learned how different races could be one in fidelity to duty, how racial differences of no consequence could lock foes in eternal race hatred, how love could bring together a man and a woman from alien cultures, how evil could exist parallel to good, and how the power of empathy can transcend racial lines. No matter the world from which they come, people need not be strangers to one another. Captain Kirk discovered a constant throughout the galaxy: all intelligent life forms seek purpose and meaning in their lives.

So, what is the better pathway forward? Well, authenticity, purpose, and meaning provide a better way of being in the world than the racism of "antiracism." Living against prejudice and bigotry is something everyone can and should practice in life. Don't essentialize races or stereotype or judge people based on their skin color. Don't be Julie's dad, and don't be Robin DiAngelo. Be wise about the unique soul of every spirit one encounters in life. It is a simple thing we all should do in life—do unto others as you would have others do unto you. The Golden Rule is a core tenet of almost all religions and ethical traditions for a reason—it is the best principle ever imagined for governing our conduct and building a healthy society.

But how specifically might one live in purpose and meaning so that every individual's relationship with life is respected? As a way to conclude our correspondence, we lay out the following ten principles that we abide by for creating a better consciousness about race—for the coming of a better time.

1. *Never use slogans, even if others do. Use precision and depth to better understand others. It is better to use three hundred thousand words to convey precisely what you mean than thirty slogan words that may mean anything to anyone.* For example, if a diversity trainer asks that you think only in *allyship*, raise your hand and say, "I have friends, not allies, in life. I'm not at war with the world, and neither are my friends." The language of warfare is inappropriate when talking about your friends, relatives, neighbors, and fellow citizens.

2. *Never slur a group of people based on their race—and never assign a racial category to a group that is not explicitly defined by race. Individuals may be worthy of condemnation, but racial groups are not.* For example, if you are driving by a Blue Lives Matter rally and your family member remarks that the protesters are white supremacists, say we know nothing about the inner lives and hearts of the protesters. It will not do to collectively demonize a group of people, no matter the racial makeup of the group. By extension, do not demonize individuals absent clear evidence that they are prejudiced or bigoted.

3. *Don't allow yourself to become a caricature to gain profit and office. Do not live your life as an avatar for the collective agenda of others.* For example, if you find yourself competing in an oratory contest before an audience hungry for extremist rhetoric and tales of victimization, don't feed red meat to the crowd. There is no self-respect in spouting dogma to win the prize.

4. *Seek out differences in friendships and engage the larger world.* For example, if you are a young white Jewish professional, why not live with a black Christian roommate? If you are a black college student, why not pledge Sammy, as opposed to Alpha Phi Alpha? You will never be as young again as you are now. Be ever wonderful and curious about others. Never stay as you are in this world of abundance. Be

who you are—the wonderful, delightful, intelligent, strong-willed, difficult, and beautiful you.

5. *Live in the present, never the past, or even better, live in the future. We create our tomorrow with our vision today.* For example, if you are a black college student being pressured to go to a Historically Black College and University for law school, don't be afraid to pursue your goals and dreams elsewhere. It is not 1790 or 1950 anymore. The history of American slavery does not define you, nor does Jim Crow. There is something liberating in making one's peace with the past and being able to focus on the future. To paraphrase Forrest Gump, "Before one can move on in life, one must let go of the past."

6. *Don't let others define you.* For example, if you are a black male on an American schoolyard in the South, or a white female in Asia, know that your worth has nothing to do with the color of your skin or gender but with the content of your character. Don't make your decisions based on what people who treat you poorly say or what the 76 percent think. If you think for yourself and are true to yourself, you will be seen by your friends and family as genuine and authentic.

7. *Let your search for purpose and meaning in life trump your desire for power, domination, or revenge.* For example, if you are reading a history that casts everyone from one group as oppressor and everyone from another group as oppressed, consider that the author is writing with an ideological agenda, is not writing to uncover any truths, and is not writing for you. Don't allow your race or gender to be weaponized through the use of slogan words or the dissemination of half-empty historical narratives. People are most happy, content, and honest when they have an internally (or some might say divinely) directed calling—not an externally directed one that demands belittling, hurting, or demonizing others for validation. Beyond that, it doesn't matter what your specific calling is. What is important is that the calling secures you against the chaos of the outside world—that it immunizes you against pathological ideologies and slogan words that claim utopia is just a cancellation away.

8. *Do not deny the full scope of your ancestry or family.* For example, if you are an Old American, you almost certainly have family connections across the color line. Embrace them, no matter how distant they are, and recognize our joint inheritance. On average, black Americans are one-quarter European, and Latinos are almost two-thirds European.* No matter your race, you may find black cousins who have outachieved your white cousins by a stretch, or white cousins who fought for the rights of black Americans. No matter your race, you will inevitably find cousins who value family connection over racial identity—and any number of ancestors who built this country for the better.

9. *Lift others up until they prove they do not want to be lifted up.* For example, if you have the means, make an effort to help others better themselves, whether by extending financial assistance or even educational or employment opportunities. Often, people require only a helpful hand to be pulled from a life of bad circumstances and poor choices. But also recognize that everyone has their own individual agency. For those who accept handouts but refuse a hand-up, there is only so much we can do.

10. *Seek out truth and understanding wherever possible—even when others are unwilling to do the same.* For example, if you have questions and concerns about an idea or policy, no matter how popular, do not be afraid to express your principled concerns. At times, this may take courage, because sometimes it's easier to simply remain silent. But if you are too afraid or hesitant to stand up for your principles and values, who will?

The aim of a good, noble life is to work toward a Blessed Society in which divisions melt away, but mutual understanding, trust, and tolerance can never be established if divisions remain hidden and are not first recognized. They will also not go away by defining people by their immutable characteristics and reconstituting the sins of the past. What has transpired can never be undone. Yet, what is to come is ours to imagine

---

* Lizzie Wade, "Genetic Study Reveals Surprising Ancestry of Many Americans."

and realize. Together, we need not fear what lies beyond the horizon's edge.

To the next generation,

Wink & Jen

Jen's Postscript

Dear Readers,

Since Wink and I wrote these letters, and before publication, the tensions in my marriage reached a crescendo that was no longer tenable—neither for my soon-to-be ex-husband nor me. As my work to bridge divides continued to develop, the divide at home only deepened. Wink has walked beside me on this incredibly painful journey.

As I sit reviewing our letters prior to publication, I ask myself—would I change anything I've written given what I know now? Is everything I wrote about my life at home null and void? While I may have chosen different stories to tell, stories I will tell in our future correspondence, our letters remain unedited, except for points of clarity (and grammatical snafus) per our publisher's request.

For now, as I sit with this heartbreak, I hesitate to say too much. This situation—like life more generally—continues to unfold in unpredictable ways. What I will say is this: while my husband and I may not have made it due to different values and choices, those values and differences really came into focus with our changing political and cultural climate, so fraught with a sectarianism that continues to amplify.

In many ways, it was the gradual unveiling of these very differences that first spurred me to write. Differences that persuaded me to investigate the divisions in our country as they played out daily in our home. And for that, I am grateful. If I am to be completely honest, however, these "unreconciled differences" that emerged in my home dampen my optimism for our country. Can a love for a country and an "American ideal" succeed where a love of family fails?

Truth be told, my husband and I both love this country, but it is in the expression of these ideals where we vary wildly. Needless to say, I will not fly the thin blue line flag at my new home. Not because I've done an about-face, as I stand behind our decision at the time not to cower to the prevailing narrative of ACAB (*All Cops Are Bastards*—another lovely slogan). Rather, it is simply not my flag. It symbolizes his commitment, and one that I still honor, but I am not a LEO and will soon not be the wife of one either.

I honor the courage to stand up to one's principles and values, even when they go against the grain. And yet, the anger and vitriol that can accompany our viewpoints make it impossible to lean into different perspectives, drawing us further into our tribal enclaves. As we sink deeper into these *affinity groups*, the dangers of breaking ranks within these groups are as dire as communing with "the enemy." Traitorous, even.

As I do the necessary work on myself to navigate the divorce—and there is a lot to do—I often find myself lonely, my little tribe in disarray. The urge to fend off this loneliness leads me to consider the tribal urge to find other areas of belonging. But through this correspondence and my friendship with Wink and other similar "dissidents," I have changed. I know this to be true, not only because I feel it to be so, but also because my husband tells me as much, and he is right.

And so, I work to be content with a loneliness that I know is most "oppressive" in the time between my letters to Wink. Letters that remind me that we belong in this "truth in between" that has no flag of allegiance, but instead many banners of friendship.

And, when all else fails, I have my pug. And dogs don't do dogma.

Jen

Wink's Postscript

Dear Readers,

When Jen shared the collapse of her marriage with me, I felt hollowed out inside.

I reached for clumsy words of comfort. The picture in my mind was one of incongruence—as she and I grew closer in spirit, Jen grew apart from her life partner. Whatever words I offered with the best of intentions left me bereft, knowing whatever I said would not mend the ache in Jen's heart. Sadly, life is not a fairy tale. Who could have foreseen when we started this correspondence that Jen's moment of emotional breakdown, her *Good Will Hunting* moment, would be her marriage?

Jen is not alone in this world, as she well knows. As one relationship comes to a close, a new universe of fellow dissidents comes into view for my friend. Hold on tight, Jen, to us all who dream of a better time—David Bernstein, Erec Smith, Izabella Tabarovsky, Sheena Mason, Charles Love, Wilfred Reilly, and many others. You are never alone in this great enterprise we call classical liberalism. Sometimes your mind may go to sad places of loneliness.

I, too, know the feeling of loneliness, of feeling unknown by a spouse on matters of race. Are my experiences universal or particular to the black experience? It is an interesting question. On the one hand, it is race that has proven to be the proverbial pebble in our family shoe. My spouse and I grew up in different places and times. There was no overlap between life in 1970s Brooklyn and 1960s Hickory Hill. My wife did not take for granted an ancestral picture on the church wall as I did. Nor did she grow up on a street named after her family as I did. My wife was the product of private schools for most of her childhood, not brand-new suburban schools emblematic of the New South. These different transformative experiences were overlooked in the glow of early romance. However, as with most marriages, the universal truth is that repressed values and attitudes will come to the surface over time. All families can relate to the unforeseen consequences of childhood memories in parental lives.

How did Francesca Johnson phrase it in the letter she left for her children? She speaks in a language that all of Middle America can understand: "I could let this die with the rest of me, I suppose. But as one gets older, one's fears subside. What becomes more and more important is to be known—known for all that you were during this brief stay. How sad it seems to me to leave this Earth without those you love the most ever really knowing who you were."

We know one another, Jen, and that is real love.

Wink

Afterword

When Wink and Jen approached me to write the afterword for *Letters in Black and White*, I felt honored—and hesitant. As a first-generation Soviet-Jewish immigrant who grew up behind the Iron Curtain and whose American journey didn't start until the age of twenty, what insights could I possibly offer on the subject of race relations in America? With my personal and professional interests grounded in Soviet and Jewish history, who was I to comment on this exchange, which seemed so distinctly, and exclusively, American?

And then I opened the book.

As I read, I found myself relating to their conversation from places that were deeply familiar to me.

Their exchange on the remembrance and meaning of suffering resonated deeply with me as an heir to the memory of the Holocaust and Stalin's repressions.

Their discussion about the toppling of Confederate statues in America brought to mind the pulling down of Soviet monuments in Eastern Europe and the unexpected historical memory dilemmas it produced.

Their conversation about the pros and cons of reparations recalled for me the controversies that accompanied Israel's founding Prime Minister David Ben-Gurion's Holocaust reparations agreement with German Chancellor Konrad Adenauer.

As I read Wink's letters embracing his family history in full, including ancestors who were enslaved and those, both white and black, who owned slaves, I thought about post-Soviet Russia, where conversations of reconciliation and retributive justice were hopelessly snagged by the fact that multitudes of families counted both victims and perpetrators among their members.

Wink and Jen's conversation about the importance of incorporating stories of resilience and overcoming into a group's collective memory alongside stories of oppression and suffering made me think of the inspiration I derive from the unfathomable courage of the heroes of the Warsaw Ghetto Uprising and the resistance of Soviet Jewish dissidents.

As an immigrant who had to discard part of her original identity and forge a new one in America, I found myself relating to the watershed moments of their lives: ones that life throws at us without asking our permission, and those that we intentionally bring into our lives in the process of becoming.

As a refugee from a Communist society, I found myself nodding to their exchange about how collectivist ideologies have come to dominate America in recent years, pushing aside the values America once held dear and which drew me and countless other immigrants to this country—those of liberty and individual rights and freedoms.

What I expected to be an exclusively American conversation turned out to be something much broader. In it, the particularity of America's race relations broadened into the discussion of the universal questions of the human condition. Few writers can do this. I believe that Wink and Jen succeeded thanks to their conviction that no matter how different we are from one another, we all share fundamental values as members of the human species. It is to that shared aspect of our humanity that they appeal.

It's strange to think how radical this perspective feels in America today. In today's American culture, we are instructed to draw lines and retreat into our separate social "bubbles." We are urged to "stay in our lane" and warned against committing "cultural appropriations." We fear being condemned in the court of public opinion for one inartful word and losing our jobs, careers, and reputations as a consequence. The choice to stay silent behind closed doors, alone or with those who think like us, feels so much safer.

It is a choice and perspective that Wink and Jen reject completely. By appealing to our shared humanity, they've chosen to step outside the narrow ideologies of the moment. Instead of erecting barricades, they invite their readers into the process of building a shared sense of meaning. They bring their authentic selves into their exchange, trusting that this authenticity will produce a genuine understanding and connection.

By doing so, they have given us, their readers, permission to do the same. They invite us to follow their example and have conversations that connect rather than polarize. They invite us to reject clichés and rehearsed and facile arguments in favor of depth and nuance. They invite us to re-up our belief in the human spirit. I sincerely hope that many of their readers will follow their example.

Izabella Tabarovsky
Senior Advisor, Kennan Institute (Wilson Center)

Acknowledgments

We are honored and humbled and blessed to have Erec Smith and Izabella Tabarovsky write our foreword and afterword, respectively. They are true friends and fellow dissidents. We do not stand alone in our aim for a better way of being in the world.

For Helen Pluckrose, who published the article in *Areo Magazine* that gave start to our correspondence, and for her support that led to this book. And for Iona Italia, who took over from Helen and continues her support of our correspondence.

From a place of deep appreciation, we thank Martin Seligman, Phil Zimbardo, Wilfred Reilly, and Charles Love, who believed in our mission and cheered us on as we started to compile our correspondence.

Our friends at Counterweight, including Harriet Terrill and Isobel Marston, supported and published our joint contributions and sharpened our own views and perspectives.

Our friend Eric Leroy, who had the patience to read our letters from the start and engaged us honestly, openly, and often harshly—thank you for it all.

A hearty thanks to friends who read portions of this manuscript over the years with finesse, skill, insight, rigor, and welcome honesty—Anna Russell, Luis Anguiano, Dan Wolf, Mary Burkey Owens, and Desi-Rae.

A tip of the proverbial hat to each other as fellow correspondents on the front lines of a haunted present and the coming of a better time.

And finally, to Kurt Volkan at Pitchstone Publishing, who took a chance on a correspondence that, to our knowledge, is the first of its kind to be published as a book.

Winkfield Twyman, Jr.

Eighty years before I drew my first breath, you had laid the foundation for me and my family and my cousins. I never knew you in the flesh, but I grew up in the family church you founded. I began school on property you had once owned. Your echoes were ever present throughout Hickory Hill in the 1960s. And for all these blessings and much more, I give thanks to my grandma's grandfather, our founding father, Daniel Brown.

To Rosa Nell Brown Twyman Jackson: One day I got into a fight with my best friend, Kevin Robertson, on Irvington Street. I was seven years old and in the second grade. I may have won the fight, but you were waiting for me at your home on Terminal Avenue. I walked in the front door and confessed to the fight. You sternly told me, "We do not fight in our family. That is not who we are!" You set me right for life, and your stern discipline echoes in the man I am today. I was blessed to have you as a grandma, and your spirit lives on in my memory.

I had fifteen uncles, and that meant I heard fifteen different opinions about any topic under the sun. I learned to disagree without being disagreeable from Uncles Robert Daniel Twyman, Sr., Willie Earnest Twyman, Sr., James Scott Twyman, Clinton McCormick Twyman, Sr., and William Womack.

I learned I was loved as family from Aunts Charlotte Twyman Day, Mattie Womack, Amy Wilson Twyman, and Juanita Twyman.

I am grateful to Drs. Tony and Jennifer Lawrence, my Maryland family, for the hours of stimulating conversation over the years.

To Meredith Valmon and Ellyn Rainey for being family, and to Mr. and Mrs. Walter Lawrence for entrusting me with documents from our family's past.

Mom, Aunt Juanita once told me you were the hardest working person Juanita had ever met. That comment stayed with me through the years. I had more opportunities than you did in life as an orphan, and I devoted myself to working harder than even you did to right wrongs in your days. Life has been good to me, and I wish you could have seen your grandchildren, Tripp, Matthew, and Caroline, all beautiful and accomplished in their own special ways. You would be so proud, mom. I see your profile in Caroline every day. One day, we will meet again and rejoice in how amazing it is to be loved.

Myra, I remember a snowy day in January 1965. I skipped up the steps to the front door of the Green House. Dad opened the screen door, I walked inside, and there you were resting on mom in the bedroom. You were my first memory, one moment out of a lifetime, until you passed away all too soon. Your poetic gift for the poignant is ever present in this manuscript.

Dad, this book is dedicated to you for a very good reason. You saw my very best self in your world. And I saw my very best self in the larger world beyond Jean Drive, Virginia State College, and Howard Law School. As I have grown older, I have learned how dads are never of the life and times of sons. We can be stubborn in what we think is best but, if we are too stubborn, we risk severing the ties that bind. I have learned the hard way as a dad, and now I have more understanding for you back in the summer of 1983. Let's agree to disagree and accept one another's vision for life before it is too late. I only have one dad, and you only have one son. Let's love one another even if we don't understand one another.

To Tripp and Matthew: You guys are my reason for living. You are the aim of my exertions. Even before you were born, I was thinking about the schools you would attend. You make me proud—strong Twyman men, the two of you. When I pass away one day, it will be well with my soul because of the sons I brought into the world.

All of the people I call cousins have informed my sense of self over the years. Some, like Bruce and Calvin, knew me before I knew myself on Twyman Road. Others like Bill and Elizabeth never knew of me until the magic of genetic genealogy. I adore my cousins from near and far—Rosa Nell Grace, Elizabeth Twyman Anderson, Bruce Twyman, Elaine Christian Twyman, Bill Twyman, Gene Twyman, James F. Twyman, Nathan Twyman, Kiernan Twyman, Deb (Andrew) Maddox, Patty Kelley, James Edwin Smith III, Samuel Hayes III, Brenda Yurkoski, Calvin Twyman, Geneva Austin, Toni Twyman, Bob Twyman, Todd Patrick Twyman, Nia Twyman, Alicia Twyman, Tina Mae Womack, Nancy Wheeler, Nancy Williamson who has a wonderful soul and spirit, Rukiya Wilkins, Maurice Dodson, Mark Brown, Shannon Christmas, Vaden Robinson, Jr., and Abraham Lincoln Day, Jr.

Here's to my Friends (not allies) in my life story: Kevin Robertson, Janet G. Davis, Trina Branch, Terry Nicholson, Steve Skiena, Nadine, Madeline, Lisa Wilson Edwards, Rodney Akers, Anthony Farley, Professor Sheena Mason and her idea of "Racelessness," Rachel Myers, Susan Willis, Christine Hickman, John Carr, Jimmie & Candy Heyward at Oak Lawn, the memorable Julie, and the mysterious Julia.

I want to thank the many librarians and archivists who answered my many questions over the years with documents, words of advice, and shared curiosity: Elizabeth A. Baldwin, Deputy Clerk, Circuit Court, Charlotte County, Virginia; Hugh Burkhart, Associate Professor, Coordinator of Instruction and Undergraduate Learning, Copley Library, University of San Diego; Diane Dallmeyer, Administrative Assistant, Chesterfield Historical Society of Virginia; Virginia Dunn, Archives Library Reference Services Manager, The Library of Virginia; Cassandra Farrell, Map Archivist, Archives Reference Services, The Library of Virginia; Victoria Garnett, Assistant, Digital Collections, The Library of Virginia; Pattie Grady, Research Volunteer, Chesterfield Historical Society of Virginia; Robert (Bob) Kuhlthau, Volunteer Assistant, Albemarle Charlottesville Historical Society; Leeta D. Louk, Clerk of the Circuit Court, Madison County, Virginia; Regina D. Rush, Reference Librarian, Albert and Shirley Small Special Collections Library, University of Virginia; and Courtney Thompson, Reference Archivist, Archives Reference Services, The Library of Virginia.

During the week of July 29, 2017, I traveled to Charlottesville, Virginia, in search of my Twyman past. I found myself driving along a country road toward Buck Mountain Episcopal Church in Albemarle County with the weight of racial anxiety on my shoulders and curiosity in my heart. My 5x great-grandfather, George Twyman III (1731–1818), had served as the first Moderator (and Recording Secretary) of the church, but would I be welcomed in the year 2017 as racial tensions brewed in Charlottesville? I made eye contact with Chaplain Connie Clark ("Please, call me Connie") and saw acceptance and felt the warmest embrace imaginable. I felt an infinite stream of possibility in the coming of a better time.

As a young man with more hope and drive than money in my pocket, I met several elders who inspired me for a lifetime: Professor Edward Ayers, Honorable Jim Benton, Honorable Henry L. Marsh III, Professor Waldo Martin, and the incredible lawyers and staff of the law firm Hill, Tucker and Marsh.

My contributions to this manuscript are a lasting testament to my first and second-grade teachers—Mrs. Lucille Walker and Mrs. Dorothy Taylor. Without their stern and far-sighted instruction, I might have veered off onto a bad path in life. May every child come across a Mrs. Walker and Mrs. Taylor early in life when the stakes are highest.

May every writer come across a Connie Morgan in life. The courage to write can fail a writer. In those moments of hesitation, wisdom steps in and whispers authenticity. Connie, you helped me understand that, while logic is the beginning of wisdom, the destiny of wisdom is an open mind.

Years ago, my mom-in-law, Carol Lawrence Rainey, was named Brooklyn Chapter of the NAACP Woman of the Year. I am the privileged beneficiary of her wisdom as the mother of my wife, my partner for life. And the same goes for my children, who have grown up under the active and involved vision of a one-in-a-million grandmother. It doesn't get better in life, and yet, we have lived in united purpose for our most precious cargo in life while at odds when it comes to race. Mom, there's an old song I used to listen to in high school down in Chester, Virginia, a world away from Flatbush Avenue in Brooklyn. And the Dave Mason song went, *"There ain't no good guy, there ain't no bad guy. There's only you and me and we just disagree."* Let's leave race alone 'cause we can't see eye to eye. And together we usher in a higher love for the kids and our grandchildren's grandchildren. Izabella might even use the term *rapprochement*.

My lovely wife, you attended many school, youth sports, and Jack and Jill functions alone over the years, and I appreciate your patience. Thank you for allowing me the space to write whatever it was I was working on. You take care of me when I am lost in the depths of research and writing.

Caroline, you are fated to live a wonderful life, and cousins feel it. Listen to all of your ancestors and bring into the world not despair but hope in the coming of a better time. I can't believe I am the dad of a lifeguard. Stay ever wonderful, delightful, intelligent, strong-willed, difficult, and beautiful sweet Caroline.

Cousins, come closer and listen to me. It is amazing how amazing my life has been. One day, I will return to the land of our ancestors and kiss the ground on Twyman Road and give thanks.

Finally, the matter of this book being what it is, I feel duty-bound to applaud Dave Orland, who runs a book club where people can disagree without being disagreeable, and The Book Group Mavens, a point of light in San Diego.

Jennifer Richmond

I was always drawn to writing, but it was hard. I figured if it was a gift of mine to write, it would've come naturally. And so, while I wrote theses, a dissertation, and innumerable analyses and articles, I buried my desire to *really* write. To write life plainly, as Wink would say. Until one day.

One day the whisper to write turned into a more urgent plea. The day my son came home sounding like a Twitter feed with little critical thought or reflection, the writing began in earnest. As he sought to navigate between two very different households with wildly divergent ideologies, I realized it was up to me to help him find the "truth in between." With this commitment, we started to poke at the places we were most uncomfortable. We actively sought voices with whom we disagreed.

As I sought the origins of polarization in my research and writing, namely in our political divisions, it became apparent that our discussions around race were a major wedge driving these disagreements. To learn more, I signed up for some diversity training. And, the rest is history, as they say.

If you told me five years ago that I would be writing a book on race, I wouldn't have believed it. I am an international relations specialist and a China scholar. At many intersections in my writing, I queried whether I had chosen the right path. I spent a lifetime learning Chinese language, culture, politics, and economics. How did I get here?

As I sat at this crossroads, I realized that it was my understanding of systems and structures so different from our own that gave me a unique angle and perspective on the growing tensions in America. It was these experiences that made me so passionate about seeking solutions to the fraying of the fabric of our society. And I had a lot of help along the way.

This book is for the next generation. This book is for my son. Finn has supported me through this exploration, even when my writing and research bordered on the taboo that could tarnish him by proxy. After the thin blue line flag disagreement, he provided comfort and company for me when on my mental holiday away from home, all while approaching both his father and stepfather with love and understanding at a time when their ideals couldn't be further apart. He stands in the gap.

This book is also for earlier generations. My dad, whose struggle with cancer began about the same time as this correspondence, is my fearless editor, sounding board, and discussion and debate partner. Even as his cancer made speech difficult, we continue to communicate through a love of both country and family. For a love of what can be. His courage gives me a foundation.

A foundation that my mom nurtured throughout my life. Through the roller coaster of life, both past and present, she encourages me to hold my hands in the air, instead of white-knuckling it through the ride. One day at a time, one day at a time is her forever-mantra. Through one letter at a time, I have been able to not only weather but also even enjoy the ride. Or at least most of it.

This book is for my generation. For my sister, who has supported me without judgment through mental health crises, family squabbles, and even Covid disagreements. My ex-husband and soon-to-be ex-husband, who, even in disagreement, have taught me so much about myself and encouraged my growth, whether they meant to or not.

For Vera Fischer, my shelter from the storm.

And my family and friends who held me in love even when our varying ideologies and viewpoints could've rendered us asunder—you renew my optimism: Pam, Billy, Christian, Caitlin, Cole & Kenny Cossaboon; Brian, Bodhi, August & Liam Rogers & Leif Thurmond; Sue Richmond & Sam & Emily Smith; M. Ann Pritchard; Cecil Greenstreet; Kea Worthen; John Wood, Jr (and the broader Braver Angels organization); Cindi McGaughan; Kasey Solesbee; Stacey Kilfoy; Julie Knap; Jamie Carpenter; Julia Roadman; Lana Russell; Anne-Marie Gonin; Christine Yonge; Kristine Crump; Cristia Moore; Peter Zeihan; Wayne Watters; Susan Copeland; and Don Kuykendall.

Appendix I:
"Diversity Drop-Out"

Austin, Texas prides itself on being a very progressive, liberal city. One of the mayor's crowning achievements has been putting together a task force on Institutional Racism and Systemic Inequities. As part of this effort, the city promotes diversity training for the general public.

As someone who has spent a lifetime exploring culture, I jumped at the opportunity to better understand diversity dynamics. My most recent endeavor has been to encourage people across ideological, racial, and gender differences, to break away from the Twitter banter of 280 characters and engage in authentic discussion and debate through letters. I presumed this training was my chance to have these conversations in real time and face to face, in a setting explicitly designed for such a purpose. I was wrong.

Ultimately, the only way to root out and rectify institutional racism and systemic inequity is through education, and the Mayor's initiative deserves applause. However, promoting voluntary programs that are inevitably attended only by adulatory (mostly affluent and white) participants, who already subscribe to antiracism efforts, won't have an enduring effect. Instead, it advances a familiar echo chamber unable to resonate outside its narrow (and dare I say, privileged) confines. Despite Austin's honorable educational efforts, real change is not accomplished through diversity training and the pedantic social identity theorizing that has little practical application to raising educational standards in low-income schools—where the real battle begins.

My first surprise was the theme of the training. Instead of focusing on diversity, the central subject was *white identity*. This was not a bait and switch *per se*—understanding white identity and the often invisible forces that shape culture is necessary to combat institutional racism—but diversity and creating unity through diversity was never a topic. To be fair, the title of the training was "Beyond Diversity."

The primary exercise was to determine our *white privilege* scores. We carried our scores around with us as badges, which determined where we stood in a literal line-up. With our numbers held out in front of us, we were told, without talking, to find our place in line according to our score. Quiet weeping pierced the hushed and somber atmosphere, as a few whites observed the segregated queue.

Speaking one's truth—whatever that entails—was also encouraged. Apologies, often wet with more tears, received a warm reception. I shifted nervously in my seat, a sheen of perspiration on my brow, as I listened to the internal debate in my brain on the wisdom of speaking *my* truth. While never one to dismiss an invitation to speak, I ultimately decided that what I had to say would likely be dismissed, and would therefore be a waste of emotional energy. *You're here to learn*, I reminded my conflicted brain, *not to challenge the program.*

Then the facilitator asked for divergent views, and my hand shot up before my brain had the chance to interject. Dumb hand. My sweaty palm gripped the mic, and I began to speak. What follows is more or less what I said, minus the citations and the gloss of hindsight.

Culture matters. Better understanding white identity and culture is of great value, especially when, as designers of the dominant culture, we assess other cultures through a lens fogged with our own preconceptions. However, assigning blanket identities to a culture or race results in gross-oversimplification, which then leads to wedge issues, designed to create discord, rather than opportunities to generate empathy and partnership.

In our society—particularly in some areas of academia—we've come to accept either/or distinctions: either you're with me, or you're against me. At the slightest hint of disagreement, we can retreat to our *safe spaces* to avoid discomfort. Nowadays, we can easily dismiss those with diverse views as racist, or a slew of other epithets, to quickly shut down even the most benign of conversations or inquiries. When you throw out the *r-word* people come running, as if to the scene of a train wreck, to assess damage and salve wounds, sometimes with a thinly veiled delight in the electric atmosphere.

Race is a delicate topic, and black voices especially have been historically met with hostility. This traumatization can create a sensitivity that needs to be acknowledged. What is at risk, however, is the fostering of a *victimhood culture*—an umbrella culture that threatens to cover us all. John McWhorter calls this new trend "third-wave antiracism," which is a "call to enshrine defeatism, hypersensitivity, oversimplification and even a degree of performance."

This new culture, with its roots in the postmodern movement, transcends racial boundaries. As Michael Aaron notes, the postmodern movement "eschews objectivity, perceiving knowledge as a construct of power differentials rather than anything that could possibly be mutually agreed upon." The postmodern urge to deconstruct all discourse to a power struggle leaves us with few options to craft real solutions to many of our problems and, most importantly, to racism. There will always be a struggle. Societies the world over are unequal in innumerable ways. And struggle on we must, but when the struggle becomes the goal, we miss real opportunities for change.

Under such circumstances, it is hard for someone to *speak their truth*, as you have encouraged. The slightest misstep in the minefield of race discussions can cause an explosion, leaving a gaping hole in any productive dialogue.

"I don't believe that all views are welcome," I concluded—and, with a trembling hand, gave back the mic.

Most people gave me a wide berth for the rest of the training, until we had to collect in *affinity groups*, based on similar white privilege scores. I don't believe my brain simply conjured up the disdain radiating from at least a few of the alabaster faces at our *high white privilege* table when they came to the unfortunate realization that I was in their cohort.

Our next exercise was to come up with a few of the top *white* characteristics. We were told that these traits were neutral—neither good nor bad. To the extent that certain races have identifiable group traits, what I saw written, at least to my sensibilities, I would classify as almost entirely negative—indeed, as bad, if not evil. Let me name a few words that stuck out: *violent, rape culture, fragile*. I have a hard time arguing with any of these, but, of course, all of these could be used to explain other cultures too. However, that wasn't part of the exercise.

But here's my favorite story. One white woman in my group was adamant that we include a *white savior complex* as a "defining aspect of white culture." To her, with a mobility issue, this was incredibly important. She besmirched white men in particular, who frequently asked if she needed any help. In line for lunch, one of the black male caterers asked if she needed any help. I had to literally bite my lower lip to stop myself from making the obvious observation. Although one person identified "the need for civility" as a *white* characteristic in this exercise, apparently, sometimes, just sometimes, kindness and civility bridge cultures.

At one point, Justice Clarence Thomas was accused of having a *white consciousness* because he didn't agree with affirmative action. Could it be that he didn't agree with a *white savior* system that may work to disadvantage blacks, and ultimately harm black consciousness by holding blacks to lower standards? To quote John McWhorter: "I know of no more vivid hypocrisy on the part of those who style themselves black people's fellow travelers than to earnestly dismiss claims that black people's average IQ is lower than other people's while in the same breath nodding vigorously that a humane society must not subject the same people to challenging tests."

I knew by this point to keep my trap shut, but this was one of the issues that I actually came to discuss. I came to better understand enduring racism and the challenges it poses. To listen to black voices and find ways to meaningfully ally with the black community. To explore and debate different views on how to bolster the strength and resiliency that has been a part of black heritage in America. However, the training was crafted in such a way as to prevent authentic dialogue among racial groups, and disagreement was met with denial.

Nevertheless, I did gain important insights from these exercises. I came to realize that the sense of *rugged individualism* that permeates the American mindset is part of a predominately *white* consciousness, a *pull yourself up by your bootstraps* mentality. We whites do have the *privilege* to adhere to such an ethos. Given that racism was institutionalized, we will need more than *personal responsibility* and *individual grit* to correct anti-black racism. How do we do it?

One of the most direct paths to correct inequity is our education system. But the system is struggling, and most acutely in schools in lower-income areas. Is this a question of resources? That is undoubtedly part of the equation, but only part.

According to a McKinsey & Co report, "By one measure we get 60 percent less for our education dollars in terms of average test-score results than do other wealthy nations."

Prior to the dismantling of segregation, at a time where overt racism was still ubiquitous, there were a number of all-black schools that excelled, although they lacked resources. Thomas Sowell gives the example of Dunbar High School in Washington, D.C., which "sent a higher percentage of its graduates on to college than any white public high school in Washington." Today, there are several successful inner-city charter schools that are scoring above the national average. According to Sowell: "In 2013, children in the fifth grade in one of the Harlem schools in the Success Academy chain 'surpassed all other public schools in the state in math, even their counterparts in the whitest and richest suburbs,' according to the *New York Times*. Nor was this an isolated fluke. In 2014, children in the Success Academy chain of charter schools as a whole scored in the top 3% in English and in the top 1% in math."

Studies have shown that charter schools are closing the achievement gap in low-income areas. This is true not only in the United States but also in the United Kingdom, where educators like Katharine Birbalsingh are having an indelible impact on the lives of poor, inner-city, mainly black students. Given these examples, along with numerous others, we should ask: *where are we failing?*

We can talk about spending more money, raising teachers' wages, and other hackneyed solutions—with none of which I disagree—but these have not proven sufficient to address better opportunities for the students themselves. And, when options that fall outside of these traditional solutions are presented, they are not only denounced, but there is also a lot of money spent, sometimes in lawsuits, to keep these alternative solutions from going mainstream.

However, to criticize the system, especially the National Education Association (NEA), for this failure is to risk serious and severe backlash. There are good intentions baked into the system, but are these intentions in the best interest of the students, or of the organization? Like many institutions, the NEA is stuck in a path dependency that induces bureaucratic rigidity, inhibiting change.

The NEA has considerable political sway and can effectively block opposition that threatens its control of public education. Charter schools, operating outside of its purview, constitute such a threat. Also, the NEA gives considerable contributions to the Congressional Black Caucus Foundation, the Congressional Hispanic Caucus Institute, the Democratic Leadership Council, Jesse Jackson's Rainbow PUSH coalition, Al Sharpton's National Action Network, and many similar groups. Therefore, suggested changes to the system are not only in jeopardy from pushback but also risk eliciting charges of racism for critiquing an institution with strong financial ties to communities of color.

All this suggests that there are solutions out there—or at the very least different opportunities worth exploring. And yet the system remains broken.

Increasingly, our conversations have ossified around either/or false dichotomies, polarizing society and making true progress elusive. We are backsliding. Whether we are discussing concrete issues, such as school reform, or more general corrections to institutional racism, reverting to this simplicity degrades our critical thinking and our abilities to address complex issues. Furthermore, speaking one's truth, as was encouraged in the diversity training, has become a dangerous enterprise. The situation reminds me of Mao Zedong's Hundred Flowers Campaign: a solicitation for dissident views that ended in the persecution of any who accepted the invitation.

Understanding white identity is useful, but the often arbitrary assignment of a blanket identity belies the complexity of true diversity both in and among races as well as across a variety of valuable viewpoints. At best, it shuts down meaningful dialogue and critical exploration. At worst, it foments discord and disunity. Ultimately, true wisdom and progress is born out of the tension between differing perspectives, each of which lends important insight that can help us find a more sustainable path forward. To truly go *beyond diversity* we must, through authentic discussion and debate, wrestle with our various cultures and how they are shaped vis à vis one another, to focus on the social connections necessary to build a genuinely diverse and egalitarian society *together*.

Without expending the energy to take this extra step, we risk not only becoming diversity drop-outs but also ensuring institutional racism and systemic inequities persist, despite our best intentions.

Appendix II:
Record of Daniel Brown (1833–1885) and His Family in the 1870 U.S. Census

Enumerated on 30th Day of June 1870
Post Office: Manchester, Va.

Brown, Daniel	35	Male	Mulatto	Farm Laborer
Sallie A.	33	Female	Black	Keeping House
Martha I.	15	Female	Black	At House
Mason	14	Male	Black	Farm Laborer
Robert	14	Male	Black	Farm Laborer
Harriet	10	Female	Black	At School
Benjamin	8	Male	Black	At School
Goodridge	5	Male	Black	
Daniel	2	Male	Black	
Alvira Smith	15	Female	Black	Domestic Servant
Isaac D. Dickerson	25	Male	Black	Farm Laborer
Wilson Ward	19	Male	Black	Farm Laborer

Appendix III:
The Last Will and Testament
of Daniel Brown (1833–1885)

In the name of God, amen. I, Daniel Brown (free servant), of the County of Chesterfield and state of Virginia being of sound & disfearing [sic] mind & memory, do make & declare this to be my last will & testament, hereby revoking all wills by me heretofore made.

First. I devise to my son Daniel Brown as his share of my real estate, my land in the County of Chesterfield on James River known as Chester Lodge,* lately purchased by me of Mr. Henry Jenks & containing eight & three quarters acres more or less subject to all estate for life or widowhood of my wife Sally Anne Brown until he shall have arrived at the age of twenty-one years.

Second. I direct that my land in Charlotte County called Freedman's Choice, conveyed to me by John Bayley by deed duly recorded in the Clerk's Office of said County & containing one hundred & seventy five

---

Daniel Brown, Will Book 27, page 199, Chesterfield County, VA

* Chester Lodge, a farm and good dwelling house, first appears in the historical record on February 3, 1797, as the residence of Henry Randolph. Henry's son, James Williamson Randolph, who became the most prominent book publisher in Richmond, Virginia, was born at Chester Lodge on August 19, 1815. A public auction of the farm occurred in March 1837. On June 21, 1871, Daniel Brown purchased Chester Lodge from Henry Clay Jenks, a grocer in Richmond. Chester Lodge included eight acres of land comprising all the old landings on the James River at Warwick, an extinct town located seven miles south of downtown Richmond and burned to the ground by Benedict Arnold during the American Revolutionary War. The property was at the merger of Falling Creek and the James River. As of 1936, part of Chester Lodge was still standing.

acres more or less shall be sold by my executrix, to be hereinafter named, at such time for such times as she shall deem best; the proceeds thereof to be applied first to the payment of any debt that may be then due on the fall creek [sic] Place whereon I now reside, next, to the payment of any other just debt against my estate, & lastly, to the support & maintenance of herself & our children, or to the purchase of stock & supplies for the farm.

Third. I leave to my wife Sally Anne during her life or widowhood, all my property of every kind both real and personal trusting to her to take care of our children. But if she shall marry again, then I direct that she shall be only entitled to what the law allows as dower, but not including in that any charge upon Chester Lodge.

Fourth. Upon the marriage or death of my wife, then I direct that all my property of all kinds, except Chester Lodge shall be equally divided among all my children except my son Daniel Brown; it being inherited as he has Chester Lodge that he shall not share in my other land, but only in my personal property.

Fifth. I direct that not only shall my wife's interest in Chester Lodge cease, if she shall marry again; but that in any case possession thereon shall be given to my son Daniel Brown when he becomes of age; which will be on the . . . . . day of . . . . . 18. . . .

Sixth. I appoint my wife Sally Anne Brown sole executrix of this my last will & testament, & direct that she shall not be required to give security.

In testimony of all which I hereunto set my hand & seal this . . . . day of . . . . 1872. Daniel Brown, His x mark [mark of Daniel Brown]

March 3, 1885 Witnesses: Thos. J. Cheatham P. E. Temple in Chesterfield County Court April 13, 1885.

The last will and testament of Daniel Brown dec'd was preserved in Court and proved by the oath of Dr. T.J. Cheatham and P. E. Temple, subscribing witnesses thereto and ordered to be recorded. Teste: Marcus A. Cogbill, Clerk

Appendix IV:
Inventory & Appraisement of Personal Estate of Daniel Brown (1833–1885)

Pursuant to an order of the County Circuit Court of Chesterfield County at the April Term, we having been appointed appraisers to value the personal property of Daniel Brown, dec. and having been duly sworn, respectfully submit the following:

One brown mule	Bill	$100.00
" dun "	Tom	$100.00
" black "	George	$50.00
" bay mare	Kate	$50.00
" " "	Dolly	$125.00
" Buffalo Cow		$25.00
" Red Cow	Sarah	$35.00
" Yearling		$6.00
Six (6) hogs		$85.00
Six (6) pigs		$12.00
Three (3) sheep		$15.00
Fifteen (15) Fowls		$4.00
Three (3) Wagons		$90.00
Two (2) Carts		$10.00
One (1) buggy & harness		$25.00
" (1) Flint stone		$1.00

Chesterfield County, Will Book 27, 1883–1889, Microfilm Reel 332, pp. 217–219, Inventory & Appraisement of the Estate of Daniel Brown, dated 7, May 1885 with filing date of 12 May 1885.

Three (3) Double plows	$10.00
" (3) Single "	$3.00
Two (2) Cultivator	$2.50
One (1) Corn Planter	$5.00
Inventory Balance Forward	$703.50
One (1) Lassow	$3.00
Two (2) Wheel barrows	$5.00
Set of hoes, forks & shovels	$1.50
Set of wagon harness	$5.00
Set of old harness & cart saddle	$3.00
Set mechanics' tools	$5.00
One (1) Grain cradle	$2.50
" (1) Fan Mill	$15.00
" (1) Thrashing Machine	$25.00
" (1) Mower	$15.00
Nine (9) bbls (barrels) Flour	$27.00
Set old bbls (barrels)	$1.00
One hay frame	$5.00
Set old wagons	$3.00
Set Lumber	$50.00
One (1) Straw Cutter	$5.00
Set Black Peas	$2.50
Set blade ladder	$10.00
One (1) Old Straw Cutter	$1.50
" (1) Calendar Clock	$15.00
" (1) Mahogany Table	$5.00
" (1) Bureau	$3.00
Two (2) Chests	$1.00
One (1) pair Andirons	$ .50
Set chairs	$1.00
One (1) Sideboard	$1.00
One (1) Boar	$10.00
One Desk	$1.00
" (1) sewing machine	$8.00
" (1) Bureau	$2.50

" (1) Bed stead & bedding $8.00
" (1) Mirror $1.00
" (1) Cooking Stove $3.00
Set of Cutlery $ .50
Set of Crockery $1.00
One (1) gun $5.00
"   (1) Feather tick [unclear] $8.00
     =====
     $963.00

May 7, 1885   H.G. Watkins
     William Johnston } Appraisers
     P.C. Touple

I accept the foregoing as a true inventory & appraisement of the personal estate of Daniel Brown dies.

her
Sarah A. X Brown Ex. Tx.
mark

I have reviewed the foregoing inventory & appraisement and found the same in proper form.
     May 11, 1885   P.V. Cogbill Circuit Clerk
     Chesterfield County Court

In Chesterfield County Circuit Clerk's office, May 12, 1885: The foregoing inventory & appraisement was filed & [unclear]

     Teste
     Marcus A. Cogbill, Clerk

Appendix V:
Children and Grandchildren
of Daniel Brown (1833–1885)

Children

1. Robert Daniel Brown (1860–1934) & Amy Wilson Brown (1862–1940)

    Grandchildren

    William H. Brown (1882–?)
    Mary Lou Brown Carver (1885–1944)
    Earnest Brown (1888–?)
    Laura Elizabeth Brown Wright (1890–1970)
    Jerad Brown (1892–?)
    Jesse Brown (1892–?)
    Jennie Brown (1893–?)
    Nora Brown (1893–?)
    Nellie Brown (1895–1895)
    Walter Brown (1897–?)

---

* According to family oral history, Daniel Brown had sixteen children, but this listing of seventeen children born to Daniel Brown and his wife Sarah (Sallie Anne Nell) Cole/Giles is derived from both family oral history and family trees on Ancestry.com. Research is ongoing, but this discrepancy is not unexpected given the high rates of infant mortality at the time and the possibility that a child who passed for white may have later become lost to the family. We also can trace Brown's paternal ancestors back to the family's arrival in North America: (1) Daniel Brown (1783–after 1860), (2) Samuel Brown (1746–1808), (3) Thomas Brown (1726–after 1762), (4) Francis Brown (1700–1755), (5) William Brown (1685–1706), (6) George Brown (1642–1706), (7) Col. William Browne (1600–1664) (arrived in Virginia in 1622).

       Bettie Ellen Brown Glenn (1897–1989)
       Rosa Nell Brown Twyman Jackson (1897–1983)
       Hattie Brown (1899–?)
       Jessie Brown (1900–1964)
       Martha Brown (1901–1982)
       Cora Brown (?–?)

2. Martha Jane Brown (1855–?)

3. Mason Brown (1856–?) & Agnes Thomas Brown (1878–?)
   Grandchildren
   Sarah Brown Jones (1899–1924)

4. Harriet Brown (1860–?)

5. Benjamin Brown (1862–1941) & Mary E. Wilson Brown (1872–?)
   Grandchildren
          Cora Brown (1893–?)
          Cara Brown (1896–1938)
          Edward Ashley Brown (1896–1944)
          Lottie Hazel Brown Banks (1898–1962)
          Ruby Brown Scott (1900–1984)
          Armatean Brown Funn (1903–1997)
          Nornctuose Brown (1905–?)
          Benjamin H. Brown (1906–1932)
          Leslie Theodore Brown (1908–1971)
          Lillie Brown (1908–?)

6. Hatty Brown Austin (1862–?) & Wilson Austin (1861–?)
   Grandchildren
          Bertha Sophia Austin (1884–?)
          Maude E. Austin (1888–1978)

7. Goodrich R. Brown (1865–1949) & Josephine Webb Brown
   Grandchildren
          Claude Brown (1894–1939)
          Clifford E. Brown, Sr. (1896–1970)
          Lustrenia Brown Austin (1896–?)
          Lena Brown Patterson Samuels (1899–?)
          James Brown (1902–?)
          Emily Brown Friend (1906–?)

Sarah (Salle) Brown (1908–?)
Daniel Webster Brown (1913–?)

8. Joseph L. Brown (1870?–)

9. Daniel Webster Brown (1872–1946) & Sarah Branch Tucker (1877–1941)
   Grandchildren
   Carrie Araminta Brown Walker (1905–1989)
   Esther Virginia Brown (1907–1989)
   Robert Goodrich Brown (1910–1976)
   John Webster Brown (1913–1972)
   Daniel Russell Brown (1915–1977)

10. Eliza Brown (1873–1893)

11. Emma J. Brown (1873–1946) & Walter Funn (1873–1896)
    Grandchildren
    Lloyd B. Funn (1895–1899)
    Oscar Leandrew Thompson Funn (1896–1949)

12. Richard Brown (1877–?)

13. Cora Brown (1878–1970)

14. William Isaac Brown, Sr. (1884–1940) & Edna Harris Brown (1885–)
    Grandchildren
    Antionette M. Brown (1913–1935)
    William Isaac Brown, Jr. (1915–1982)
    Alvin Goodrich Brown (1917–2000)
    Clarence Woodrow Brown (1920–?)
    Ulysses Benjamin Brown (1928–?)
    Robert Monroe Brown (?–1924)
    Emma G. Brown (?–?)

15. Anna Brown (?–?)

16. Edward Brown (?–?)

17. Theodore Brown (?–?)

Appendix VI:
William Richmond Deed

State of North Carolina
Caswell County

Know all men by here presents that I William Richmond of the county
and state aforesaid, for and in consideration of the natural love and affection which I have and bear unto my beloved son Adam S. Richmond
of the county and state aforesaid, do give and bequeath and by these
present, have given, and bequeathed unto the said Adam S. Richmond,
one negro woman Phillis; and her eight children (viz) Bazzillia, Dinah,
Tiller, Moses, Sampson, Tailor, Judith and Hannah; with all their natural
increase; I do give and deliver unto the said Adam S. Richmond, to have
and to hold for his own future use, benefit, and behoof; and I the said
William Richmond do hereby bind myself any heirs and assigns to war-
rant and forever defend the wright, and title to the said negroes as above
described and set forth, unto the said Adam S. Richmond his heirs and
assigns, against myself my heirs and assigns, them and all and every other person or persons whatsoever lawfully claiming or to claim the same
or any part thereof in witness my hand and seal this 2 day of March in the
year of our Lord one thousand eight hundred and thirty two.

Signed sealed and delivered in the presence of
Abner Stanfield

INDEX

ABOUT THE AUTHORS

Winkfield Twyman, Jr., is a former law professor and writer who seeks understanding across the color line in America. Born in Richmond, Virginia, he currently lives in San Diego, California.

Jennifer Richmond has worked in international relations for more than twenty years. She is the founder of Truth in Between and a cofounder of the Institute for Liberal Values. She lives in Austin, Texas.